P9-DHI-188

WRITERS AT WORK

Seventh Series

Previously Published

WRITERS AT WORK
The *Paris Review* Interviews

THIRD SERIES

Edited by GEORGE PLIMPTON and introduced by ALFRED KAZIN

William Carlos Williams	Saul Bellow
Blaise Cendrars	Arthur Miller
Jean Cocteau	James Jones
Louis-Ferdinand Céline	Norman Mailer
Evelyn Waugh	Allen Ginsberg
Lillian Hellman	Edward Albee
William Burroughs	Harold Pinter

FOURTH SERIES

Edited by GEORGE PLIMPTON and introduced by WILFRID SHEED

Isak Dinesen	John Dos Passos
Conrad Aiken	Vladimir Nabokov
Robert Graves	Jorge Luis Borges
George Seferis	John Berryman
John Steinbeck	Anthony Burgess
Christopher Isherwood	Jack Kerouac
W. H. Auden	Anne Sexton
Eudora Welty	John Updike

FIFTH SERIES

Edited by GEORGE PLIMPTON and introduced by
FRANCINE DU PLESSIX GRAY

P. G. Wodehouse	Joyce Carol Oates
Pablo Neruda	Archibald MacLeish
Henry Green	Isaac Bashevis Singer
Irwin Shaw	John Cheever
James Dickey	Kingsley Amis
William Gass	Joseph Heller
Jerzy Kosinski	Gore Vidal
Joan Didion	

SIXTH SERIES

Edited by GEORGE PLIMPTON and introduced by
FRANK KERMODE

Rebecca West	Kurt Vonnegut, Jr.
Stephen Spender	Nadine Gordimer
Tennessee Williams	James Merrill
Elizabeth Bishop	Gabriel García Márquez
Bernard Malamud	Carlos Fuentes
William Goyen	John Gardner

Writers at Work

The *Paris Review* Interviews

SEVENTH SERIES

Edited by George Plimpton
Introduction by John Updike

VIKING

VIKING
Viking Penguin Inc., 40 West 23rd Street,
New York, New York 10010, U.S.A.
Penguin Books Ltd, Harmondsworth,
Middlesex, England
Penguin Books Australia Ltd, Ringwood,
Victoria, Australia
Penguin Books Canada Limited, 2801 John Street,
Markham, Ontario, Canada L3R 1B4
Penguin Books (N.Z.) Ltd, 182–190 Wairau Road,
Auckland 10, New Zealand

First published in 1986 by Viking Penguin Inc.
Published simultaneously in Canada

The interview with Arthur Koestler is reprinted by
permission of The Sterling Lord Agency, Inc.
Copyright © 1984 by Arthur Koestler

LIBRARY OF CONGRESS CATALOGING IN PUBLICATION DATA
Writers at work.
1. Authors—20th century—Interviews.   I. Plimpton,
George.   II. Paris review.
PN453.W738   1986   809'.04   86-5474
ISBN 0-670-80888-1

Printed in the United States of America by
R. R. Donnelley & Sons Company, Harrisonburg, Virginia
Set in Avanta

Contents

Introduction

*T*he Paris Review interviews, of which this is the seventh hefty collection, offer the writer some special temptations: as much tape, time, and space as he* wants to fill; interviewers more knowledgeable and piquantly interested than your usual harassed professional journalist; and the opportunity to peruse and edit the transcript, to eliminate babble and indiscretion and to hone finer the elicited aperçus. This editorial process has evolved to the point that in this volume we are told how Philip Larkin conducted his interview entirely by mail, John Barth made his shorter every time it was returned to him to make it longer, and Milan Kundera concocted his, in the interviewer's somehow enabling presence, with "typewriter, scissors, and glue." Even among those writers submissive to the old-fashioned question-and-answer procedure, signs of resistance were noted. John Ashbery gave his interviewer an "impression of distraction, as though he wasn't quite sure just what was going on or what his role in the proceedings might be." Arthur Koestler complained of a cold, moaned when the tape recorder was set up, refused to be photographed, and came fully alive only when he suddenly emitted "a very peculiar noise, a wailing

*The androgynous "he"—read "he or she" throughout.

falsetto half-yodel" that beckoned his wife to bring more malt whiskey to lubricate his ordeal. Kundera, we are told, "hates to talk about himself," and some such disclaimer figures in almost every one of these thirteen encounters. And yet, in the thirty years since *The Paris Review* began to offer its temptations, few writers of distinction have finally resisted, and this *Writers at Work* series now forms an unparalleled roll call of the century's literary lights. Malcolm Cowley, who heads up, by right of seniority, this present volume, in 1957 introduced the first, whose senior interviewee was E. M. Forster, whose baby was Françoise Sagan, and whose middle-aged voices included those of William Faulkner, Thornton Wilder, James Thurber, Alberto Moravia, Georges Simenon, and Nelson Algren.

As Alfred Kazin pointed out in introducing the third volume of this series, wise men such as Socrates and Buddha were interrogated in antiquity, and Boswell interviewed Johnson and Eckermann, Goethe. But until the twentieth century, it was generally assumed that a writer had said what he had to say in his works. Among the causes of the uneasiness so drolly noticeable in these writer-interviewer tussles is the fear, far from unjustified, that the writer's words as distractedly dictated, under random verbal prodding from a stranger, into a tape recorder, will be taken as a worthy substitute for the words he has with such labor and love and hope of imperishability written down and ushered into print. Writers take words seriously —perhaps the last professional class that does—and they struggle to steer their own through the crosswinds of meddling editors and careless typesetters and obtuse and malevolent reviewers into the lap of the ideal reader. So to clutter the written record with an interview seems something of a desecration, or at the least a misuse, of language, and spendthrift besides. Also, one of the satisfactions of fiction or drama or poetry from the perpetrator's point of view is the selective order it imposes upon the confusion of a lived life; out of the daily welter of sensation and impression these few verbal artifacts, these narratives or poems, are salvaged and carefully presented. The creative writer uses his life as well as being its victim; he can control in his work the self-presentation that in actuality is at the mercy of a thousand accidents. Philip Larkin's poetry, for instance, does not stammer, and Raymond Carver's tirelessly polished stories ("It's something I love to do," he says, "putting words in and taking words out") have nothing of the messiness of their milieux. Also again: an interview, in our age of fast cultural food and the thirty-second sell, may give its consumer a sensation of duty done by that particular author. Milan Kundera and Philip Roth, in the following pages, are especially zealous in directing attention away from themselves to their written work, and in acting as their own best critics. But any interview, however stringently controlled, however many months go by in its adjustment and elaboration (months and months, in Roth's case), remains intrinsically informal instead of formal and perforce grapples with the questions someone else asks rather than (as in the practice of art) the groping, truly interesting questions that one asks oneself.

Art of many sorts stems from a pose, from an unlifelike convention that releases inhibition and permits an absentee, as it were, enactment of human truths suppressed in normal social workings. Posing as Venus or Eve or Euphrosyne, a young woman in the most muffled of Victorian times could display her naked body to the artist and thence to his audience of gallery-goers. Music and dance put on parade ecstasies otherwise confined to the intimacy of the bedroom or the prayer stall. The writer, even the lyric poet, in picking up his pen and posing at his desk puts on a disguise that frees him to speak. Our consumeristic appetite for interviews such as these thirteen derives in part from the hope that the disguise will slip, the constructed authorial persona will be poked away, and the "real" person behind the words will be revealed as ignominiously as a shapeless snail without its shapely shell. Roth (whose defense of the free-world writer against the charge of triviality is worth the price of this book in itself) takes the opportunity to explain how manipulated, how invented, how aesthetically determined are the autobiographical-seeming first-person novels that have made his fame. "What may be taken by the innocent for naked autobiography is, as I've been suggesting, more than likely mock-autobiography or hypothetical autobiography or autobiography grandiosely enlarged." The writer is an impersonator, he insists, and cites many examples, most fondly the personally generous Jack Benny's radio impersonation of a miser called Jack Benny: "It excited his comic imagination to do this," and as a writer you need to "torture and subvert" your own biography to give it "that dimension that will excite your verbal life." Edna O'Brien, when faced with the blunt question "Is the novel autobiographical?," usefully distinguishes between emotions, which the author must have experienced, and incidents, which are often fabricated. "But any book that is any good must be, to some extent, autobiographical because one cannot and should not fabricate emotions." John Ashbery, asked, "Is there a close connection between life and poetry?," makes the distinction along a somewhat different plane: "In my case I would say there is a very close but oblique connection. . . . I don't want to bore people with experiences of mine that are simply versions of what everybody goes through. For me, poetry starts after that point. I write with experiences in mind, but I don't write about them, I write out of them. I know that I have exactly the opposite reputation, that I am totally self-involved, but that's not the way I see it." May Sarton confides that "I'm only able to write poetry, for the most part, when I have a Muse, a woman who focuses the world for me," but quickly Platonizes the revelation: "She may be a lover, may not. In one case it was a person I saw only once, at lunch in a room with a lot of other people, and I wrote a whole book of poems." Importuned by the autobiographical question, William Maxwell calmly answers, "I don't feel that my stories, though they may appear to be autobiographical, represent an intention to hand over the whole of my life. They are fragments in which I am a character along with the others. They're written from a considerable distance. I never feel exposed by them in any way." Writers, who have developed ways of profitably using their lives and what of the world their lives permit them to see, have perhaps less than the normal need to boast and to boost the ego; the package has already been delivered. "I have always been averse to talking about myself," Ashbery simply states.

Along with our reprehensible interest in the "real" people behind the impersonations goes a curiosity about their working "secrets," the magic that has enabled them to be writers while the bulk of humanity, each soul laden with its story to tell, is denied access to print. There can be few surprises in this line: manuscript accumulates pretty much by way of the same patient labor as other products. It *is* surprising that Ashbery composes his poems right on the typewriter, and that Raymond Carver for years was so pressed for space and peace that he would write sitting in his car, and that Eugene Ionesco dictates like a pasha of industry: "I sit comfortably in an armchair, opposite my secretary. Luckily, although she's intelligent, she knows nothing about literature and can't judge whether what I write is good or worthless. I speak slowly, as I'm talking to you, and she takes it down." Unsuspected depths of the writing travail are revealed by Carver's "twenty or thirty drafts of a story" and "forty or fifty drafts" of a poem, and by Roth's six months of eight-hour days that produce at the end one page ("Usually it doesn't come to more than one page") of sufficiently lively sentences, and by Larkin's optimum average of three poems per year, and his last fallow decade—truly his last, for Larkin, like Koestler, has met his death since being interviewed. With eerie prescience he serenely estimated, while still in his early sixties, that "It's unlikely I shall write any more poems."

Beyond the trivial mechanics of tools and schedule, the engines of creation are difficult to inspect; Kundera's concern with musical counterpoint, Barth's early baptism in "the ocean of rivers of stories," Roth's search for "the liveliness," Ionesco's faith in dreams as "reality of its most profound"—these fascinating sidelights do not illuminate the fierce practicality of composition, the translation of one's own interests, by way of a superior structural sense and a certain detached selflessness, into language interesting to others. The theories and enthusiasms behind significant art are available as well to intelligent artistic dullards. Ashbery, the most diffident and fatalistic of those who here discuss the artistic process from the inside, quotes Kenneth Koch: "It's rather hard to be a good artist and also be able to explain intelligently what your art is about. In fact, the worse your art is, the easier it is to talk about."

What can be talked about, with no fear of compromising one's own privacy or the private throes of imagination, is the past; these interviews seem most relaxed and valuable in their living glimpses of figures now legendary. Who now, besides Malcolm Cowley, is left to describe how "You forgave Hart [Crane] a great deal because he was so kind and helpful. But then he'd get drunk and start throwing furniture out of the window. Or he'd stagger around the house with a lighted kerosene lamp"? In a few offhand words Cowley brings Hemingway, Faulkner, Pound, Fitzgerald, and Ford Madox Ford back to human scale, wheezing after girls, telling stories in the backwoods manner, sneaking alcohol in the kitchen, filling a room with their enthusiasms. Few of us can look forward to being a "national scholarly resource" on Cowley's scale, but we all become living archives, witnesses to what can no longer be witnessed. Koestler, asked if his friend George Orwell was a happy man, testifies with startling force: "That was the last thing he was." Maxwell remembers the old *New Yorker* art meetings, when Harold Ross would "lean forward and peer at the drawing with his lower lip sticking out." May Sarton once saw Virginia Woolf enter a party in London: "She came into the room like a dazzled deer and walked right across—this was a beautiful house in Regent's Park—to the long windows and stood there looking out. My memory is that she was not even introduced at that point, that she just walked across, very shyly, and stood there looking absolutely beautiful." Tristan Tzara is a name that, for Americans at least, has all but melted into cultural history; but Ionesco movingly recalls: "I met Tzara at the very end of his life. He, who had refused to speak Romanian all his life, suddenly started talking to me in that language, reminiscing about his childhood, his youth, and his loves." Even the close-mouthed Larkin loosened up when he remembered the youthful Kingsley Amis and his funny faces, "his Edith Sitwell face, and so on." A whole lost world of New York poets comes back in Ashbery's recalling:

Actually the one poet I really wanted to know when I was young was Auden. I met him briefly twice after he gave readings at Harvard, and later on in New York saw a bit of him through Chester Kallman, who was a great friend of Jimmy Schuyler's, but it was very hard to talk to him since he already knew everything. I once said to Kenneth Koch, "What are you supposed to say to Auden?" And he said that about the only thing there was to say was "I'm glad you're alive."

And out of her deep acquaintance with Robert Lowell, Elizabeth Hardwick distills a revealing sexual insight: "He liked women writers and I don't think he ever had a true interest in a woman who wasn't a writer—an odd turn-on indeed and one I've noticed not greatly shared."

It is the female interviewees in these pages who, perhaps not surprisingly, most warmly extol literature in general. Hardwick testifies: "As I have grown older I see myself as fortunate in many ways. It is fortunate to have had all my life this passion for studying and enjoying literature and for trying to add a bit to it as interestingly as I can. This passion has given me much joy, it has given me friends who care for the same things, it has given me employment, escape from boredom, everything. The great gift is the passion for reading. It is cheap, it consoles, it distracts, it excites, it gives you knowledge of the world and experience of a wide kind. It is a moral illumination." Edna O'Brien remembers with rapture her first encounters with the writing of Hemingway, Joyce, and Woolf; she regrets that "literature is no longer sacred" and ends by asserting that it is "the next best thing to God." May Sarton also speaks of her poetry in religious terms: "In the inspired poem something is given," and each new surge of her poetry requires a Muse whereby "the deepest source is reached." The men are more guarded (and none is quite as willingly shrewd and amusing as Miss Hardwick in discussing the writings of others, the "literary scene") but each of them at some point lets slip a pledge of allegiance, a confession of pleasure and pride that circumstances have enlisted them in this vocation:

COWLEY: Writing becomes its own reward. What do you need from others—except a little money—if you have satisfied the stern critic in yourself?

KOESTLER: (*Stands and walks to bookcase.*) Whenever I get depressed, which I often do, I come over here and look at this. My comforter. If ever I wonder what on earth it was all for, here is the evidence. The thirty books I've written plus all the translations.

MAXWELL: If you get it all down there's a serenity that is marvelous. I don't mean just getting the facts down, but the degree of imagination you bring to it. . . . Writing fiction was, and still is, pure pleasure.

IONESCO: People who don't read are brutes.

LARKIN: I can't understand these chaps who go round American universities explaining how they write poems: it's like going round explaining how you sleep with your wife.

ASHBERY: Of course, my reason tells me that my poems are not dictated, that I am not a *voyant.* I suppose they come from a part of me that I am not in touch with very much except when I am actually writing. The rest of the time I guess I want to give this other person a rest, so that he won't get tired and stop.

KUNDERA: A novel is a meditation on existence, seen through imaginary characters. The form is unlimited freedom. Throughout its history, the novel has never known how to take advantage of its endless possibilities.

BARTH: Nearly every writer I know was going to be something else, and then found himself writing by a kind of *passionate default.* . . . After I had written about a novel's worth of bad pages, I understood that while I was not doing it well, *that* was the thing I was going to do.

ROTH: What I want is to possess my readers while they are reading my book—if I can, to possess them in ways that other writers don't. Then let them return, just as they are, to a world where everybody else is working to change, persuade, tempt, and control them. The best readers come to fiction to be free of all that noise, to have set loose in them the consciousness that's otherwise conditioned and hemmed in by all that *isn't* fiction.

CARVER: Good fiction is partly a bringing of the news from one world to another. That end is good in and of itself, I think. . . . It just has to be there for the fierce pleasure we take in doing it, and the different kind of pleasure that's taken in reading something that's durable and made to last, as well as beautiful in and of itself.

Such testimonials to the intrinsic worth and beauty of their activity are worth eliciting, in an age when so many men and women resent their work and regard it ironically. An artist of any sort, in our society and most others, is a privileged person, allowed to stand apart from some of the daily grind and supposed to be closer to the gods, to have access to the divine sources of tribal well-being. Once everyone participated in the dance, and submitted to the signifying tattoo. As the gods recede, the distances between the artist and the other tribal members grow greater, and to lessen the distance, perhaps, interviews like these are sought and, however uneasily, granted.

—JOHN UPDIKE

1. Malcolm Cowley

Malcolm Cowley was born August 24, 1898, in a farmhouse in the western Alleghenies, near the village of Belsano, the son of a homeopathic physician. His college years at Harvard were interrupted by his service as a munitions-truck driver with the French army in 1917. After two financially difficult years in Greenwich Village, he was awarded a small scholarship to France, earning a diploma at the Université de Montpellier. From 1929 to 1944 Cowley was an associate editor of *The New Republic*, succeeding to the post held by Edmund Wilson. Since then he has been closely associated, as a literary advisor, with the Viking Press, where he edited the first series of *Writers at Work* in 1957.

His most widely read work, *Exile's Return* (1934; revised 1951), is celebrated as the classic account of the brilliant new writers who appeared after World War I, the so-called Lost Generation (though Cowley deplores the easy label). Ernest Hemingway, Hart Crane, F. Scott Fitzgerald, and William Faulkner were among his friends, and he has described their works and days in a series of books, including *The Literary Situation* (1954), *A Second Flowering* (1973), *—and I Worked at the Writer's Trade* (1978), and *The Dream of the Golden Mountains* (1980). He was largely responsible for revising Faulkner's reputation at a time when most of his novels were out of print. Besides being a literary historian, a critic, a memoirist, and the author of fifteen (to date) books, Cowley has lectured and taught widely. A two-time president of the National Institute of Arts and Letters, he was for ten years chancellor of the American Academy of Arts & Letters. Cowley lives, with his second wife, in a converted barn in Sherman, Connecticut.

MOTHER AND SON

My mother died in Pittsburgh on the evening of Thanksgiving Day, that is, on November 25, 1937. If she had lived three weeks longer sh would have been 73.

She died in the Wallace Building, three stories of grimy yellow br in the commercial center of the district known as East Liberty. Even at night streetcars grumbled past two sides of the building. It had s on the ground floor, some of them expensive, though *even these* had taken to changing owners. The upper stories contained a few cramped apartments like ours, but were mostly occupied by music teachers--voice, piano, v olin--and by a few unprosperous physicians who lived next to their of- fices. Every two or three years there was a fire in the building, but it was always brought under control. During one fire Mother stood shi ering in the street *beside my father* and watched firemen playing their hoses on the roo "Oh, Doctor," she said, "I forgot to empty the pan under the icebox." She emptied the pan next morning when they went back to the apartment and found it not much damaged except by smoke.

She had lived in the Wallace Building since it was spanking new a she was a bride. She died there in a little room lined ceiling-high w my father's books, which she never opened, and dimly lighted by an ai shaft. She died of a heart illness that, in its acute form, had last a little more than three weeks, although it went back to another atta two years before, *as always,* when she was spending the summer in the country. T first attack would have killed an ordinary woman, but Mother had brou herself through it by her pure determination to live. In her extreme pain she had sometimes moaned "Mamma, Mamma," as if begging for solac

First page of a Malcolm Cowley autobiographical piece entitled *Mother and Son.*

Malcolm Cowley

This interview was conducted in two places dear to Malcolm Cowley, and which suggest the two main areas of his literary life. One conversation took place in the Harvard Club's Card Room, a cubbyhole in the New York club's upstairs warrens. Cowley often lunches at the club on the days when he comes into New York from his Connecticut home to perform his editing duties at Viking Press. A second talk held at Cowley's Connecticut home, where he is freer to do his own writing. Cowley's manner is brisk, his voice hearty. He wears a hearing aid, but that is his only visible concession to his years.

Thomas H. Guinzburg, who was Cowley's former publisher and employer at the Viking Press, wrote the following upon reading this interview: ". . . fellow readers will gain the strong impression Cowley is determined to resist the constant invasions of his time. Do not believe him. Malcolm has always given ample time to any of us who were perceptive enough to seek it, frequently delaying his own more valuable projects in the process. Cowley missed the golden payday when editors suddenly became stars and found themselves negotiating their names onto book jackets and title pages. Nor did he ever adopt the 'New York' scene. He and his wife, Muriel, continue to live and work in Sherman, Connecticut, and from his one-man assembly line there continues to pour out our most accurate impressions of the life and times of American twentieth-century writing and publishing."

INTERVIEWERS: How would you compare the lot of writers today with when you started?

COWLEY: In many ways things are easier now for writers. Sixty years ago there were no such things as writing fellowships; there were no Guggenheims . . . very few prizes. There were almost no teaching posts for writers. So the would-be writers came to New York and tried to get a job on a newspaper. Usually they ended up in an advertising agency, or they starved in the Village. Free-lance work was paid for at the rate of about a penny a word for reviews. *The New Republic* and *The Dial* paid two cents; that was high, and besides, you were always glad to be printed in those magazines.

The only chance for higher pay was with fiction, in the glossies. These had enormous circulations for that time, and they were paying good rates for fiction. *The Saturday Evening Post* went up to $4,000 per story with F. Scott Fitzgerald, and I don't think that was absolutely their top rate. A couple of other writers earned up to $50,000 every year writing short stories. Fiction was the field and remained so until the disappearance of the family magazine in the thirties and forties, one after the other going, until now it is the devil's own job to get fiction published, even for people who are very good at it. But still, by and large, the writer has an easier time of it than a few decades ago.

INTERVIEWERS: What about the poets?

COWLEY: There's been an enormous change. As late as 1930 there were only a few men and women who supported themselves as poets. One was Robert Frost and another was Oscar Hammerstein II. We had great respect for e.e. cummings because he lived as a poet, but even he got a little money from his mother. T. S. Eliot was a bank clerk, and then worked with Faber & Faber, the publishers. Robert Frost managed to support himself after *North of Boston* by readings, and by lecturing at universities. He rather blazed a trail in that respect. Now, a lot of poets are poets primarily. Many of them may teach or read their poetry to keep up, but probably two or three hundred people in the United States if asked their trade would say "poet."

INTERVIEWERS: Do you regret not having concentrated more fully on your poetry?

COWLEY: Yes, I have regretted it very much. The shift, for me, was the essential middle-class feeling that I had to support myself.

INTERVIEWERS: What were you paid for *Blue Juniata?*

COWLEY: I got an advance of $125 and no further payments.

INTERVIEWERS: That was why you didn't go on?

COWLEY: I wanted to go on writing poetry, but I always had the feeling that I couldn't write any poem that didn't come to me. I didn't say to myself, "Go spend two hours and write a poem." Perhaps I should have. Of course, if I'd had a few more dollars I would have written more poetry. Book reviewing didn't help. Odd: being an editor didn't interfere with my writing; it was being an editor *and* a book reviewer. You find that you put everything you've got into anything you write. There may not be so much left over.

INTERVIEWERS: There are many excuses for not writing.

COWLEY: Pipes are one of the best. I can use one even to keep from talking. And there's always a letter to be written. One of the great penalties of having been around for a long time is that there is hardly a genuine letter in the mail I receive. It's rare that one of my letters isn't a request for information about somebody on whom the requester is doing a dissertation. Jesus! Well, at least I don't have Edmund Wilson's great arrogance of sending back a printed card saying that he won't do it. I do reply. I generally refer them to other sources.

INTERVIEWERS: You're probably considered a soft touch.

COWLEY: I keep hoping I'll be compensated in some way. Once I wrote a piece that tried to sum up the joys and vexations of being eighty, but I left out one of the worst vexations— which is to become a national scholarly resource. I never expected to become a national scholarly resource—but you can't escape the destiny of your dotage. Simply by having outlived your great contemporaries, you find that you have a field all to yourself; or if you don't have a field, at least you have a stable in one corner of the field. Hundreds of scholars then come into the field who are writing dissertations, monographs, biographies—all sorts of things—and for each one they want to have a little reinforcement, a little supplement; they want to have a word straight from the horse's mouth. So they come to me and say, "Well, you are the horse—won't you please share your memories? Won't you please answer this little questionnaire of five single-spaced typed pages?" or, "Won't you let us put your memories on tape?" There is no enrichment from this sort of thing. Not one of them thinks of filling the horse's feed-box with oats or of putting a little hay in the manger. They assume, I guess, that a horse can just forage for himself—if he has time; certainly nobody gives him an offer to earn an easy living by putting himself out to stud.

INTERVIEWERS: You're making us feel guilty. Do you mind if we ask you about Gertrude Stein's remark, "You are all a lost generation"?

COWLEY: Oh, it's simple as all get-out. Gertrude Stein was having her Model-T Ford repaired at a garage in the south of France. The mechanics weren't very good; they weren't on the job—in fact, I think they were on strike. The proprietor said to Miss Stein, "These young men are no good—they are all a lost generation"—*une génération perdue.* So an unknown French garageman should get credit for that remark. Of course, Miss Stein deserves credit for picking up on the phrase.

INTERVIEWERS: Is it possible the garageman was referring to "a lost generator"?

COWLEY: Her French was better than that.

INTERVIEWERS: Was there a special sense, a feeling, about being an artist, or writer, at that time?

COWLEY: The writers had an odd advantage in being born around 1900. The century had turned, so as they grew older they began to feel that it was their century—new, unprecedented. This doesn't mean that they all thought they were wonderful people, but they did think that their lives represented the fate of the new world, no less. That feeling is very strong in Scott Fitzgerald, for example, and in other writers, too; there's something of it in Dos Passos and cummings.

INTERVIEWERS: What were some of the English-language magazines in Europe when you arrived?

COWLEY: The first one that I ran into in Paris was *Gargoyle,* edited by two characters from Greenwich Village, Arthur Moss and Florence Gilliam. Then, in 1921, Gorham D. Munson and Matthew Josephson arrived, and they got out *Secession.* Matty became a friend of the French Dadaists; he was wonderful at making acquaintances. Next he got a job on *Broom,* which Harold Loeb had started and published in Rome; then, with Matty as managing editor, the magazine moved to Berlin, where everything was fabulously cheap. Matty had a salary of one hundred dollars per month, for which he had a triplex apartment and riding lessons for his wife.

After that came the other magazines. The great Paris magazine was Eugene Jolas's *Transition.* There was an extremely vivid sense that a new type of writing was coming along. Something had to change after the war that had shaken civilization;

here were all these people who regarded the older magazines as stuffy, commercial, not giving a voice to younger people. So the magazines were started partly with the idea that a new generation was coming onto the scene, and that they should have periodicals that spoke for them and introduced new talents. Ernest Walsh did that in *This Quarter.* Ford Madox Ford started *The Transatlantic Review* and was very much interested in the younger Americans.

INTERVIEWERS: Did you ever see Pound in Paris?

COWLEY: I went to see him a couple of times, but I was a little uneasy with him. Pound always had some new discovery or enthusiasm; he was always finding the lowdown on something. On one of my visits to his little apartment, he announced loudly, "I've got the lowdown on the Elizabethan drama! It was all cribbed from these books," and he carried out two huge volumes of the Venetian State Papers. Well, it *was* a real discovery: the plots of several Elizabethan plays *did* come out of the Venetian State Papers.

INTERVIEWERS: Why did Hemingway have such an apparent dislike for Ford Madox Ford?

COWLEY: Hemingway had the bad habit of never forgiving anyone for giving him a hand up. That may have been the problem between them. Ford was a character; he was a liar, not for his own profit, but just because he had a very faint hold on actuality. He told beautiful stories of English literary life, in which he knew everybody, had a hand in everything, and his hand grew larger as he told the story. He had a roving eye for younger women, whom he especially liked to fascinate. He came to this country after the breakup of his marriage to Stella Bowen. I can remember on one occasion he came up to Robber Rocks—a place back in the woods near the New York–Connecticut line which was the country headquarters for Allen Tate, Hart Crane, and others—where a lot of young wives were around at the party. They would be fondled by Ford, and then escape him up the stairs. Ford, heavy and wheezing by that time, would follow them to the head of the narrow stairs, and the door would close in his face. He would wheeze back down, and a while later he'd follow another young woman until she took refuge behind a locked door.

INTERVIEWERS: Do you think collecting in such colonies is of value to a writer? It doesn't seem to be done as much these days.

COWLEY: Perhaps that is true. But I think young writers always collect, and that is a good thing, because the persons they learn from, their real professors, are other writers of the same age. That particular neighborhood, near Robber Rocks, was cheap. The Rocks was owned by Slater Brown, but others rented rooms from a woman called Aunt Addie Turner, who lived in a great barn of a house that had once been a boys' school. She rented out parts of it for eight dollars a month. A few miles over the Connecticut line was another group—Josephine Herbst, John Hermann, Nathan Asch, and a couple of others.

INTERVIEWERS: What sort of boarder was Hart Crane?

COWLEY: He was rather difficult. You forgave Hart a great deal because he was so kind and helpful. But then he'd get drunk and start throwing furniture out of the window. Or he'd stagger around the house with a lighted kerosene lamp.

INTERVIEWERS: I take it that for him alcohol acted as a stimulus to the creative process?

COWLEY: One of the reasons why Hart, and many writers, turn into alcoholics is that early in their lives they find that getting drunk is part of the creative process, that it opens up visions. It's a terrible sort of creative device, because three out of four who involve themselves in it become alcoholics. But it does open up doors in the beginning. Hart Crane would even make a first draft when he was drunk; he'd come out and read it, and say, "Isn't this the greatest poem ever written?" It wasn't. But then he would work over it patiently, dead sober, for several weeks, and it would amount to something. Not the greatest poem ever written, but still extraordinary.

INTERVIEWERS: Did Crane get any help from his family?

COWLEY: Hart's father had been quite wealthy until 1929. He invented the Lifesaver candy with a hole in it. "Crane's Chocolates" used to advertise in *The Saturday Evening Post.* But Hart was estranged from his father after his parents were divorced. The father remarried after the Crash and started a quite fashionable country restaurant named Canary Cottage in Chagrin Falls, outside of Cleveland. Still, he couldn't have helped Hart much.

INTERVIEWERS: Did Faulkner write under the influence of alcohol?

COWLEY: I rather think he did in his early years. He always hesitated to admit it, but I'm sure that a good many of his things were written when he'd been drinking. It didn't break him. And he did an extraordinary amount of revision, but he would try to preserve the integrity of that original vision, so that his rewriting was not so much line for line as it was shifting episodes and characters.

INTERVIEWERS: What did his manuscript pages look like? Did he make many corrections on the galleys?

COWLEY: He made them in the case of one book, *Sanctuary.* Otherwise his corrections were usually made in typescripts.

INTERVIEWERS: Writers so often complain about the horrors of writing.

COWLEY: Almost all of them are certainly procrastinators, but a few people really like to write. Kay Boyle used to say that she loved the smell of paper. Anthony Trollope trained himself to turn out forty-nine pages of manuscript a week, seven pages a day, and he was so rigorous about keeping to that exact number of pages that if he finished a novel halfway through the last day, he'd write the title of a new book and "Chapter One" on the next page and go right on until he'd done his proper quota of seven pages.

INTERVIEWERS: Do you think American writers are more prone to procrastinate than British writers?

COWLEY: American authors are more self-conscious than the British . . . a little more preoccupied with what the critics will say. The writer's problem is largely one of self-esteem. He thinks, "Is what I am writing worthy of the picture I have formed of my talent?" A lot of writers have only one book in them. Margaret Mitchell wrote *Gone With the Wind*—then she never even tried to write another book. A lot of writers keep publishing what is essentially the same book with different titles.

INTERVIEWERS: Can success be harmful?

COWLEY: They tell me that success is a terrible test of people. Thank God I've never had to undergo it. But nationwide success with money pouring in will kill lots of writers. Ross Lockridge, who wrote *Raintree County*, and Thomas Heggen, the author of that novel about a ship, *Mister Roberts*, both committed suicide. It was always said that Gilbert Seldes's review of *The Great Gatsby*, which was ecstatic, probably damaged Scott Fitzgerald. The trouble is that after something like that, every work has to count . . . every word has to live up to this marvelous praise. The poor author gets stage fright.

INTERVIEWERS: Are the creative impulses involved in writing poetry and essays vastly different?

COWLEY: There is a different process involved: the poem has to start with an emotion. After that, you call on the same parts of your mind during the creative process, but the beginning is quite different. With the essay you start out with a given or chosen subject. The poem comes to you.

INTERVIEWERS: Are there mnemonic devices to get you going on a day's work?

COWLEY: A lot of people use walking. I wonder if the decline of walking will lead to a decline of the creative process.

INTERVIEWERS: Do you see a relationship between unhappiness and poetic creativity?

COWLEY: To the extent that poems may be born from a straining of one's senses and imagination to a degree to which they couldn't be strained in ordinary life. I was reading F. Scott Fitzgerald's correspondence the other day. Scott and Zelda's difficulties were ones that I never had to face; I never had to drive myself to drink in order to get my imagination working. Actually, I found my imagination worked best on fatigue. That's another form of intoxication . . . to set yourself writing, and keep on writing until after two or three hours the subconscious takes over. It's certainly safer than alcohol. The trouble with alcohol is that you can't keep it up.

I went to visit the Fitzgeralds when they were living outside of Baltimore—a place called "La Paix." Scott said to me, "I'm on the wagon, but I got you a pint of whiskey from my bootlegger; I'm on water." So we talked, or mostly *he* talked, and every once in a while he'd go out to the kitchen to get another glass of water. His talk became more belligerent, sometimes incoherent, until finally he said, "You know, that water I've been drinking all evening—it's half grain alcohol." I said to myself, "Oh . . . surprise!"

INTERVIEWERS: So alcohol is of no use?

COWLEY: Sometimes Edmund Wilson said a glass of whiskey would get him started on a piece—would help with the start and perhaps the finish. But usually the writer is sober when he writes. He had better be. John Cheever used to say he could tell from a writer's work if he'd had a drink.

INTERVIEWERS: It's been reported that you discovered John Cheever.

COWLEY: Nobody ever discovered John Cheever; he discovered himself. But what you ask about was as close to discovery as an editor can hope for. I was the junior editor on *The New Republic* in 1930. A manuscript came in marked for my attention; it was a story on yellow copy paper called "Expelled from Prep School." I read it with great interest and carried it to Bruce Bliven, the managing editor. Bruce said, "Well, it's a little long. Cut it down by half and we'll take it." We did take it. A couple of months after that, John Cheever himself appeared. He was eighteen. His brother had given him an allowance of ten dollars a week to try to be a writer in New York. That memoir was the first I read of John's. He began writing stories—published in small magazines that didn't pay . . . always stories about seven thousand words in length, very fresh and good, too, but with no hope of their being published by magazines that paid money.

One Friday night when John was at our house for dinner, I told him, "Tomorrow, write a story of one thousand words. Sunday, write another, and Monday write another, three and a half pages, and do the same thing on Tuesday." Wednesday was my day at *The New Republic* for seeing contributors, so I said, "Bring them all in on Wednesday and I'll see if I can't get you some money."

Well, this sounds like wise old Nestor telling a young author what to do. But I knew John; nobody else could have invented four stories in four days. But on Wednesday he brought in four thousand-word stories. *The New Republic* didn't print fiction, but I thought one of them could be considered local color. So I got that one accepted, and I sent the other three stories to Katharine White at *The New Yorker*. She took two of them, and John was launched on his career as a professional writer.

INTERVIEWERS: Who worked with William Faulkner at Random House?

COWLEY: A succession of people, but they didn't really work with him at first. I don't think they always read proofs of his novels, at least in the late 1930s, because some of them are marred by errors in grammar that Faulkner would have been glad to have pointed out to him, and would have fixed up. But he absolutely could not have stomached receiving a critique on the whole concept of a book—the sort of thing that Maxwell Perkins at Scribners might have put together—and he certainly would not have written a book to order.

INTERVIEWERS: And yet he spent those years in Hollywood.

COWLEY: Cynically. He didn't think he was actually any good in Hollywood. He was able to work consistently with only one director, and that was Howard Hawks. One thing that has never been published about Faulkner is that he thought his best movie was *The Southerner,* the Jean Renoir film, for which he did not get movie credit. He was under contract to Warner Brothers and could not let it be known that he had worked for another studio.

INTERVIEWERS: What about your own remarkable identification with Faulkner's work?

COWLEY: I shouldn't be given all the credit for rescuing Faulkner from neglect. There were always men of letters in this country—Conrad Aiken, Robert Penn Warren, and a couple of others, Caroline Gordon, especially—who were enthusiastic about Faulkner's writing. But it is true that public estimation of his books sank so low that by the middle of the war, only one book, *Sanctuary,* was not out of print; his publishers had donated the plates of his other novels to the war effort to be melted down and to make copper jacketings for bullets. The publishers were very patriotic. So at that time I had the strong feeling that Faulkner had to be brought back. I had done a Hemingway Portable for the Viking Press, a book that came early in their series of Portables. I had suggested, "Why not a Faulkner Portable?" Viking replied, "We don't think Faulkner has sufficient public to justify a Portable." That wasn't enough for me. Fortunately, through Matty Josephson I had been offered a contract to write a history of American literature. I always hated big undertakings—the sort of thing he suggested—so I thought I'd break it down and do one author at a time. Since I'd been reading Faulkner and believed that among the writers of his generation his public reputation was the one most out of line with his extraordinary talent, the choice was compulsive. I took about ninety single-spaced pages of notes. Then I began writing an essay which got to be too long for any magazine to print as a whole. So I "beefed" it— I got that phrase from George Milburn, a writer and a good one, too, who came from the back country in Oklahoma. He told me that he had beefed a novel by cutting it into steaks and selling them to *The New Yorker.* I beefed the essay on Faulkner and sold chunks of it to three magazines.

At the time I was helped financially by an extraordinary piece of good luck. It was during the war. The phone rang, and the voice at the other end said, "This is Stanley Young. How would you like to be supported for five years?" I wrote him, "Well, I'd like that fine, but I'm getting along all right. Why don't you make that offer to Kenneth Burke?"—who was my oldest friend. Stanley said, "Oh, no. We'll think about Kenneth later. In the meantime, we'd like you to figure out how much it would take you to live for five years." He went on to explain. "This is an idea of Mary Mellon's, of the Pittsburgh Mellons. You come in and have lunch with Mary and if you pass muster this idea of hers will go through."

So I had lunch with Mary Mellon. I think I drank too many martinis. I talked very much and excitedly. So it went through. For five years I received, under contract with Mary Mellon, fifty-five hundred dollars per year, which seemed a great deal of money to me.

Four other people got this arrangement. Then it was decided the plan wasn't working. When Mary Mellon died, Paul Mellon closed out all the contracts, which he was quite right to do. As a matter of fact, I was the only one of the five authors who carried through on the aim of the plan. It enabled me to do a great deal of work on authors, including Faulkner, while at the same time being rather standoffish about publication.

Of course, it could have been an opportunity to write poetry, but I kept remembering that the arrangement was only for five years. At the end of that time I would still have to live mostly by writing for magazines. So I "beefed"—cut steaks and roasts from—the long Faulkner essay and published them.

One day Marshall Best of the Viking Press called and said, "It seems to us that Faulkner's work is attracting a good deal of attention in magazines. We're thinking of going ahead with the Faulkner Portable." I said, modestly, "Yes. It is attracting a good deal of attention." I had this idea of putting together an outline of the Yoknapatawpha County saga in the Portable. I also had an idea that Faulkner might help me on this with advice. It turned out he was most eager to do so.

So we worked through this, discussing by letter what should go in and what should stay out—a correspondence published in a book called *The Faulkner–Cowley File*. At the end of it Faulkner wrote and added a biographical dictionary of the Compson family. When the Portable came out, Faulkner inscribed a copy to me, writing, "Damn you, you've done what was supposed to be the occupation of my declining years." Apparently, that's what he had wanted one day to do himself.

INTERVIEWERS: Was the Faulkner Portable an immediate success?

COWLEY: The Portable couldn't have started a renewed interest in Faulkner's work if it hadn't been for Caroline Gordon, who did a front-page review for *The New York Times,* and Robert Penn Warren, who reviewed it for *The New Republic* in an article so long that it had to be published in two issues. From that time on, Faulkner, who had been completely beneath the dignity of English departments to talk about, began to be studied by graduate students.

INTERVIEWERS: What was your personal relationship with Faulkner?

COWLEY: Beginning in 1944 we had quite a correspondence. I wrote him a letter saying I wanted to do a piece about his work. I hoped to meet him. After four or five months he answered from Hollywood. He explained that when he got letters from strangers, first he opened them to see if there was return postage. If there was, he used the stamps. As for the letters, he'd drop them in a drawer and then, he said, every six months or so he'd open the drawer and begin to read the letters. Mine had been luckier; it had only waited in the drawer three or four months. He wrote me that the idea of finishing his career without having attracted any more attention than he had done so far was painful and, yes, he would be grateful to have a long essay written about him, but he didn't want any personal details included. He wanted to live anonymously. He wrote me in one of his letters that he wanted his tombstone inscribed, "He wrote the books and he died."

INTERVIEWERS: Did you know that there is an odd typographical error on his tombstone in Oxford, Mississippi? It reads, "Belove'd Go to God." It was probably supposed to say "Belovèd Go to God," but the carver misread the accent mark for an apostrophe.

COWLEY: I think he would have smiled at that.

INTERVIEWERS: Was he a good storyteller in person?

COWLEY: He would tell a story very much as stories were told on the "gallery," as they call it, of a little one-room store in Mississippi—men squatting on their heels in overalls and chewing tobacco. He didn't chew tobacco, but he told stories the way backwoods storytellers told them, which was very entertaining. He wasn't one of them, but he fit in. In Oxford they called him "Count No 'Count."

INTERVIEWERS: Did Faulkner know Hemingway?

COWLEY: Hemingway and Faulkner never met, but they read each other and profited by the reading, Faulkner especially. It's largely a question of emulation that causes writers to appear as if in groups. Even if they never meet, they read each other.

INTERVIEWERS: Hemingway's life has always been closely linked to his work. Now that his private letters have been published, what effect do you think they'll have on his reputation?

COWLEY: His reputation as a man will go down because there's a great deal of malice, rivalry, and plain falsehood in his letters. All his weaknesses of character come out, and in the published letters they're not balanced or driven from your mind by his tremendous personality. He had a gift for charming people by giving them his undivided attention. As he said, so few people know how to listen. That's one way he charmed people, by listening. At the same time he was always suggesting expeditions and adventures, so that in personal relations he had an enormous charm that doesn't come through in the letters.

INTERVIEWERS: It's difficult to reconcile this charm with the impression one gets from the letters.

COWLEY: Well, he wrote those letters very often late at night when he couldn't sleep. Frequently he wouldn't mail the letters because they told too much. But I think if you sit back from that collection of printed letters and consider what he's saying, you can begin to get a picture of his charm, because for each of the persons he was writing to he had adopted a different story. He was projecting himself into their different personalities.

INTERVIEWERS: I recall Selden Rodman's comparing Hemingway to Byron and saying that Hemingway's genius was essentially comic.

COWLEY: Comic isn't the word. He was never a comic writer. He was often a satirist, and a cruel one.

INTERVIEWERS: What would you say was the essence of his genius?

COWLEY: A sort of restoration to literature of various primal qualities. There's almost the quality of a medieval lyric in much of Hemingway's writing. It's fresh. If you read *Le Morte d'Arthur,* the chapter that begins with the month of May at King Arthur's court, there's a freshness in it that one finds again in Hemingway.

I think he is a lyric writer, more or less. He always had trouble with plots because he wasn't so much filling out a plot as he was making a journey or progression, day by day. Later he would try to fit that into a plot. If it came out well, it came out very well indeed. At other times he stumbled off the path, as in two or three of his unpublished manuscripts.

INTERVIEWERS: Despite these difficulties with plot, he was a very good storyteller?

COWLEY: As a storyteller in company he was amazing. He was even more amazing in the matter of simple vitality. When he came into a room, he filled it, as people say.

INTERVIEWERS: Were his ethics as great as his vitality?

COWLEY: As a writer his ethics were very strong . . . that is, his ethics governing the relationship between his "me" and the product of "me"; it would be hard to find any higher. But as a man in relation to other writers—Dos Passos, for instance—his ethics were lower than a snake's belly.

INTERVIEWERS: This question of ethics in relation to fiction seems to be a current critical concern. What is your opinion of John Gardner's contention, in *On Moral Fiction,* that fiction must point out a moral, or that the worth of fiction can be assessed in terms of the ethic it espouses?

COWLEY: He's got hold of a half-truth. Any fiction should be a story. In any story there are three elements: persons, a situation, and the fact that in the end something has changed. If nothing has changed, it isn't a story. Almost every story, therefore, becomes a fable, because the change is usually for better or worse. And if the reader extends the applicability of this change from a particular set of events to another, then he's drawn out of the story a fable with a moral. And, of course, every work of fiction involves moral judgments concerning the characters . . . judgments that the author reveals by his style or his choice of details, if in no other fashion.

There is another sense as well in which not only fiction, but all kinds of writing, are moral. Almost every work set on paper involves a choice. The writing of one page might involve hundreds of moral decisions. "Shall I use this word, which easily comes to hand, or shall I stop and search my mind for a slightly better word?" Those are aesthetic decisions which almost always have a moral element. Choosing the hard over the easy is already a moral choice.

INTERVIEWERS: Faced with moral considerations, can you as a critic render a positive judgment of a book's aesthetics while at the same time disliking its meaning?

COWLEY: I can do that, yes. I might wish that the author had a different set of morals. And I can also make my judgment by not reading the book—a very easy way to get around it.

INTERVIEWERS: What do you find yourself reading nowadays?

COWLEY: I too often pick up magazines. I read *The Nation, The New Republic, The New York Review,* and sometimes *The New Yorker,* against which my complaint is that the articles are too long. If I get hooked on one, the evening is shot.

INTERVIEWERS: Has there been a change in the character of the publishing houses?

COWLEY: It's always been a strange profession; publishers and editors seem to change jobs more than men in other professions. They go from house to house like baseball players . . . except they're not sold, or traded. Those who really change places are the publicity directors . . . musical chairs!

INTERVIEWERS: What about the relationship between the editor and the author?

COWLEY: These days there's a good deal more directed writing in which bright young publishers or editors dream up an idea for a book and then think of somebody to write it. Part of the creative process, at least in nonfiction, has moved over from the writer to the editor.

INTERVIEWERS: What would someone like Maxwell Perkins have made of this trend?

COWLEY: Perkins wasn't much interested in nonfiction. But with fiction, he took a tremendous hand . . . concerned with motivation, the handling of scenes, and the overall picture of a book . . . so much so that he was capable of writing ninety pages of directions and suggestions. He did this for Marcia Davenport's *The Valley of Decisions*. She put Max's directions to the left of her typewriter and her original manuscript on the right; she looked at Max's directions, then at the manuscript, and she retyped the book. It subsequently became very successful.

INTERVIEWERS: What are the distinguishing attributes of a good publishing house editor?

COWLEY: The first ingredient would be a nose for good writers. And then loyalty to the writer once he found him. The most loyal editor in the whole game was Pat Covici at the Viking Press, who was loyal to his authors in a way that made the authors completely loyal to him. He did this with his interest, his confidence, his offer of whatever help they needed. Steinbeck wrote a whole volume of letters to Pat when he was working on *East of Eden*.

INTERVIEWERS: What about an editor's attitude towards public taste?

COWLEY: If an editor begins to let the concept of catering to the public weigh on him he becomes, to me, a bad editor. An editor should have an idea of what meets his own taste; that should provide the criterion. The whole notion of divining the public taste has been one of the deadliest ideas of publishing. When *True Confessions* was at the height of its success, a new fiction editor was picked every month. She would be one of the typists in the office, preferably the youngest, because it was felt that if she followed her own honest feeling about what was good, that was what the public wanted. After a month or so, she would become too sophisticated and then they would fire her as the fiction editor and take on another typist. That was cynicism carried to the extreme, but it may well have produced better results than an editor guessing at what the public might like.

INTERVIEWERS: What has been the most rewarding aspect of your long career in literature?

COWLEY: Writing becomes its own reward. What do you need from others—except a little money—if you have satisfied the stern critic in yourself? For me the most rewarding moments have been those when I knew that a book was finished at last and ready to be printed. I remember one such moment; it was when I finished the revised edition of *Exile's Return,* in 1951. I had worked on the revision happily, being a revisionist by instinct, and most of the manuscript had gone to the printer. But there was a necessary appendix still to come, and it had to reach the Viking Press by a certain date or else the book would be postponed to another season. I have the story in an old notebook. (*There is a long pause while Cowley finds and pages through the notebook.*)

The date for Viking was March 30, 1951. I finished and sealed and addressed the appendix at half-past eight in the evening of March 29. In those fortunate days there was a mail car on the train that left Pawling at 9:05, and letters given to the clerk were delivered in New York the following morning. Pawling was a dozen miles from our house, over back roads. I drove there with Muriel and our son Rob and missed the train by three minutes. Then I raced it fifteen miles south to Brewster, at the risk of wiping out the family. This time the train was pulling out of the station just as we pulled in. I raced it again to Croton Falls, where Rob ran hard and gave my big envelope to the mail clerk just as the wheels of the engine started to turn. At last the book was out of my hands, finished to my satisfaction, and I was exultant. We drove home slowly while I sang old songs in a cracked voice.

JOHN McCALL
GEORGE PLIMPTON
Spring 1981

2. Arthur Koestler

Arthur Koestler was born September 5, 1905, in Budapest. From 1922 to 1926, he studied math and science at the University of Vienna, where he became deeply involved in the Zionist movement, ultimately leaving for Palestine without taking his degree. He held various odd jobs throughout the Middle East before becoming the Cairo correspondent for the German *Ullstein Verlag*; later he became the foreign editor of that publication.

From 1931 to 1938 Koestler was a member of the German Communist Party, and during that period he lived for a year in the Soviet Union. While reporting on German and Italian involvement in the Spanish Civil War, he was captured by the Fascists and condemned to death as a spy. The British Foreign Office was able to obtain his release but only after three months of harrowing uncertainty, later recounted in *Spanish Testament* (1938) and *Dialogue with Death* (1942).

After leaving the Communist Party, he wrote his first novel, *The Gladiators* (1939), concerning the Spartacus slave revolt in Rome. In 1940 he wrote *Darkness at Noon,* his most popular novel and the last written in German. Two later novels, *The Invisible Writing* (1954) and *The God That Failed* (1950), chronicle his involvement—and disillusionment—with the Communist Party. Other works of fiction include *Arrival and Departure* (1943), *Thieves in the Night* (1946), *The Age of Longing* (1951), and *The Call Girls* (1972).

Koestler lived in England from 1940 on, becoming a British subject in 1948. In 1965 his longtime secretary, Cynthia Jeffries, became his third wife. She and Koestler died together in March 1983 in a suicide pact. The following interview was the last Arthur Koestler granted before his death.

among my closest friends; the idea of the anthology was conceived one late
evening when he and his wife Zita were staying with us in ~~North Wales~~ Bwlch Ocyn. They
were also among our first weekend guests in Verte Rive, together with Michael
Foot (another close friend of the period) and his wife, ~~Silix~~ Jill. Dick
was a brilliant, outgoing and warm personality, but he was also an incurably
opportunistic politician, as his diaries while a Cabinet Minister quite
plainly reveal~~ed~~. Thus it is amusing to read in his Introduction, to the book after
describing that evening in Wales when the project had been hatched: "We were
not in the least interested... in swelling the flood of anti-Communist
propaganda". That of course was precisely what we were interested in, but
for a Labour M.P. in those days it just wouldn't do to say so in as many
words. At any rate, The God That Failed (the title was invented by Dick)
became a kind of household word and seemed to have been quite effective in
"swelling the flood of anti-Communist propaganda", to judge by the number
of reprints and foreign translations.

~~Verte Rive solved the problem where~~ to live, at least for the time
being; it did not solve that other problem, what to live for — in other
~~words what type of book to write.~~ ¶ When I finished my piece for The God That
Failed, I thought I had at last done with writing on political subjects for
the rest of my life. I had been labouring under the same illusion when I
fled London for ~~that lonely sheep farm in~~ Wales to write Insight and Outlook,
~~an essay on the creative process in science, art and humour~~ In the preface I had promised
the reader a second volume "which is in preparation and will, it is hoped,
appear twelve months after the first." But all I had to show for ~~£~~ Volume
Two was a chaotic jumble of notes, the mere sight of which gave me indigestio
After a hopeless struggle I had to shelve Volume Two "for the time being".
In actual fact, it never saw the light of day. Its place was taken by The
Act of Creation, published fifteen years later. In 1949, I was obviously not
ready to embark on that rather ambitious undertaking. ~~They left me free~~ and so I was
wheeling in a vacuum as it were. ~~I embarked on an autobiography, but after~~ This is when — in July 1949 — a new
arrival from Pretoria (entered) unobtrusively my life. ~~the first chapter got stuck. Mamaine's illness added to my depression: she~~
~~was in a London nursing home under the care of a specialist for asthma whom~~

———————————————————————————————————————

*Macmillan, London, and New York, 19. (see Chapter).

Arthur Koestler

The Koestler drawing room is predominantly green with deep green walls. It has an Empire flavor, and there are interesting pieces of Egyptian sculpture in it. On the coffee table are Barbara Pym's Quartet in Autumn *and* The Dancing Wu Li Masters: An Overview of the New Physics.

Koestler is wearing the costume of the old Left—rough materials tending to light rather than dark, in his case to greenish, with nothing matching anything else: checked shirt, wool cardigan, tartan tie, tweed jacket, etc.

Sitting very uneasily in a pool of lamplight, Arthur Koestler seemed low. His wife, Cynthia, had opened the front door of their house in London's Montpelier Square. A gentle, soft, sad woman wearing no makeup, she had explained that Mr. Koestler was not at his best; he was recovering from a "viral infection," which is how the Koestlers describe a cold. She is much

*younger than he and began to work for Koestler in 1949.
Cynthia had watched him divorce two previous wives—Dorothy
in 1950, Mamaine in 1953—before taking her place officially
at his side in 1965. She has the slightly numb Buddhist detach-
ment of one who has spent a lifetime in surrender of her will
to another.*

*From the pool of lamplight Koestler mumbles about not
being too well. He casts about in the air a bit, rather abstract-
edly, then suddenly says, "I used to be a journalist—what is the
peg for this interview?"*

*It is evident that he dislikes being interviewed and, indeed,
consistently refuses. "And I'm recovering from a viral infection," he moans as the tape recorder is set up. He dislikes tape
recorders because, he says, he rambles when he talks. He dislikes
appearing on television and radio, "because my accent is too
thick and it embarrasses me." When asked about allowing a
photographer to come and take a picture, he cocks his head on
one side, frowns, and says, "I'd prefer to avoid it." One feels the
list of his dislikes is an extended one.*

INTERVIEWER: What do you dislike most of all?

KOESTLER: Stupidity more than anything. Including my own.

INTERVIEWER: You were born in Budapest in 1905. Into
what kind of family?

KOESTLER: Typical Central European Jewish middle-middle.
My father was Hungarian, my mother Viennese. I reviewed a
book once, *Last Waltz in Vienna.* It was about a family such
as mine, before the extermination. It's about the humdrum,
day-by-day life before the ceiling fell in.

INTERVIEWER: The ceiling?

KOESTLER: 1939, 1942 mostly, Auschwitz.

INTERVIEWER: What did your father do for a living?

KOESTLER: He was an industrialist. He had too much imagination. He financed disastrous inventions like the envelope-
opening machine. He said too much time is wasted opening

envelopes and big businesses need these machines. So one day a huge machine came into the house. It would have covered half that wall. The inventor came with it. He looked like one of Snow White's seven dwarfs the way he hopped around his machine. It was plugged into the electricity, turned on, there was an enormous clattering and shuddering, then flames started to lick here and there about it and we all got terribly scorched. Another invention he financed was radioactive soap. You must remember the time, 1918-ish, when curative properties were indiscriminately ascribed to radioactivity. The soap was supposed to make you glow with health and vitality, but it didn't catch on.

INTERVIEWER: You were at the university in Vienna in the twenties—did you know Freud?

KOESTLER: I interviewed him in 1938 in London. He died in Hampstead soon after.

INTERVIEWER: Was he important to you?

KOESTLER: When you grew up in Vienna you sucked in the ideas of psychoanalysis like mother's milk. My personal discovery of Jung was much later.

INTERVIEWER: Do you feel like an exile?

KOESTLER: When I go to France or Austria, then I feel that I'm abroad, that I'm British to the core. But when I get back here, then I feel a bit of an exile.

INTERVIEWER: An exile from where?

KOESTLER: Central Europe. No, let's say Europe in general because I spent thirteen years of my life in France.

INTERVIEWER: You were in a concentration camp there for four months—was that a useful experience?

KOESTLER: I was in a Spanish prison before that, in a death cell where I didn't know when my turn to be shot was coming. Afterwards the French camp was easy to bear. It taught me among other things the relativity of freedom. Solitary confinement is rock bottom, it's absolute unfreedom. I was in solitary most of the time.

INTERVIEWER: Was that frightening?

KOESTLER: In fact, I preferred solitary to sharing. It depends on the individual. But it's generally considered rock bottom.

INTERVIEWER: Have you ever felt you were going mad?

KOESTLER: No.

INTERVIEWER: What would be madness for you?

KOESTLER: At the University of Michigan there was an awfully nice English psychiatrist. It was because he was so nice that I first took the psilocybin mushroom there instead of at Harvard, although I knew Timothy Leary before he went into drugs. I had what is called a very bad trip.

INTERVIEWER: What did you dislike about it?

KOESTLER: Well, it was extremely frightening. When I was under, I noticed that the nice English psychiatrist had a scar on his neck—from a mastoid operation perhaps. His face went green and the scar started gaping as a wound and for some reason I thought, "Now at last the Gestapo have got me." Or was it the KGB? It was one of the two. The psychiatrist had a standard lamp and the base of it suddenly developed bird's claws. Then I flipped for a moment into normality and told myself, "You are hallucinating, that's all—if you touch the claws they'll go away." So I touched them. But they didn't go away. Not only a visual but also a tactile hallucination. It was very frightening. So when you ask me what madness is—it is when your perceptions are dramatically deviating from reality. That is not a scientific definition, however. When I came back from this experience of induced schizophrenia, the aftereffects lasted for several months. Timothy Leary went round the bend, of course. I came to the opposite view to Huxley's. These things have no particular spiritual value but they might have clinical value. For example, I think every psychiatrist should have a session with mescaline or LSD in order to know what a psychosis is like, what hallucinations are like. It should be part of the psychiatrist's curriculum.

INTERVIEWER: Why did you choose to go to England in 1940?

KOESTLER: My father was an Anglophile. He had business contacts here, frequently came to England, and told us tales. I had an English "Miss," as it was called—you say "Governess." Then I did journalism for the *News Chronicle*. I was their war correspondent in Spain and Palestine. And when in the war France collapsed in a most shameful way, I had only America or Britain. America was still neutral. So I came to England and enlisted. I had to join the Glorious Pioneers— "Digging for Victory," as their slogan went.

INTERVIEWER: George Orwell thought that a great insult to you, that you couldn't join the real army.

KOESTLER: It was the only regiment open to foreigners, although the French could go into the Free French Army, and the Poles had their own units too.

INTERVIEWER: You lived in Wales for a while.

KOESTLER: North Wales, three years, just about long enough. Then on and off to America after the war. But unlike many men in circumstances similar to mine, I didn't put down roots there. When I was in America, it became very obvious to me that I am a European.

INTERVIEWER: What do you like about England?

KOESTLER: The question should be reformulated. What *did* I like about England when I settled here? And what's my feeling now? These are different things.

INTERVIEWER: Are they dramatically different?

KOESTLER: No. It is a continuum. When I settled here, Europe was kaput. England was the only country left. What appealed to me was what Orwell described, those anonymous crowds, gentlemen with walking sticks, old maids bicycling to Holy Communion through the fog and the mist. A nation of darts players, pigeon fanciers. That in 1940 was still very close to the truth.

INTERVIEWER: The British Empire notwithstanding.

KOESTLER: Gentle knobbly faces with bad teeth and so on. Then history made a perverse somersault and it turned out that England was the only country that lost the war. In England you began to have phenomena like skinheads.

INTERVIEWER: You have a farmhouse in Suffolk. Why choose Suffolk?

KOESTLER: We had a house in the Austrian Tyrol for twenty years. Until ten years ago. I loved it. Then the tourists caught up with us and the village was ruined. I chose Suffolk to be near Cambridge. Also, I love the climate of East Anglia. You feel very braced by it and vigorous in the daytime, and at nighttime you sleep like a dormouse. Dry continental climate blowing over from Siberia.

INTERVIEWER: You opposed Fascism, then you ditched Communism.

KOESTLER: No, I didn't. Communism ditched me by turning into Stalinism.

INTERVIEWER: Do you have faith in any political philosophy?

KOESTLER: Nothing very original or specific now.

INTERVIEWER: Do you vote? Are you excited by the prospect of voting next time?

KOESTLER: I couldn't be more unexcited. I vote to participate, to play the game. That's all. Please don't let's talk about politics.

INTERVIEWER: Am I being too formal? I get the feeling that I'm being a bit wooden.

KOESTLER: You're doing all right, coping with a strange alien and feeling your way.

INTERVIEWER: Who was the saintliest man you ever met?

KOESTLER: I've met a lot of saintly people. I walked beside a saint in India. He was the head of the Boodan movement, which tried to persuade rich landowners to give their land to the poor. But Indian saints are quite different from Western ones. There were no hospitals until the British came, no concern for the poor. In India a saint is absolutely impervious to suffering—physical or economic.

INTERVIEWER: Who was the most exciting man you ever met?

KOESTLER: One was certainly Vladimir Jabotinski, an extremist Zionist leader. He's dead now. He was in Israel for a couple of years but the British didn't like him at all. Enormous leadership and charisma, an ability to make things happen, but beloved as well as followed.

INTERVIEWER: Do you believe in occultism?

KOESTLER: Do you mean hidden wise men in Tibet? No, no.

INTERVIEWER: Did you ever meet Gurdjieff or Aleister Crowley?

KOESTLER: No.

INTERVIEWER: Are you a religious man?

KOESTLER: Not in a denominational way. I'm attracted by mysticism.

INTERVIEWER: The Society for Psychical Research, ESP— that sort of thing?

KOESTLER: I do believe that the evidence for telepathy, for example, is overwhelming and that it is a part of reality that is above science. Science allows us to glimpse fragments of reality. There is another level, for the understanding of which our brains are not programmed. In other words, there are concepts, such as infinity in space and in time, which science cannot fathom. These concepts belong to a level of reality which is above our heads.

INTERVIEWER: Do you suffer from insomnia?

KOESTLER: No. I used to sleep seven hours a day. Now it's closer to nine, which is one of the disappointments of old age —they always promised one would sleep less. I sleep very well and always have, even in prison. (*Picks up a magazine clipping.*) Look at this. Did you ever see a magazine called the *New Musical Express*? It turns out there is a pop group called The Police—I don't know why they are called that, presumably to distinguish them from the punks—and they've made an album of my essay "The Ghost in the Machine." I didn't know anything about it until my clipping agency sent me a review of the record.

INTERVIEWER: It was in the hit parade.

KOESTLER: What's that it was in?

INTERVIEWER: The best-seller list for pop records. Didn't you get a copy of the record?

KOESTLER: No. I've had no contact with the group.

INTERVIEWER: But obviously you are pleased.

KOESTLER: A rather difficult book has become the inspiration for a pop group. It came as a great surprise to me. I'm slightly tickled by it.

INTERVIEWER: Do you write very easily?

KOESTLER: No. Very hard.

INTERVIEWER: Was German your first language?

KOESTLER: I was bilingual—Hungarian and German. I believe I'm the only writer who *twice* changed the language in which he writes, from Hungarian to German at seventeen years old, and from German to English at thirty-five. Since 1940 I have written only in English. But in any language it is a struggle to make a sentence say exactly what you mean.

INTERVIEWER: Is English better suited to your purposes than German?

KOESTLER: Oh yes, much. English has a muscularity with the fat massaged away. German is a very woolly language. French has a so-called Cartesian lucidity, but it's deceptive because it misses so much, a pseudolucidity because . . . no, cross that out, it's getting too complicated.

INTERVIEWER: What imaginative writers are important to you?

KOESTLER: No comment. That's list-making.

INTERVIEWER: What kind of food do you like?

KOESTLER: French.

INTERVIEWER: Are you a good cook?

KOESTLER: I used to be in my bachelor days.

INTERVIEWER: Do you watch television?

KOESTLER: Occasionally. Selectively.

INTERVIEWER: Cinema?

KOESTLER: Less and less. You can't go by car to a movie because of the parking problems. Which means hanging around for taxis—especially afterwards. For me, it's very rare that a movie nowadays is worth all the complications of getting there and back.

INTERVIEWER: Do you have a video machine?

KOESTLER: No.

INTERVIEWER: You should get one. What was the last film which excited you?

KOESTLER: *Close Encounters of the Third Kind* was the one I continued to remember afterwards.

INTERVIEWER: What are your vices?

KOESTLER: (*A very long pause.*) Is smoking a vice? I drink the normal amount. Malt whiskey usually. (*An even longer pause.*) Funny, I can't think of any vices. I'm trying but I can't.

INTERVIEWER: You try to be good. Do you succeed?

KOESTLER: Look at that Viking ship over there made out of balsa. For twenty years now there has been something called the Arthur Koestler Award for Prisoners, awarded to prisoners competing with paintings, model-making, writing, etc. It isn't much publicized because there's no point in doing so. That's my do-gooding side.

INTERVIEWER: What are your failures?

KOESTLER: Let's come back to what makes a good man. I don't know what makes a good man. I was active in the campaign for the abolition of capital punishment.

INTERVIEWER: Amnesty International?

KOESTLER: I'm a member, of course, but just in the normal way. I'm vice president of the Voluntary Euthanasia Society.

INTERVIEWER: Who is the president?

KOESTLER: There isn't one.

INTERVIEWER: Did he kill himself?

KOESTLER: No, there just isn't one at the moment.

Koestler, quite by surprise, begins to make a very peculiar noise, a wailing falsetto half-yodel. "Hoo-ooo-oo." I look about me but detect no obvious reason for it. Here it goes again. "Hoo-oo-ooooo!" with a sort of impatient upcurl in the tail of it. Eventually Cynthia appears up from her private lair downstairs and stands a touch tautly in the doorway of the drawing room. The wail, presumably, is her summons.

KOESTLER: Can we have some more drinks, angel? Because I want to get on with this. (*Two large watered malt whiskeys are eventually produced.*)

INTERVIEWER: Do you take holidays?

KOESTLER: I sometimes displace myself to a sunnier climate but I always take the office with me.

INTERVIEWER: Where to?

KOESTLER: The South of France, the Austrian Tyrol. I'm always working, you know. Nine-thirty until one. I have much reading to do and I'm a very slow reader, one of my misfortunes. If I'm reviewing a philosophical book it takes me a week to read it.

INTERVIEWER: What are the pleasures of reviewing?

KOESTLER: You force yourself to read very carefully and it triggers off unexpected trains of thought. Also you find yourself reading books you wouldn't normally read.

INTERVIEWER: You've resisted the temptation to become a guru figure, but do you get an enormous amount of "problem" mail?

KOESTLER: A huge amount. I don't answer the crank letters. The temptation to become the prophet is very great and very dangerous—it has to be resisted.

INTERVIEWER: Going on television once a week and telling

people the answer to life—that sort of thing?

KOESTLER: That does happen to people, you know, and it's very bad. My novel *The Call Girls* has something to do with this. I'm ambivalent about the mail in the morning. It's an awful bind. The fan mail is hell. But no fan mail would be a worse hell.

INTERVIEWER: Are you musical?

KOESTLER: I listen to music a lot, not very discriminatingly. Not at the opera or at concerts, but on the records. It's one of the few remaining joys in life, you know.

INTERVIEWER: Are you going to write about the silicon chip?

KOESTLER: I don't think so.

INTERVIEWER: Do you read newspapers?

KOESTLER: I read *The Times* and the heavy Sunday papers. I read *The New Scientist,* plus some technical stuff. Over half my work is reading up, you know.

INTERVIEWER: How long have you lived in this house?

KOESTLER: Since 1952.

INTERVIEWER: You were good friends with Orwell. Was he a happy man?

KOESTLER: That was the last thing he was.

INTERVIEWER: What about yourself?

KOESTLER: I'm a happy man only when work goes well.

INTERVIEWER: Will you keep on writing?

KOESTLER: You know, I would like to die in harness.

INTERVIEWER: What are you working on at the moment?

KOESTLER: Don't want to talk about that. Superstition. Vices . . .

INTERVIEWER: Oh good, you've thought of one.

KOESTLER: I'm a workaholic.

INTERVIEWER: An obsession with not wasting time.

KOESTLER: If I stop working and just try to enjoy myself, I get very neurotic and guilt-ridden. Orwell was the same. Like the man who, if he stops running, becomes afraid. Or the shark which must move to breathe. But I love playing games like Scrabble. That's not wasting time because it's an effort. Like climbing mountains, which I used to do too. Everything which is an effort is virtuous, is work, and is worth doing.

INTERVIEWER: Does your family try to persuade you to work less?

KOESTLER: My family is just my wife, Cynthia, and one dog —it used to be two dogs. Cynthia used to be my secretary, so she's part of the work too. A most stabilizing factor in marriage: shared work. (*Stands and walks to bookcase.*) Whenever I get depressed, which I often do, I come over here and look at this. My comforter. If ever I wonder what on earth it was all for, here is the evidence. The thirty books I've written plus all the translations. Forty-two different languages including English. Croatian, Ukrainian, Norwegian, Telugu . . . Russian? Oh yes, in *samizdat,* of course. Naturally, *Darkness at Noon* is my most popular book in Russia. I must have had something to say. There must be something in it after all.

INTERVIEWER: What makes you doubt there was something in it?

KOESTLER: If a writer loses his doubts then he's finished.

INTERVIEWER: Does there come a point when one has to stop doubting?

KOESTLER: Yes, death. But not until. When a writer loses his uncertainties he loses his humility—then he's finished. He'll just go on writing the same book like an idiot.

INTERVIEWER: Looking at that wall of books, are you searching for an answer?

KOESTLER: Oh yes. There is a British astronomer called Sir Thomas Gold. He tells a story of when he was going round America on a lecture tour explaining the Big Bang theory. There's a very old lady at one of the lectures who says, "Mister, I've got a much better theory about the universe. There's a huge tortoise with a thin covering of earth on its back—that's the universe." And Tommy Gold says, "But what is the tortoise standing on?" And she says, "On a much bigger tortoise, of course. It's no use arguing, Mister. It's tortoises all the way down." That just about sums it up. The cosmological quest— an infinite series of recessions. Ha!

DUNCAN FALLOWELL

3. William Maxwell

William Maxwell was born in Lincoln, Illinois, on August 16, 1908. He received his B.A. from the University of Illinois in 1930, and an M.A. from Harvard in 1931. Aside from a short time on the English faculty of the University of Illinois, from 1931 to 1933, Maxwell has lived most of his adult life in New York City, where he has enjoyed a long relationship with *The New Yorker* magazine, serving as a fiction editor from 1936 to 1976.

Maxwell's parallel careers as a writer and editor span half a century. He wrote his first novel, *Bright Center of Heaven* (1934), during the Depression; his most recent book, *So Long, See You Tomorrow* (1980), won the American Academy of Arts and Letters' William Dean Howells Medal for the most distinguished work of American fiction published during the preceding five years, and the American Book Award for Fiction (paperback) in 1982. In 1984 he was awarded the Brandeis University Creative Arts Medal for Fiction. Other novels include *They Came Like Swallows* (1937), *The Folded Leaf* (1945), *Time Will Darken It* (1948), and *The Château* (1961). In addition, Maxwell has published two collections of short fiction, *The Old Man at the Railroad Crossing* (1966) and *Over by the River and Other Stories* (1977); a study of his family heritage, *Ancestors* (1971); and a fantasy for children, *The Heavenly Tenants* (1946). He has edited the letters of Sylvia Townsend Warner, published in 1983, and has contributed many book reviews and stories to *The New Yorker*.

In 1963 he was elected to the National Institute of Arts & Letters and from 1969 to 1972 served as president of that organization. Maxwell lives with his wife in New York City.

~~CHAPTER 19~~

~~Their breakfast was brought in to them by a tall, full-bosomed woman of forty, with carrot-colored hair and a beautiful carriage. "Bonjour monsieur dame," she said, and raised the front wheels of the~~ teacart and then the back, so that ~~the wheels~~ they did not touch the telephone cord When she had gone back to the kitchen, Harold said, "There are plates and cups for three, which can only mean that he is having breakfast with us."

"You think?" Barbara said.

"By his own choice," ~~Harold~~ said, "since there is now someone to bring him a tray in his room."

They sat and waited. In due time, Eugène appeared and drew the armchair up to the tea cart.

It was a beautiful day. The window was wide open and the sunlight was streaming in from the balcony. Eugène inquired about their evening with Sabine, and then said, "It is possible that I may be going down to the country on Friday. A cousin of Alix is marrying. ~~They live outside of Paris.~~ And if I do go---as I should, since it is a family affair---it will be early in the morning, before you are up. And I may stay down for the weekend."

They tried not to look pleased.

He accepted a second cup of coffee and then asked what they had done about getting gasoline coupons. "But we don't need them," ~~Harold~~ said and so, innocently, obliged Eugène to admit that he did. "I seldom enjoy the use of my car," he said plaintively, "and it would be pleasant to have the gasoline for short trips into the country now and then."

He reached into his bathrobe pocket and brought out a slip of paper on which he had written the address of the place they were to go to for gasoline coupons.

"How can we ask for gasoline coupons if we don't have a car?" Harold

and the telephone, like a spoiled child that cannot endure the conversation of the grownups, started ringing. Eugène left the room. When he came back, he

Page from the working manuscript of William Maxwell's *The Château*.

William Maxwell

William Maxwell was interviewed in his East Side New York apartment. He wore a tie and blazer for the occasion. A tall, spare man, he sat on the edge of a low sofa, his knees nearly touching his chin. Twice he rose and went to the walnut bookcase, once for Virginia Woolf's Between the Acts, *and then for Eliot's* Four Quartets, *which he studied patiently for the lines he needed. At the end of the living room, two large windows looked out on the street, eight floors below, where one could see the morning traffic, but not hear it. The spacious room was furnished austerely—two vases of flowers stood on the mantel, a piano occupied one corner. The decor did not suggest Maxwell's profession. The rapture with which he recited Eliot did.*

One of his colleagues at The New Yorker, *Brendan Gill, has supplied the following report on his friend:*

"In this interview William Maxwell at one juncture urges

that the subject under discussion veer away from The New
Yorker, *on the grounds that the magazine has been almost done
to death, in one book or another. No doubt a book that I once
wrote is one of the death-dealing volumes that Maxwell has in
mind, but no matter—let me offer a brief quotation from my*
Here at The New Yorker *(a title suggested, by the way, by the
editor of the magazine, William Shawn; I would never have
dared to propose it on my own):*

One day in my office I was showing Maxwell a Roman coin that I had
purchased at Gimbels. With thousands of similar coins, it had been
buried in the sands of Egypt by Ptolemy's army paymaster, in order
to keep it from falling into the hands of the rapidly approaching
Caesar. Maxwell jiggled the coin in his palm. "The odds," he said,
"are on objects."

   *True enough, but since Maxwell made the remark well over
thirty years ago and since he and I are both in rude health and
are evidently convinced that we have outwitted the need ever to
die, we may be said to be doing not so badly, either as objects
or subjects. And though Maxwell will enter history as a distinguished American author of the middle years of the twentieth
century, he will also enter it in the reminiscences of many of his
fellow authors as an exceptionally sympathetic and adroit editor.
When I first met him, forty-five years ago, he was serving as
Katharine White's assistant, but he looked so young and so
readily abashable that I mistook him for an office-boy. I was right
about his being young; I was wrong about his being abashable.
He has a gentle voice to match his seemingly gentle heart, and
yet I was to discover that on some level of his being he is as tough
as nails. Maxwell said once of Shawn that he combines the best
features of Napoleon and Saint Francis of Assisi; it is often the
case when one makes such a comment about an associate that
it will prove, at bottom, autobiographical. Unlike Shawn, Maxwell has been a joiner of organizations and has been happy in*

the acceptance of honors from the hands of his peers; at the same time, he is a loner. If he is a clubman, he is a clubman who eats and drinks by himself. Dr. Johnson would have stared askance at him, not in the least to Maxwell's dismay.

Over the years, how much Maxwell taught me about the art that I was trying to master and that was forever turning out to be more difficult than I had expected! How reluctant he was to reject a piece until every means of salvaging it had been explored! For a long time, Maxwell and I occupied adjoining offices in the squalid rabbit-warren of The New Yorker; *now and again in those days I would hear the faint, mouse-in-the-wainscot rustle of a note being slipped under my door. Opening the note, I would encounter five or six hastily typed words from Maxwell, in praise of something I had written. Snobbish as it is sure to sound, on* The New Yorker *we write not so much for readers out in the world as for one another, and it has always been for Shawn and Maxwell and Mitchell and Hamburger and the rest of my colleagues that I have written; on the occasions when a note from Maxwell appeared under my door, I felt ten feet tall and befuddled with joy.*"

INTERVIEWERS: *So Long, See You Tomorrow* comes nineteen years after your previous novel. Why this gap?

MAXWELL: Nothing but being an editor probably, and working on other people's work. Which interested me very much. I had marvelous writers to work with. Quite a lot of me was satisfied just to be working with what they wrote. Besides, I write terribly slowly. The story "Over by the River" was started when the children were small and my older daughter was twenty when I finished it—it took over ten years. Undoubtedly if I knew exactly what I was doing, things would go faster, but if I saw the whole unwritten novel stretching out before me, chapter by chapter, like a landscape, I know I would put it aside in favor of something more uncertain—material that had a natural form that it was up to me to discover. So I never work from an outline. In 1948 we came home from France and I walked into the house, sat down at the typewriter with my hat still on my head, and wrote a page, a sort of rough statement of the book I meant to write, which I then thumbtacked to a shelf and didn't look at again until it was finished. To my surprise everything I had managed to do in the novel was on that page. But in general the thing creeps along slowly, like a mole in the dark.

With *So Long, See You Tomorrow* I felt that in this century the first-person narrator has to be a character and not just a narrative device. So I used myself as the "I" and the result was two stories, my own and Cletus Smith's, and I knew they had to be structurally combined, but how? One day I was in our house in Westchester County, and I was sitting on the side of the bed putting my shoes on, half stupefied after a nap and thinking, If I sit on the edge of the bed I will ruin the mattress, when my attention was caught by a book. I opened it and read part of a long letter from Giacometti to Matisse describing how he came to do a certain piece of sculpture—*Palace at 4 A.M.* —it's in the Museum of Modern Art—and I said, "There's my novel!" It was as simple as that. But I didn't know until that moment whether the book would work out or not.

INTERVIEWERS: Much of your work seems to some extent autobiographical. Is autobiography just the raw material for fiction, or does it have a place in a novel or a story as a finished product?

MAXWELL: True autobiography is very different from anything I've ever written. Edmund Gosse's *Father and Son* has a candor which comes from the intention of the writer to hand over his life. If the writer is really candid then it's good autobiography, and if he's not, then it's nothing at all. I don't feel that my stories, though they may appear to be autobiographical, represent an intention to hand over the whole of my life. They are fragments in which I am a character along with all the others. They're written from a considerable distance. I never feel exposed by them in any way.

As I get older I put more trust in what happened, which has a profound meaning if you can get at it. But what you invent is important too. Flaubert said that whatever you invent is true, even though you may not understand what the truth of it is.

When I reread *The Folded Leaf,* the parts I invented seem so real to me that I have quite a lot of trouble convincing myself they never actually happened.

INTERVIEWERS: How do you apply that to character? What is the process involved in making a real person into a fictional one?

MAXWELL: In *The Folded Leaf,* the man who owned the antique shop bore a considerable resemblance to John Mosher, who was the movie critic at *The New Yorker.* He was a terribly amusing man whom I was very fond of. Nothing that John ever said is in that book, but I felt a certain security at the beginning in the identification. Then I forgot about Mosher entirely, because the person in the book sprang to life. I knew what he would do in a given situation, and what he would say . . . that sudden confidence that makes the characters suddenly belong to you, and not just be borrowed from real life. Then you reach a further point where the character doesn't belong to you any longer, because he's taken off; there's nothing you can do but put down what he does and says. That's the best of all.

INTERVIEWERS: Virginia Woolf was an influence in your early work, wasn't she?

MAXWELL: Oh, yes. She's there. Everybody's there. My first novel, *Bright Center of Heaven,* is a compendium of all the writers I loved and admired. In a symposium at Smith College, Saul Bellow said something that describes it to perfection. He said, "A writer is a reader who is moved to emulation." What I wrote when I was very young had some of the characteristic qualities of every writer I had any feeling for. It takes a while before that admiration sinks back and becomes unconscious. The writers stay with you for the rest of your life. But at least they don't intrude and become visible to the reader.

INTERVIEWERS: Well, all young writers have to come to terms with their literary fathers and mothers.

MAXWELL: And think what *To the Lighthouse* meant to me, how close Mrs. Ramsay is to my own idea of my mother . . . both of them gone, both leaving the family unable to navigate very well. It couldn't have failed to have a profound effect on me.

INTERVIEWERS: What exactly is the force that makes you a writer?

MAXWELL: Your question reminds me of something. I was having lunch with Pete Lemay, who was the publicity director at Knopf and is now a playwright, and he said that he had known Willa Cather when he was a young man. I asked what she was like and he told me at some length. It wasn't what I had assumed and because I was surprised I said, "Whatever made her a writer, do you suppose?" and he said, "Why, what makes anyone a writer—deprivation, of course." And then he begged my pardon. But I do think it's deprivation that makes people writers, if they have it in them to be a writer. With *Ancestors* I thought I was writing an account of my Campbellite forebears and the deprivation didn't even show up in the first draft, but the high point of the book emotionally turned out to be the two chapters dealing with our family life before and after my mother's death in the Spanish flu epidemic of 1918. I had written about this before, in *They Came Like Swallows* and again in *The Folded Leaf*, where it is fictionalized out of recognition, but there was always something untold, something I remembered from that time. I meant *So Long, See You Tomorrow* to be the story of somebody else's tragedy but the narrative weight is evenly distributed between the rifle shot on the first page and my mother's absence. Now I have nothing more to say about the death of my mother, I think, forever. But it was a motivating force in four books. If my mother turns up again I will be astonished. I may even tell her to go away. But I do not think it will be necessary.

INTERVIEWERS: But to what extent can writing recover what you lose in life?

MAXWELL: If you get it all down there's a serenity that is marvelous. I don't mean just getting the facts down, but the degree of imagination you bring to it. Autobiography is simply the facts, but imagination is the landscape in which the facts take place, and the way that everything moves. When I went to France the first time I promptly fell in love with it. I was forty years old. My wife had been there as a child, and we were always looking for two things she remembered but didn't know where they were—a church at the end of a streetcar line and a château with a green lawn in front of it. We came home after four months because our money ran out. I couldn't bear not to be there, and so I began to write a novel about it. And for ten years I lived perfectly happily in France, remembering every town we passed through, every street we were ever on, everything that ever happened, including the weather. Of course, I was faced with the extremely difficult problem of how all this self-indulgence could be made into a novel.

INTERVIEWERS: Do you have an ideal reader in mind when you write? I've heard it said that a writer writes for himself and strangers.

MAXWELL: I think I write for myself, and I'm astonished that strangers are moved by it. I know that nobody else's praise or approval is enough for me to say, "All right, I don't have to worry about it any more" . . . I have to be satisfied myself that there is nothing more I can do to make it better.

INTERVIEWERS: But you must imagine readers.

MAXWELL: Oh yes, of course. While I'm writing I think I would like so-and-so to read this; but so-and-so changes from time to time, according to what I'm writing.

INTERVIEWERS: Will you talk about something while you're working on it?

MAXWELL: Oh no, that would be a serious mistake.

INTERVIEWERS: Why?

MAXWELL: Because more often than not the writer who talks about something he's working on talks it right out of existence.

INTERVIEWERS: Let's go back to what you were saying about recreating experiences in your fiction. What about writing that comes entirely from the imagination?

MAXWELL: I would love to be able to do that. Just open the door and invite everybody in.

INTERVIEWERS: Have you ever tried?

MAXWELL: I've tried in shorter things, in those tales that are neither fables nor fairy tales. I just hang over the typewriter waiting to see what is going to happen. It begins with the very first sentence. I don't will the sentence to come; I wait, as actively passive as I can possibly be. For some reason the phrase "Once upon a time" seems to be essential. Then, if I am sufficiently trusting, the rest of the story follows, and the last sentence is straight from the first. I also did it, to a considerable extent, in *Time Will Darken It.*

INTERVIEWERS: But would you suggest that would-be writers wait for something to drop into their heads? Isn't this a refutation of the theory that writing is ninety percent perspiration and ten percent inspiration?

MAXWELL: If they just sat and waited, maybe nothing would happen. Maybe they'd fall asleep. I think they should read— to learn how it is done—writing, I mean—and in the hope that what they read will in some way make their own experience available to them.

INTERVIEWERS: Do your best sentences come from on high, or are they the product of much working and reworking?

MAXWELL: There's something in the *Four Quartets* about language that doesn't disintegrate. That's what I try to do—

write sentences that won't be like sand castles. I've gotten to the point where I seem to recognize a good sentence when I've written it on the typewriter. Often it's surrounded by junk. So I'm extremely careful. If a good sentence occurs in an otherwise boring paragraph, I cut it out, rubber-cement it to a sheet of typewriter paper, and put it in a folder. It's just like catching a fish in a creek. I pull out a sentence and slip a line through the gills and put it on a chain and am very careful not to mislay it. Sometimes I try that sentence in ten different places until finally it finds the place where it will stay—where the surrounding sentences attach themselves to it and it becomes part of them. In the end what I write is almost entirely made up of those sentences, which is why what I write now is so short. They come one by one, and sometimes in dubious company. Those sentences that are really valuable are mysterious—perhaps they come from another place, the way lyric poetry comes from another place. They come from some kind of unconscious foreknowledge of what you are going to do. Because when you find the place where a sentence finally belongs it is utterly final in a way you had no way of knowing: it depends on a thing you hadn't written. When I wrote those fables and sat with my head over the typewriter waiting patiently, empty as a bucket that somebody's turned upside down, I was waiting for a story to come from what you could call my unconscious. Or it could be from the general unconscious. Often before poets write a poem they begin to hear the cadences of it, and then they begin to hear humming in their ears, and there are other strange manifestations, and then finally words. The last is the words.

INTERVIEWERS: Are story writing and novel writing two vastly different enterprises?

MAXWELL: When I'm writing a novel, there's a sense that I have something more important by the tail; the reason for writing the novel is often that I don't know exactly what I do have. Sometimes I'm sustained by a metaphor or an image. In

The Folded Leaf, I knew that the suicide attempt was the climactic part of the novel but I didn't know how I was going to get there; the image that sustained me throughout the whole of the writing was that of walking across a very flat landscape toward the mountains; when I got to the mountains the necessary scenes would occur. In *They Came Like Swallows,* I felt the book had to be like a stone cast into a pond. And a second stone, and a third—with the ripples moving outward from inside the first ones but never overtaking them.

INTERVIEWERS: How do you know when it's time to write another novel? Is it some sort of instinctual act, like the impulse that impels birds to migrate?

MAXWELL: I expect to live forever, and therefore I never get worried about what I ought to be writing, or about anything undone. In the case of *So Long, See You Tomorrow,* I was sitting at my desk, and something made me think of that boy I had failed to speak to, and thinking of him I winced. I saw myself wincing and I thought, "That's very odd indeed that after all these years you should have a response so acute; maybe that's worth investigating." And so that's what I set out to do.

INTERVIEWERS: You wrote somewhere that *So Long, See You Tomorrow* was a futile way of making amends. Was it really futile? Can't fiction make amends for real life?

MAXWELL: Forgiveness is in the hands of the injured, not the injurer. I don't know. Would you forgive me?

INTERVIEWERS: I would, sure.

MAXWELL: Well, that's comforting.

INTERVIEWERS: You said that your mother's death made you a novelist. When did you first start writing?

MAXWELL: I sometimes think that children, without knowing it, are projected into the unlived lives of their parents. My mother's sister told me that when my mother was twelve years old she used to go up into the attic and "write on her novel." So perhaps I am a projection of my mother's unlived literary life. When I first began to write I was a freshman in a small-town high school. I wrote a story about an aristocrat during the French Revolution who hid in a clock. If there were any French aristocrats in central Illinois in my boyhood I didn't know them. But at least we had a grandfather's clock in the front hall. Then we moved to Chicago and I wrote a little for the high school magazine. In college I began to write poetry. I'm not a poet, though. I've never written anything that comes from the place poetry comes from.

INTERVIEWERS: Is it a different place?

MAXWELL: When I was at Harvard I got to know Robert Fitzgerald, and I used to show my poems to him. In spite of the fact that I was older than he was—I was a graduate student and he was a sophomore—I had enormous respect for him. He was better educated than I was, and intransigent, and he despised anything that wasn't first rate. One day he looked at my poem and then he looked at me, rather in the way you look at children who present a problem, and he said, "Why don't you write prose?" I was so happy that he thought I could write anything that I just turned to and wrote prose—as if he'd given me permission to try. The prose took the form of fiction because I do like stories and don't have a very firm grasp on ideas.

INTERVIEWERS: How long was it after you began to write prose that you became sure you would be a writer?

MAXWELL: Oh, it began in pure pleasure. I left Harvard and went back to Urbana, and was rooming in the house of a woman who was teaching at the University of Illinois. A professor at Yale, a friend of hers, was doing a series of biographical essays; he sent her a two-volume life of Thomas Coke of Holkham—Coke introduced in Parliament the bill to recognize the American colonies, and was also an important agriculturist—and asked her to do a forty-page condensation that he could work from, and she split the job with me. She wanted to save me from becoming an English professor. I was then twenty-three. She let me have all the big scenes and she concentrated on the agriculture, which she said interested her. It did not

interest me. The book was full of interesting people—for example, Lady Mary Coke, who was Coke of Holkham's aunt. She
dressed her footmen in pea-green and silver livery and suffered
from the delusion that the Empress Maria Teresa was trying
to take her servants away from her. When she was depressed
she would fish for goldfish in the ornamental pond in front of
her house. And in her old age she slept in a dresser drawer.
Anyway, I had so much pleasure in working with this material
that I began to write my first novel, *Bright Center of Heaven*,
because I didn't want the pleasure to end. Writing fiction was,
and still is, pure pleasure. Oh, I ran out of steam from time to
time. After I got to *The New Yorker*, particularly when I was
working five days a week and seeing both artists and writers,
I wrote less and less and almost stopped writing altogether. But
then I quit *The New Yorker* in order to write. It was a genuine
parting; I left fully intending never to return. But something
always brought me back. I never came back five days a week,
though. If I hadn't worked at *The New Yorker* there might
have been more books, but I'm not sure if they would have
been as good. Writing part-time forced me to write slowly, and
I think I was more careful. I write much more slowly now than
I used to.

INTERVIEWERS: Why? What does age do to a writer?

MAXWELL: I think it makes you more serious. It makes you
more aware of other people's lives. You see more from the
inside: the troubles, the sorrow, and the unfairness. And then
when you accept the idea that life is good, no matter how
unlucky you are, you get a firmer insight into it.

INTERVIEWERS: What about your schedule? When do you
work?

MAXWELL: Well, I don't want to be uncooperative, but are
you sure you want to ask that?

INTERVIEWERS: It *is* sort of a boring question.

MAXWELL: If you have any reason in the world for wanting
to know, I'll tell you . . . I like to work in my bathrobe and

pajamas, after breakfast, until I suddenly perceive, from what's on the page in the typewriter, that I've lost my judgment. And then I stop. It's usually about twelve-thirty. But I hate getting dressed. The cleaning woman, who may not approve of it, though she's never said, my family, the elevator men, the delivery boy from Gristede's—all of them are used to seeing me in this unkempt condition. What it means to me is probably symbolic—you can have me after I've got my trousers on, but not before. When I retired from *The New Yorker* they offered me an office, which was very generous of them because they're shy on space, but I thought, "What would I do with an office at *The New Yorker*? I would have to put my trousers on and ride the subway downtown to my typewriter. No good."

INTERVIEWERS: Maybe once you got there you could strip down.

MAXWELL: I don't think it would work. It isn't the same as going straight from the breakfast table.

INTERVIEWERS: Do you find certain environments more conducive to good work than others?

MAXWELL: I'm just as able to work on Cape Cod as here in New York or in Westchester. I prefer small messy rooms that don't look out on anything interesting. I wrote the last two sections of *They Came Like Swallows* beside a window looking out on a tin roof. It was perfect. The roof was so boring it instantly drove me back to my typewriter.

INTERVIEWERS: Do you isolate yourself totally when you're working?

MAXWELL: I don't mind interruptions, unless there are terribly many of them. When the children were small, they came and sat on my lap and punched the keys as I did, but they soon lost interest. My younger daughter told me recently that when she was a child she thought the typewriter was a toy that I went into my room and closed the door and played with. Once when I was typing with great concentration she touched one of the releases, and the carriage shot out from under me. I roared at her, and she went and knelt like an Arab under the dining room table, with her face against the floor, and would not accept the apology that I, also kneeling like an Arab, with my face next to hers, sincerely offered. In general I don't mind domestic sounds. I find them reassuring.

INTERVIEWERS: Do you keep a notebook?

MAXWELL: No, I never have. I like the insecurity and the danger of not keeping a notebook. I've tried writing notes down on file cards, but I find I never look at them again.

INTERVIEWERS: Do you think there's such a thing as writer's block?

MAXWELL: There's such a thing as loss of confidence.

INTERVIEWERS: Have you ever experienced it?

MAXWELL: I've come close. There was a period after I left *The New Yorker* for the first time, when I thought I knew enough about writing stories to be able to make a living by it, but it turned out that every idea I had for a story was in some way too close to home. The stories I did write weren't bought. I began to feel that my hands were tied. I guess, though, I have always believed that if the material interested me enough to want to write about it, then it was all right; it wouldn't go away and so I should just keep working on it. Updike said once, riding in a taxi—he was talking about the reviewers, who had been scolding him for not writing what they thought he ought to be writing—"All I have to go on," he said, "is something I caught a glimpse of out of the corner of my eye." That seemed a very nice way of describing the way material comes to you. That glimpse, it's all you have. I don't think a writer's block is anything more than a loss of confidence. It certainly isn't a loss of talent.

INTERVIEWERS: Do you find it gets easier or harder to write as you get older?

MAXWELL: I think it's easier when you are young. My first novel was written on a farm in Wisconsin. Very Chekhovian, that farm was. I wrote in a room that had been converted from a water tank next to the windmill. Some of the characters were derived from people living on the farm at the time, so it was a handy place to be. I would come for lunch and they would make remarks I had put in their mouths that morning. Which wasn't really mysterious, because if you are conscious of character—in the other sense of the word—you can't help being struck by how consistent people are in everything they do and say. I finished the book in four months, with the help of Virginia Woolf, W. B. Yeats, Elinor Wylie, and a girl on the farm who was also writing a novel. When somebody said something good we would look at each other and one of us would say, "I spit on that," meaning, "keep your hands off of it."

The farm was ten miles out of Portage, where Zona Gale* lived. Nobody reads her now or knows who she was, even, but they did then. I had known her since I was sixteen years old. She was a kind of fairy godmother to me. I took my manuscript to her. I wanted to know if I had written a novel or not. When she gave it back to me she said that she had been unable to sleep and had read until four in the morning, and then gone downstairs to her study looking for the last chapter. I was too thickheaded to understand what she was trying to tell me, and said, "No, that's all there is." Twenty years after it was published I reread the book and saw the chapter she went downstairs looking for. The next novel was more difficult, and the novel after that was even more painful. By pain I don't mean the agony of writing, I mean the uncertainty of not knowing what you're going to do or how you're going to do it. It was awfully slow. One book took ten years, one four, and my last, though not very long, took two years.

INTERVIEWERS: When you write a novel, do you try to stick to the chronological narrative as you're writing, or do you jump around?

---

*She was a Wisconsin novelist and playwright—her *Miss Lulu Bett* won the Pulitzer Prize.

MAXWELL: I don't really depart from the "and then . . . and then" of the storyteller, but if I am lucky I know what the last sentence is going to be. And sometimes I realize that a rounded-out scene early in the novel has shut the door too soon on something. So I take part of that scene away, and use it later on in the book. It is the death of a novel to write chapters that are really short stories.

INTERVIEWERS: Do you have a favorite novel?

MAXWELL: I think *The Folded Leaf*. It may be for personal reasons—the whole of my youth is in it. Also, when I was working on it, in my mind's eye I kept seeing the manuscript burning in the fireplace; I was so sure nobody would be interested in it.

INTERVIEWERS: You taught for two years. Did you care much for that?

MAXWELL: I liked it. I taught freshman composition. It was lovely when you found students who responded to things you were enthusiastic about. Teaching them to punctuate properly and to analyze the periodic sentences in Matthew Arnold's "Gregarious and Slavish Instincts in Animals" was something else again. But that wasn't what drove me away from teaching. What drove me away was a silly novel by Robert Nathan called *One More Spring*, about some people who went to live in a toolshed in Central Park. The gist of the book was that life is to be lived, and, well, it is, of course. Anyway, that book made me restless with my prospects. I saw myself being promoted from assistant to associate to full professor, and then to professor emeritus, and finally being carried out in a wooden box. This was 1933, and only an idiot would have thrown up a job at that point. But I did anyway. And I floundered for several years.

INTERVIEWERS: Do you think the writing of fiction can be taught?

MAXWELL: I expect you can be taught to write a clean, decent sentence.

INTERVIEWERS: After teaching you started editing. How did you first come to work at *The New Yorker?*

MAXWELL: Do we have to go into *The New Yorker?* There have been all those books. The subject has been done to death, almost.

INTERVIEWERS: Maybe we could talk about it just a little.

MAXWELL: I needed a job in order to stay in New York. Eugene Saxton at *Harper's* wrote to Katharine White about me, and she astonished him by replying that there were not many openings at *The New Yorker* at that time, but that she would talk to me. This was 1936—the Depression—and nobody had heard of an opening anywhere in years. In the course of my interview with Mrs. White she asked me what salary I would require. Some knowledgeable acquaintance had told me I must ask for thirty-five dollars a week or I wouldn't be respected; so I swallowed hard and said, "Thirty-five dollars." Mrs. White smiled and said, "I expect you could live on less." I could have lived nicely on fifteen. A few days later I got a telegram from her asking me to report for work on the following Monday at the salary agreed upon—thirty-five dollars a week.

In those days—it is no longer true—fiction, humor, and art were handled by the same editors. The artists brought their work in on Tuesday and it was looked at by the Art Meeting on Wednesday afternoon. At the Art Meeting were Harold Ross, Mrs. White, Rea Irvin, Wolcott Gibbs (until he gave up his place), Mrs. White's secretary, who took notes of the proceedings, and an office boy named Wilbur, whose mind was on basketball. The editors sat on one side of a big table, with knitting needles. The covers and drawings were placed on a stand by Wilbur; Ross would lean forward and touch the parts of the drawing that were unsatisfactory with the end of his needle. I too had a knitting needle, which I did not use for quite some time. Occasionally Mrs. White would say that the picture might be saved if it had a better caption, and it would be returned to the artist or sent to E. B. White, who was a whiz at this. Ross would lean forward and peer at a drawing with his lower lip sticking out and say, "You can't tell who's talking." Or he would say, "Bird Rock"—a remark that mystified me until I learned that many years before this *The New Yorker* had published a drawing of a seagull standing on a rock and a man saying to another man, "They call it 'Bird Rock.' " It had become a generic term for an undesirable form of humor. A great deal of what was put before the Art Meeting was extremely unfunny. Gibbs was repelled by the whole idea of grown men using their minds in this way and seldom said anything. Rea Irvin smoked a cigar and was interested only when a drawing by Gluyas Williams appeared on the stand.

On Thursday the artists returned to find out what had happened at the Art Meeting. Someone had to convey this information to them. Gibbs felt he had been doing it long enough, and so I was taken on. It was called "seeing artists." The first time they paraded in one after another I was struck by the fact that they all looked like the people in their drawings. George Price looked like the man who floated up near the ceiling of that disreputable apartment week after week; Otto Soglow looked like his Little King. Cotton was kind and fatherly. Alajalov wore yellow kid gloves. Some artists were too important to be entrusted to me. Peter Arno and Helen Hokinson were seen by Mrs. White. I noticed that they didn't look like the characters they drew.

INTERVIEWERS: Then from the Art Meeting you graduated on to the editorial board?

MAXWELL: Yes. Only it wasn't called that. I sat in a big room where the secretaries were; there wasn't even an office for me. But it was a wonderful place to be, because I was right beside the door of Katharine White's office. She moved with majestic deliberation, and between the time she got up from her desk and the time she put her foot on the catch that released her door so that it would swing shut I learned a lot about the workings of the magazine. I remember when Gibbs's parody profile of Henry Luce was going to the printer. Time-Life was in an uproar about it; there was a continuous procession of people in and out of Mrs. White's office. I sat taking in snatches of the excitement.

When the door was closed I sat and worried about how long it would take them to decide it was not worthwhile to go on paying me thirty-five dollars a week. On Mondays and Fridays I had nothing whatever to do but stare at a Thurber drawing above my desk—until Mrs. White suggested that I get the scrapbooks from the office library and read them. She also gave me a pile of rejected manuscripts and asked me to write letters to go with those that showed any promise. After she had gone over my letters she called me into her office and said, "Mr. Maxwell, have you ever taught school?" It was a fact that I had kept from her in our interview: instinct told me that it was not something you were supposed to have done. Anyway, from her I learned that it is not the work of an editor to teach writers how to write.

One day Wolcott Gibbs asked me if I'd like to try some editing. He handed me a manuscript and walked away, without explaining what he meant by editing. I didn't think much of the story, so I cut and changed things around and made it the way I thought it ought to be. To my surprise Gibbs sent it to the printer that way. And I thought, "So that's editing." The next time he gave me a piece to edit I fell on my face. I straightened out something that was mildly funny only if it wasn't too clear what was going on. Gibbs was kind, and said that my editing revealed that there wasn't very much there, but I got the point. In time I came to feel that real editing means changing as little as possible. Various editors and proofreaders would put their oar in, and sometimes I had to change hats and protect the writer from his own agreeableness, or fear, or whatever it was that made him say yes when he ought to have said no. What you hope is that if the writer reads the story ten years after it is published he will not be aware that anybody has ever touched it. But it takes many years of experience—and love— to be able to do that.

INTERVIEWERS: Why was this drawing by Thurber in front of you?

MAXWELL: It was drawn right on the wall. A self-portrait. His drawings were everywhere, all over the office. There was one drawing on the nineteenth floor by the watercooler of a man walking along happy-as-anything and around the corner a woman is waiting for him with a baseball bat, ready to swing. One night some fool painter came in and painted over every last one of them. It was a tragedy. Brendan Gill talks about how difficult Thurber was. On the other hand, there's that story of the maid at the Hotel Algonquin who was straightening up his room and found, written in shaving soap on the bathroom mirror, the words "Thurber is a bastard." For that you can forgive quite a lot. Of course, what it comes down to in the end is that an artist is loved for his work, not his sweet disposition.

INTERVIEWERS: What was the chemistry of working with Harold Ross? Why was it so exciting?

MAXWELL: It had to do with his personality. And being taken into his confidence. People don't often strike me as being larger than life-size, but he did. He was not the unintelligent oaf he has sometimes been portrayed as being. He was clearly in command of the magazine. And he saw things through a prism of humor. I remember his telling me with amusement that his mother used to touch her hair here and there with her hand before she answered the telephone. Also, he was so decent. And, up to a point, much too trusting. It was like having a terribly funny father. He had a personal relationship with everybody in the office, including Wilbur, the office boy. Once, during a period when I had left the magazine to write a novel, I met him on 43rd Street at about one o'clock, and he said, "Maxwell, what are you doing in town?" and I said, "I came in to go to the theater." It didn't occur to me to explain that my ticket was for the evening performance. He went on to the office and told somebody, "I met Maxwell on his way to a matinee. I don't understand it. I thought only women went to matinees." He was genuinely disturbed, and didn't know whether he was under a misapprehension about matinees or about me. What he cared most about, I think, was writers— about bringing them along. So long as they didn't try to proselytize in *The New Yorker,* it didn't matter to him what their political opinions were; it was their talent that interested him. I also think he thought that people with talent didn't in general know enough to come in out of the rain, and he was trying to hold an umbrella over them.

INTERVIEWERS: It must have bothered him terribly when those feuds began—as with O'Hara, for instance.

MAXWELL: Before the feud with O'Hara, Ross worried that O'Hara would manage to get some sexual innuendo into the magazine that the editors had failed to recognize. As he once or twice did. O'Hara as a person amused Ross. Perhaps because they were all young together. O'Hara thought up the idea (based on need) that if he turned in a story and it wasn't accepted he should be paid five hundred dollars anyway. The trouble was, O'Hara could write a story a day without half trying. So instead of the five hundred, Ross went out and bought a large, inexpensive watch and had it engraved, "To John O'Hara from *The New Yorker."* I don't know how the joke went over.

INTERVIEWERS: There's a story in Brendan Gill's book about your going out to O'Hara's house to read three manuscripts he had, and your getting terribly nervous when you disliked the first two. You liked the last. Which was the one you liked?

MAXWELL: "Imagine Kissing Pete." I think it is one of the best things he ever wrote. The falling-out with *The New Yorker* was over the way two of O'Hara's early novels had been reviewed in the magazine. Fadiman's review of—*Butterfield 8,* I think it was—appeared under the heading "Disappointment in O'Hara," and the pun rankled. O'Hara was not of a forgiving disposition, and the feud lasted for years. I had no part in it whatever. It all went on over my head. Finally O'Hara sent word through St. Clair McKelway that he had finished three novelettes which *The New Yorker* could see if they would send an editor out to his house in Quogue to read them. I went. I must have been out of my mind. I mean, what if none of them had been right for the magazine? Fortunately, one was. At one point I had three wonderful writers all named John: John O'Hara, John Cheever, and John Updike.

INTERVIEWERS: Could you talk a little about editing those three? How does somebody deal with a writer as distinguished? O'Hara, to start with. He was so touchy, wasn't he?

MAXWELL: Not about editing. During the first period that I edited his work I barely knew him. I inherited him from Gibbs, who had given up editing entirely to take over the theater page from Robert Benchley. I was young and inexperienced as an editor, but fortunately O'Hara had a great respect for *New Yorker* editing. When his stories were collected in a book, he always followed the edited version. What I worked on was mostly the "Pal Joey" series. I knew nothing whatever about Broadway argot, and sometimes now in the middle of the night I groan, thinking about what I may have done to them, especially in the way of cutting. In later years O'Hara would occasionally say no to a suggested change. In one story the words "George Carlin said" turned up every time George Carlin opened his mouth. I suggested in the margin of the galleys that it had somewhat the appearance of a mannerism, and would he consider using "he said" here and there in the story. He wrote me a long, rather preachy letter on style. *His* style.

Updike is an extreme perfectionist. His manuscripts are always cleanly written, and he usually makes a great many interesting changes on the galleys. When the page proofs were ready I would mail him a set and we would talk sometimes for

an hour or two on the phone . . . mostly about whether this
or that new change—his change, not mine—was for the better,
or might possibly do some damage to the surrounding sentences. It was an education in how to refine language to the
point where it almost becomes something else. The pure practiced effectiveness and verve of an Olympic athlete is what it
often reminded me of.

INTERVIEWERS: And Cheever?

MAXWELL: I don't know what service I provided for Cheever
except to be delighted with his work. He brought me *The
Country Husband* when I was sick in bed with bronchitis. I
remember the rapture of reading it.

INTERVIEWERS: Did you show your own manuscripts to any
of these three?

MAXWELL: No, but I did to other *New Yorker* writers. Frank
O'Connor came out to our house in the country for the day,
with his wife and baby, and in the course of the conversation
he extracted from me the information that I had been working
for eight years on a novel I was in despair over. "Let me see
it," he said, and I was appalled. I was not in the habit of mixing
my two lives. At that time the manuscript of what turned out
to be *The Château* filled a good-sized grocery carton. I hadn't
been able to make up my mind whether it should have an
omniscient author or a first-person narrator, whether it should
be told from the point of view of the French or the Americans
traveling in France. I was afraid it wasn't a novel at all but a
travel diary. I told O'Connor that the manuscript was in such
a shape that it was unreadable, but he assured me that he could
read anything. He had been sufficiently trusting to let me see
the rough draft of section after section of *An Only Child,* and
I didn't feel like saying that it was one thing for me to see his
unfinished work and another for him to see mine. He went off
with the grocery carton in the backseat of the car, and read
through the whole mess. Then he wrote me a wonderful letter
in which he said he didn't understand what I was up to. There

seemed to be two novels—which he then proceeded to discuss, in detail, as separate works. My relief was immense, because it is a lot easier to make two novels into one than it is to make one out of nothing whatever. So I went ahead and finished the book.

I showed the next-to-final draft of *The Château* to Francis Steegmuller, who straightened out my wobbly French in places where corrections were called for.

Before that, at a time when I had almost stopped writing entirely, I showed what I thought was a short story to Louise Bogan, and she said it was a novel, so I kept on writing about those two characters. I sent her what I wrote, chapter by chapter, through four versions, and she never said enough is enough. From time to time I got a penny postcard from her with "v. good" or something like that on it. Once she objected to a physical description, on the ground that the writing wasn't very fresh, so I sweated over it. And another time, when I was stuck, I had a postcard from her saying, "Get that boy up off the bed on the sleeping porch." When I finished the novel she found me a title for it, from Tennyson's "The Lotos-Eaters":

> *Lo! in the middle of the wood*
> *The Folded Leaf is woo'd from out the bud*
> *With winds upon the branch . . .*

I also, at times, showed my work to Harold Brodkey. I knew his first wife when she was a little girl, and shortly after they were married she brought him to our house and we became friends. During part of the time I was writing *The Folded Leaf* I was in analysis with Theodor Reik, who thought the book ought to have a positive ending. And Edward Aswell at *Harper's* thought the story would be strengthened if I combined some of the minor characters. I was so tired and so unconfident about the book that I took their word for it. Later I was sorry. And when it came out ten years later in the Vintage Press I put it back pretty much the way it was in the first place.

While I was making the corrections Harold brought me a marked copy of the book. Mostly the things he objected to were ideas I had absorbed from Reik rather than arrived at from my own experience, and I either cut or rewrote those sentences. When I was working on *Ancestors* he got so interested in the structure that I showed the manuscript to him chapter by chapter, as I had with Louise Bogan. We had a running argument: what I cared about in fiction was emotion, and though he was not indifferent to emotion he thought—I hope I am quoting him correctly—that ideas mattered as much or more. They aren't, of course, mutually exclusive. But as a result of our argufying I became aware of the extra dimension that abstract thinking brings to fiction.

Now that I think of it I have always shown whatever I was working on to somebody—most often my wife, whose opinions tend to be detached and trustworthy. When I was writing *Time Will Darken It* I found that the book was proceeding by set conversations, rather like a play. A had a conversation in the backseat of the carriage with B, and as a result B had it out with C, and when C met D on the stairs she said—you get the idea. When I started a new chapter I asked myself who hadn't talked to whom lately. It's not a bad method. Anyway, when I finished a chapter I would read it to my wife, sitting outside on the grass in the sunshine, and it was like sharing news from home.

INTERVIEWERS: So you think writers are apt to be good judges of other writers' work?

MAXWELL: Well, Updike certainly seems to be a good judge. O'Hara was very good in his letters.

INTERVIEWERS: No professional jealousies? O'Hara, who was so competitive about his writing: if he thought for a minute you were on his level . . .

MAXWELL: I don't think he thought for a minute that I was on his level, so that was no problem. No, I don't think writers are necessarily competitive. There was a period when I thought they weren't at all. Lately they have seemed more so. In any case, I felt it was important, as an editor, to play down as much as possible the fact that I also wrote. I wanted the writers I worked with to feel that nothing was more important to me than their work. And for the three days a week that I was at my desk at *The New Yorker*, nothing was.

INTERVIEWERS: Ever since the days of O'Hara, something has endured—a *New Yorker* story. Do you agree? Is there such a thing?

MAXWELL: The usual answer from the magazine is no; they point out the range and variety of the fiction writers who have been published in *The New Yorker*. From Nancy Hale to Vladimir Nabokov is a very wide sweep. Irwin Shaw when he was a young man said once that in the typical *New Yorker* story everything occurs at one place in one time, and all the dialogue is beside the point. It was not, at the time, a wholly inaccurate description. That is to say, there were lots of stories like that. Something that *is* characteristic of the writers who appear in *The New Yorker* is that the sentence is the unit by which the story advances, not the paragraph, and the individual sentence therefore carries a great deal of weight and tends to be carefully constructed, with no loose ends. And style becomes very important. Gibbs said in a memo he wrote on the theory and practice of *New Yorker* editing—"If a writer has style, leave it."

INTERVIEWERS: That memo would be an extremely interesting document to have.

MAXWELL: Gibbs was a wonderfully fast and expert editor. In those days *New Yorker* stories were short—twelve pages was a very long story. And he edited by cutting entire paragraphs. In some mysterious way they were not missed afterward. I never learned how to do this: instead I operated on the principle of never taking out anything I liked. After Gibbs left, the fiction began to get long, perhaps because he was not there to cut it. Or maybe it was just that the subjects that could be dealt with in twelve pages had been exhausted and writers were forced to take in more territory.

INTERVIEWERS: How did editing the work of others affect your own work?

MAXWELL: I expect it affected the quality of it, made it better. It could hardly hurt anybody to have to pay close attention, word by word, and sentence by sentence, to the work of writers such as those I mostly dealt with.

INTERVIEWERS: There was no chance of losing your own voice amidst theirs?

MAXWELL: Well, you could just as easily *find* your voice amidst theirs. The essays of E. B. White are a great help if you are trying to use the pronoun "I" in a way that is natural and unself-conscious.

INTERVIEWERS: Could you take time off to write your novels?

MAXWELL: No, not as a rule. Mostly I went on working at the office two or three days a week. It took much longer to write a novel that way, but it did allow me to pick up where I had left off with a fresh view of things. Ross heard that I had been working on a novel for four years and came into my office to talk to me about it. He knew that what I was working on—it was *The Folded Leaf*—was of no conceivable use to *The New Yorker,* but he didn't like the idea of a writer having to spend such a long time over something. The upshot of the conversation was that he sent me home for six months on full pay so I could finish my novel. When it was published and got good reviews, he was pleased. He felt he had a stake in the enterprise.

INTERVIEWERS: What a lovely story.

MAXWELL: Well, he was a lovely man, and it doesn't come out in the books at all. I really loved him. And two more different people than Ross and me you could hardly conceive of. There was a story, perhaps legendary, that Mrs. White so enraged him by something she said that he picked up a telephone and threw it at her. But he never even raised his voice at me.

INTERVIEWERS: Did things change when William Shawn took over as editor-in-chief?

MAXWELL: How could they not change? Gently and slowly changes have occurred. If nothing changed then the whole thing would come to an Egyptian end. Do you like Egyptian sculpture?

INTERVIEWERS: Yes. Cats.

MAXWELL: My wife loves it dearly. But when we went down the Nile I was troubled by the fact that the motifs were unchanging for two thousand years—the king of Egypt holding his enemies by the hair, in temple after temple. That's what would happen if *The New Yorker* never changed—that dead quality would creep in.

INTERVIEWERS: Do you have any advice for writers trying to get published in *The New Yorker*?

MAXWELL: I don't think anybody can write decent fiction and at the same time try to match the requirements of a magazine—maybe, but I don't think so. You do what your heart cries out to do. In my own case, I'm often in doubt about something I've written—and I think, well, if I like it, perhaps someone else will like it too. That's the final criterion— whether or not the writer likes what he has written.

INTERVIEWERS: As an editor, in deciding whether or not to read a story, how much weight do you place on the first sentence?

MAXWELL: A great deal. And if there is nothing promising by the end of the first page there isn't likely to be in what follows. I love first sentences, anyway. When you get to the last sentence of a novel you often find that it was implicit in the first sentence, only you didn't know what it was.

INTERVIEWERS: What are some of your favorite first lines? Do you collect them?

MAXWELL: No, but offhand I think of "None of them knew the color of the sky," which is "The Open Boat" and "All the sisters lay dreaming of horses," which is *National Velvet.* And the wonderful first line of *Pride and Prejudice.* "It is a truth universally acknowledged, that a single man in possession of a good fortune must be in want of a wife."

INTERVIEWERS: Do you spend a lot of time on your own first sentences? *So Long, See You Tomorrow* begins, "The gravel pit was about a mile east of town and the size of a small lake and so deep that boys of under sixteen were forbidden by their parents to swim in it."

MAXWELL: Originally the first sentence was, "Very few families escape disasters of one kind or another." When *The New Yorker* bought it, the editors were troubled by the fact that for the first twenty pages it read like reminiscence. A good many readers don't enjoy that sort of thing, and over the years *The New Yorker* had been blamed for publishing too much of it. Actually, if writers don't put down what they remember, all sorts of beautiful and moving experiences simply go down the drain forever. In any case, *The New Yorker* was afraid that readers, seeing also that it was very long, would stop reading before they discovered that it was really about a murder. So I moved things around a bit at the beginning.

INTERVIEWERS: That didn't bother you, to start at a different place?

MAXWELL: I could see that they had a point. Of course there was a certain amount of straining at the seams—any writer would feel it—but I got past that. The effect on me was as if I were shaving and some hand came and took the razor from me and did this part of my face.

INTERVIEWERS: It's nice to be shaved sometimes.

MAXWELL: And it's nice to have someone genuinely care about your work, to the point that they can do for you what you have failed to see needed doing. In my experience at *The New Yorker*, the best writers were very good-tempered about suggested changes. I can only remember one instance when the editing process broke down and the writer took back his story. Between the time that we had accepted it and the time we prepared the galleys, another story came in and was rejected, and I suspect that his anger over the galleys was really anger about the rejection. That was the only time. It's almost axiomatic—the more talented the writer, the easier he is to work with, if the editor is both sensitive and sensible.

INTERVIEWERS: Are you in the habit of writing every day?

MAXWELL: Yes. Seven days a week. An insane life, but what happiness! It's really self-indulgence. I resent any social invitation that keeps me up after ten-thirty, so that I'm not bright as a dollar the next morning.

INTERVIEWERS: What if you hadn't been a writer at all?

MAXWELL: I can't imagine, I really can't imagine. I would have been so deprived of everything I love if I hadn't been a writer. It would have been awful, awful.

JOHN SEABROOK
GEORGE PLIMPTON
Fall 1981

4. May Sarton

May Sarton was born on May 3, 1912, in Wondelgem, Belgium. Her father, a Belgian, was an eminent historian of science. Her English mother was a portrait painter and designer of furniture and fabrics. In 1929 she graduated from the Cambridge High and Latin School and joined Eva Le Gallienne's Civic Repertory Theater in New York as an apprentice actress. In 1934 she founded her own Apprentice Theater at The New School for Social Research. Her first book of poetry, *Encounter in April*, was published in 1937. Her first novel appeared the following year. At about this time, on one of her early trips to England, she met and was befriended by Elizabeth Bowen who introduced her to Virginia Woolf and the world of Bloomsbury.

During the war years, she worked for the Office of War Information in New York, writing documentary film scripts, some of which were translated into as many as twenty-six languages.

Sarton is the author of over forty books: poetry, novels, journals, and memoirs, among them *The Bridge of Years* (1946), *The Land of Silence* (1953), *In Time Like Air* (1957), *The Small Room* (1961), *Plant Dreaming Deep* (1968), *Collected Poems* (1974), and *The House by the Sea* (1977). In 1984, *At Seventy: A Journal* appeared on *The New York Times* Best-Seller List. Her most recent novel is *The Magnificent Spinster*. Sarton has received numerous honorary degrees and has taught and lectured at many colleges and universities including Harvard, Johns Hopkins, Wellesley, and Middlebury. Recently she has been honored by the Older Women's League and the Fund for Human Dignity, and is a member of the American Academy of Arts and Sciences.

May Sarton's explorations of the solitary life and different forms of female creativity have made her an influential figure in the Women's Movement. She lives in York, Maine.

Lady of the Lake

Somewhere at the bottom of the lake she lies
She is entangled among weeds and drowned
I cannot be with her there. I know she is bound
To a dead man there, and her wide-open eyes

Only a part of her surfaces in my arms
When I can bear her up for an hour
To breathe again the leaf-green summer air
The smell of hay , her village and its charms.
And I know that I can be hers forever or a while
But she can never be mine for a day or a year or a day
For she was long ago married and given away
Though she turned to me for a hour with her radiant smile.

S he floats

Somewhere at the bottom of the lake she lies is
She is entangled among weeds and drowned
            her deep self drowned.
I cannot be with her t.ere. I know she is bound,
To a dead man and her open eyes are his.
Only a part of her surfaces in my arms
When I can lift her up in/ny to the surface
            and float her there
To breathe again the life- giving summer air
Wind in the leaves, the village and its charms.
And I know that I am hers forever or a while
But she can never be mine for a year or a day.
For she was long ago married and given away.
Though she turns to me now and then a (radiant) smile.

A manuscript page from May Sarton's book of poems, *Halfway to Silence*.

May Sarton

The author of a remarkably varied body of work, May Sarton lives by herself in York, Maine, in a former "summer cottage," quite isolated, at the end of a long dirt road. The road curves through a well-kept wood ending at "The House by the Sea" (the title of one of her journals). The house, formal in design, is of pale yellow clapboard fronted by a flagstone terrace. It faces, across a rolling meadow, the deep blue of the ocean marked here and there by a line of white foam. It is a late November afternoon and growing cold. The flower beds around the house, running along the fence and at the edge of the terraces, are all banked for winter. Her little Sheltie, Tamas, alerts her to the arrival of a guest, and she comes to greet me at the gate.

Possessed of that profound attentiveness characteristic of true charm, May Sarton has, at the same time, an exuberant nature.

Her voice, full of inflection and humor, expresses the range of her personality. It has been called a "burnished" voice and it makes for spellbinding poetry readings, which she gives frequently—at places from small New England churches to the Library of Congress, and at colleges everywhere.

In the library, a fire is blazing, and Bramble, the once wild cat, is asleep on the couch. Sarton brings in a tea tray, complete with cinnamon toast and cookies. In this room, with the shelves of her work—novels, books of poems, memoirs, and journals—and the shelves of her father's works (George Sarton was the noted Harvard historian of science), under the benign gaze of Duvet de la Tour, "The Ancestor" ("always referred to as if he were the only one"), the interview begins.

INTERVIEWER: Would you say a word about your work as a whole?

SARTON: My first book was a book of poems, *Encounter in April,* followed by my first novel, *The Single Hound.* There was quite an interval before the second novel, *The Bridge of Years.* And then *Shadow of a Man.* Then it goes on and on for a long time with a book of poems between every novel. That was my wish, that the poems should be equal in number, that the novels should not be more important than the poems because the poems were what I cared about most. Much later, when I was forty-five or so, I began to do nonfiction—first the memoirs and finally the journals, which came as the last of the forms which I have been using. Altogether now I think it amounts to seventeen novels, I don't know, five or six memoirs and journals, and then twelve books of poems, which are mostly in the collected poems now.

INTERVIEWER: Has it been easy to shift amongst all these different forms?

SARTON: Sometimes the demon of self-doubt comes to tell me that I've been fatally divided between two crafts, that of the novel and that of poetry, but I've always believed that in the end it was the total work which would communicate a vision of life and it really needs different modes to do that. The novels have been written in order to find something out about what I was thinking, questions I was asking myself that I needed to answer. Take a very simple example, *A Shower of Summer Days.* The great house that dominates the novel was Bowen's Court. What interested me was the collision between a rich nature, a young girl in revolt against everything at home in America, and ceremony, tradition, and beauty as represented by the house in Ireland.

INTERVIEWER: Is it safe to assume that the rebellious young woman is based partly on you?

SARTON: Not at all. It's a complete invention. The only person who is not invented in that book is the husband of Violet, and he is based on Elizabeth Bowen's husband. The house is, as I said, Bowen's Court. I stayed there.

INTERVIEWER: And you knew Elizabeth Bowen.

SARTON: Oh, yes. I was in love with her. I've said what I really want to say about her in the portrait [*A World of Light*]. She was a marvelous friend. A very warm and giving person.

INTERVIEWER: What intrigues me in your portrait of her is that although she had a tremendous effect on you emotionally, she had no influence on you artistically. You never emulated her work.

SARTON: No. Very little influence. None. Her style is too mannered. At her best, in *The Death of the Heart*, it's marvelous, but in the later books her style became too literary in a not very attractive way to me. For instance, a sentence is very rarely a straight sentence.

INTERVIEWER: It's convoluted?

SARTON: It's convoluted and put upside down. "Very strange was the house" instead of "The house was very strange." Incidentally, Elizabeth Bowen appears in my novel *A Single Hound,* as the lover of Mark. I made her into a painter.

INTERVIEWER: We were talking, before this digression, about

why you write novels. You say you write them to find out what you are thinking, to answer a question. Could you give another example?

SARTON: In the case of *Faithful Are the Wounds,* the question was: how can a man be wrong and right at the same time? This book was based on the suicide of F. O. Matthiessen during the McCarthy era. At that time, people outside his intimate circle, and I was never an intimate of Mattie's, did not know that he was a homosexual, so that is only suggested in the novel. But what interested me was that Mattie believed that socialists and communists could work together in Czechoslovakia and had gone way out on a limb to say this was possible and was going to happen and might be the answer to world peace. Then the communists took over and the socialists were done in. It was a terrible blow to Mattie and some people thought the suicide came from that. I wrote the novel partly because I was very angry at the way people I knew at Harvard reacted after his suicide. At first, as always happens with a suicide, people close to him thought, "What could we have done?" There was guilt. Then very soon I heard, "Poor Mattie, he couldn't take it." That was what enraged me, because these people didn't care that much, were not involved. And Mattie did care. I'm sure the suicide was personal as well as political, and perhaps everything was all wound up together at that point . . . but he was right in the deepest sense, you see, only he had bet on the wrong horse. His belief that people could work together, and that the Left must join, not divide, was correct. It proved to be unrealistic. But he wasn't nearly as wrong as the people who didn't care. That's what I wrote the novel out of.

INTERVIEWER: You've spoken of the novel. Earlier, you spoke of the body of your work as a whole. Would you talk about how the different parts fit together?

SARTON: The thing about poetry—*one* of the things about poetry—is that in general one does not follow growth and change through a poem. The poem is an essence. It captures perhaps a moment of violent change but it captures a moment, whereas the novel concerns itself with growth and change. As for the journals, you actually see the writer living out a life, which you don't in any of the other forms, not even the memoirs. In memoirs you are looking back. The memoir is an essence, like poetry. The challenge of the journal is that it is written on the pulse, and I don't allow myself to go back and change things afterwards, except for style. I don't expand later on. It's whatever I am able to write on the day about whatever is happening to me on that day. In the case of a memoir like *Plant Dreaming Deep,* I'm getting at the essence of five years of living alone in a house in a tiny village in New Hampshire, trying to pin down for myself what those five years had meant, what they had done to me, how I had changed. And that's very different from the journals. I must say, I'm not as crazy about the journals as some of my readers are. I get quite irritated when people say the journals are the best thing. God knows, I've struggled with certain things in the journals, especially about being a woman and about being a lesbian. The militant lesbians want me to be a militant and I'm just not.

But as for the vision of life in the whole of my work, I would like to feel that my work is universal and human on the deepest level. I think of myself as a maker of bridges—between the heterosexual and the homosexual world, between the old and the young. *As We Are Now,* the novel about a nursing home, has been read, curiously enough, by far more young people than old people. It terrifies old people to read about other old people in nursing homes. But the young have been moved by it. Many young people write me to say that they now visit elderly relatives in these places. This is the kind of bridge I want to make. Also, the bridge between men and women in their marriages, which I've dealt with in quite a few of the novels, especially in the last one, *Anger.*

So what one hopes, or what I hope, is that the whole work

will represent the landscape of a nature which is not primarily intellectual but rather a sensibility quite rich and diverse and large in its capacities to understand and communicate.

INTERVIEWER: How do you see your novels fitting into the tradition of the novel form?

SARTON: Well, they are quite traditional. I certainly haven't broken the forms. This is true in the poetry too. I think this may be one reason I have not had a great deal of critical attention, because the critics, I mean the real critics, not just the reviewers, are interested in the innovators. I suppose that *Mrs. Stevens Hears the Mermaids Singing* is innovative in that the material had not been dealt with as openly before, or at least not quite in the same way. But the technique isn't extraordinarily radical.

I have done all kinds of things with points of view in my novels, but I prefer the omniscient view, which I used in *Kinds of Love*. I think it's better for me, and perhaps for a poet, because you are able to describe things. In a novel like *Crucial Conversations*, the point of view is that of a friend of the marriage, an observer, and there is so much you simply cannot describe. You can't describe the atmosphere, the landscape, the interior of a house, say, without being quite awkward in the way you do it. "He walked in and noticed the roses were faded on the little eighteenth-century table." It's a little self-conscious. Ever since Henry James, there has been this big quibble about the point of view. As I say, I prefer the omniscient view although it's very unfashionable and is constantly pounced upon by the critics.

And the dialogue, of course. Elizabeth Bowen has said the great thing about dialogue: "Dialogue is what people do to each other." *Anger* is a perfect example. The war between these two characters is a war of dialogue. To some extent also in *Crucial Conversations* and even in an old novel of mine, *Shadow of a Man*, which I dipped into the other day because people are reading it now that it's in paperback, a great deal happens in the dialogue.

INTERVIEWER: For which of the novels do you have the greatest affinity?

SARTON: *Mrs. Stevens*, I think, *Faithful Are the Wounds*, and *As We Are Now* would be my three . . . and *A Reckoning*. Those four. Of course, they are all very different. *Faithful Are the Wounds* is a passionate political book, and I haven't done that any other time. In *As We Are Now* I think I did succeed in making the reader absolutely identify with Caro, the old woman who is stuffed into a ghastly rural nursing home and who is trying to stay alive emotionally. I look at *As We Are Now* as a descent into hell in which there are different steps down. The first is the person being captured, so to speak, and put in jail. The final step is when genuine love is made dirty. Caro had come alive again because a gentle nurse came into this terrible place and she sort of fell in love with her. Then that love is made dirty by the people who own the home. She tries to run away at that point. That's the final step; after that she begins to go mad and suffers despair. That's when she decides to burn the place down. She has a long conversation about God with her minister. One thing I like about this book is that there is a good minister in it. Ministers are almost always treated ironically in fiction, or made into monsters of some kind. This minister really listens. He isn't trying to tell her something. He's interested in what she has to say.

INTERVIEWER: So the end represents madness, not in any way a cleansing.

SARTON: Well, it's partly a cleansing action for her. The end has been questioned, and I myself question it because she burns up innocent people in the fire. But I felt it had to end that way. The innocent people were just vegetables, and so ill-treated that one felt death was better, really. And Caro probably does feel this way, only it isn't quite sane; she has all the inventiveness of the mad person who has an *idée fixe* of how she is going to proceed.

INTERVIEWER: At what point does the end become inevitable?

SARTON: When genuine love is defiled. That's when everything goes. There is nothing left. Then she is in hell.

INTERVIEWER: And the reason for your particular affinity with the novel *A Reckoning?*

SARTON: The origin of the book is rather interesting. I wrote it before I myself had cancer, and a mastectomy. But at an earlier date I *thought* I had cancer, and for a few days while the biopsy was being done I had an immense feeling of relief that I could lay the burden of my life down, get rid of all the clutter, and for the last six months of it, simply live and look at the world . . . look at the sun rise and not do anything that I ought to do. And then when I heard that I was all right and had to pick up the burden again of answering letters and living my life, which is a very good one but very demanding, I cried. I went out to Raymond, the gardener, and said, "I'm all right, Raymond," and burst into tears.

That was the clue to the novel, you see. Then I thought, "Ah! I'm going to write it. What would it have been like if I had had cancer, and six months to live my own death?" Really, the book is about how to live as much as it is about how to die. From much that I hear about it, I know it has been a helpful book. It's used in the hospices, and in nursing homes, and often read by nurses and people who are dealing with the dying. It has been useful, there is no doubt, and that is a wonderful feeling.

INTERVIEWER: Have any particular novelists been mentors?

SARTON: Yes. Certainly Virginia Woolf. She was the novelist who meant the most to me when I was learning. But she is a dangerous mentor from the technical point of view because she can't be imitated. It's too much her own genius. My first novel is written in a very Woolfian way. There's a description of a woman walking down some steps and it's summer and it's like a pastiche of Woolf. I never did that again.

INTERVIEWER: You've written in your journals about your meetings with Virginia Woolf, but can you cast your mind back and describe the very first moment you met her?

SARTON: I had left my first book of poems at her door, with some flowers, and the darling maid opened the door just then and said, "Oh, won't you come up?" I said, "Oh, no, I wouldn't think of it." I just left the book. Elizabeth Bowen knew that I wanted to meet Virginia Woolf desperately, so she invited the two of us and a couple of other people to dinner. That was when I first met her. She walked in, in a "robe de style," a lovely, rather eighteenth-century-looking, long dress with a wide collar, and she came into the room like a dazzled deer and walked right across—this was a beautiful house on Regent's Park—to the long windows and stood there looking out. My memory is that she was not even introduced at that point, that she just walked across, very shyly, and stood there looking absolutely beautiful. She was much more beautiful than any of the photographs show. And then she discovered that I was the person who had left the poems.

She was very canny . . . she answered my gift of that book with a lovely note, which is now in the Berg collection, just saying: "Thank you so much, and the flowers came just as someone had given me a vase, and were perfect, and I shall look forward to reading the poems." In other words, never put yourself in a position of having to judge. So she never said a word about the poems. But she was delighted to find out that I was the person who had left them.

Then, later, we talked—Elizabeth and Virginia Woolf and I. The gentlemen were having their brandy and cigars in the other room. We talked about hairdressers. It was all like something in *The Waves!* We all talked like characters in a Virginia

Woolf novel. She had a great sense of humor. Very malicious. She liked to tease people, in a charming way, but she was a great tease.

INTERVIEWER: Did you feel shy?

SARTON: Of course! But she put me at ease and I saw her quite often after that. Every time I was in England I would have tea with her, which was a two-hour talk. She would absolutely ply me with questions. That was the novelist. I always felt the novelist at work. Where did I buy my clothes? Whom was I seeing? Whom was I in love with? Everything. So it was enrapturing to a young woman to be that *interesting* to Virginia Woolf. But I think it was her way of living, in a sense. Vicariously. Through people.

INTERVIEWER: But you've written that you felt a certain coldness, in spite of . . .

SARTON: Yes. She was never warm. That's true. There was no warmth. It was partly physical, I think. She was a physically unwarm person. I can't imagine kissing her, for instance, I mean on the cheek. But she was delightful, and zany, full of humor and laughter. Never did you feel a person on the brink of madness. That has distorted the image, because she was so in control.

INTERVIEWER: You were speaking of influences. Whom else would you add?

SARTON: The person who influenced me the most has been François Mauriac. I greatly admired the economy and thrust of his books. He was able to create so much between the lines. I was aiming for that. I was aiming to eliminate what at first I was praised for, a so-called "poetic style." I wanted to get rid of that and to make the poetry less obvious, to make it sharper and purer and simpler. I've worked to get a more and more clarified style, but I think this has been misunderstood in my case. Somebody said of *As We Are Now:* "A ninth-grader could have written it"—meaning the style. I mean, this person simply didn't get it! Other people did get it, fortunately. Of course, the thing that is so tremendous with Mauriac, and isn't possible for me because I don't belong to the Church, is the Catholic in him, which gives this extra dimension to everything that he wrote. I envy him that.

INTERVIEWER: How was it that you began to write the journals?

SARTON: I wrote the first one, *Journal of a Solitude,* as an exercise to handle a serious depression and it worked quite well. I did have publication in mind. It wasn't written just for me. I think it's part of the discipline. It keeps you on your toes stylistically and prevents too much self-pity, knowing that it's going to be read and that it will provide a certain standard for other people who are living isolated lives and who are depressed. If you just indulge in nothing but moaning, it wouldn't be a good journal for others to read. I also found that by keeping a journal I was looking at things in a new way because I would think, "That—good! That will be great in the journal." So it took me out of myself, out of the depression to some extent. This happened again with *Recovering.*

INTERVIEWER: You write for publication; do you have an imagined audience?

SARTON: It's really one imaginary person.

INTERVIEWER: Would you talk a little about this imaginary person?

SARTON: Well, I don't mean that when I sit down I think, "Oh, there is that imaginary person over there I'm writing for," but . . . yes! Somebody who sees things the way I do, who will be able to read with heart and intelligence. I suppose somebody about my age. It used to be somebody about forty-five; now it's somebody about seventy. But then *Journal of a Solitude* brought me a whole new audience, a college-age audience. That was very exciting because until then my work had appealed mostly to older people.

INTERVIEWER: Isn't it true that lately you have been embraced by the spiritual establishment?

SARTON: Yes, this has happened only recently and has been extremely moving to me. I have come out as a lesbian. And although I have no shame about this at all, I still feel it's quite extraordinary that religious groups would be so receptive to me, as the Methodists were, for instance. They asked me to be one of the speakers at their yearly retreat for pastors. The other speakers were religious in a way that I am not. Then, the Unitarians gave me their Ministry to Women Award last year and I was touched by what they said . . . that I'd helped women by my honesty. The Methodists also talked about honesty.

I must say it was quite brave of me to come out as I did in *Mrs. Stevens,* in 1965. At that time it was "not done." When I spoke at colleges I would never have stated, "I'm a lesbian." But this all changed in the seventies. It's marvelous now that one can be honest and open. At the time *Mrs. Stevens* was published, it was sneered at in reviews and I lost a couple of jobs. They weren't terribly important jobs but I did lose them. Now I don't think that would happen. It might if you were a professor in a college, but coming as a visiting speaker you can be absolutely open. Women's Studies have helped me enormously, there's no doubt about it. This is one way my work is now getting through.

I know of no other writer who has had such a strange career as I've had. When I started writing, the first novels were received with ovations. In 1956, I was nominated for the National Book Award in two categories, fiction and poetry. But after my fifth novel, *Faithful Are the Wounds,* the one that was nominated, this never happened again and I began to have bad reviews. I was no longer in fashion. I can't think of another writer who has had as hard a time with reviewers over a period of twenty years as I have but whose work has been so consistently read. It's word of mouth. It's people . . . every day I get letters saying things like: "I loved such and such a book and I'm buying five copies to give to people." That's how books get around. And then the public libraries. Without the public libraries, serious writers, unfashionable serious writers like me, really wouldn't have a chance. Again, I hear from people, "I was wandering around the library and saw the title *Plant Dreaming Deep*. It caught my attention . . . now I'm reading everything you've written." It's wonderful to have this happen at the age of seventy.

INTERVIEWER: Will you talk about the relationship between the poet and the Muse?

SARTON: Many of my poems are love poems. I'm only able to write poetry, for the most part, when I have a Muse, a woman who focuses the world for me. She may be a lover, may not. In one case it was a person I saw only once, at lunch in a room with a lot of other people, and I wrote a whole book of poems. Many of these poems have not been published. But this is the mystery. Something happens which touches the source of poetry and ignites it. Sometimes it is the result of a long love affair, as "The Divorce of Lovers" poems, the sonnet sequence. But not always. So who is the audience for my poetry? The audience is the loved one for me. But usually "the loved one" isn't really interested in the poems.

INTERVIEWER: You, and Robert Graves with his White Goddess, are perhaps the only modern poets to be so strongly and personally inspired by the Muse as a mythological figure. A literal figure. Do your Muses, diverse as they must be, possess any one thing in common?

SARTON: Maybe so. The word that popped into my mind when you asked the question was: distance. Maybe there is something about the Distant Admired Person. I had a curious experience in Berkeley recently, where I stayed with a friend I went to school with, the Shady Hill School, in Cambridge, Massachusetts. She had saved a book of poems that a group of us had written. We used to meet, four of us, and read our poems to each other and savagely criticize them. These poems were *passionate* love poems to our teacher, Anne Thorp, the person I'm now trying to write a novel about. I was absolutely floored by the intensity of these poems! We were completely inexperienced. In that generation there was no sex, I mean nothing like what goes on now. We were asexual because we just didn't know anything yet. But we *felt* so intensely. And I saw that I haven't changed that much. I'm not innocent in the way I was then, but my feelings have remained very much as they were.

INTERVIEWER: If Anne Thorp had possessed all those qualities you worshiped, but had been a man . . . could you have been writing those love poems to a man?

SARTON: Yes, it's possible. I just don't know. The three other people did not become homosexual. Only I among the four.

INTERVIEWER: You have spoken of poems as coming from the subconscious.

SARTON: It's not the poem that comes from the subconscious so much as the image. Also the single line, *la ligne donnée.* If I'm truly inspired, the line comes in meter and sets the form. But what comes from the subconscious is only the beginning. Then you work with it.

In the case of metaphor, it has everything to teach you about what you have felt, experienced. I write in order to find out what has happened to me in the area of feeling, and the metaphor helps. A poem, when it is finished, is always a little ahead of where I am. "My poem shows me where I have to go." That's from Roethke. His line actually reads: "I learn by going where I have to go."

INTERVIEWER: So you write novels to find out what you think, and poems to find out what you feel?

SARTON: Yes, it works out that way. In the novel or the journal you get the journey. In a poem you get the arrival. The advantage of free verse, for instance in "Gestalt at Sixty," is that you do get the journey. Form is so absolute, as if it had always been there, as if there had been no struggle. The person who sees the lyric poem on the page doesn't realize there may have been sixty drafts to get it to the point where you cannot change a single word. It has been worked for. But something has been given, and that's the difference between the inspired poem and what Louise Bogan calls the imitation poem. In the inspired poem something is given. In the imitation poem you do it alone on will and intelligence. I mean, you say something like: "It might be a good idea to write a poem about a storm down here at the end of the field when the fountains of spray come up." And so you go ahead and do it. But the difference is simply immense, as far as the poet goes. He knows, or she knows, what is inspired and what is imitation.

INTERVIEWER: Would the reader know?

SARTON: I think so.

INTERVIEWER: What about the advantages and disadvantages of form?

SARTON: Form is not fashionable these days. What's being thrown out, of course, is music, which reaches the reader through his senses. In meter, the whole force is in the beat and reaches the reader, or the listener, below the rational level. If you don't use meter, you are throwing away one of the biggest weapons to get at the reader's subconscious and move him. The advantage of form, far from being "formal" and sort of off-putting and intellectual, is that through form you reach the reader on this subliminal level. I love form. It makes you cut down. Many free verse poems seem to me too wordy. They sound prose-y, let's face it. When you read a poem in form, it's pared down, it's musical, and it haunts. Very few free verse poems are memorable. You don't learn them by heart unless they are very short. But a lyric poem is easy to remember.

INTERVIEWER: You have written poems in free verse.

SARTON: Oh, yes, a lot. I find it exhilarating.

INTERVIEWER: How do you know when you're finished?

SARTON: That's the problem. I can go on revising almost forever. But with form, at a certain point it's all there. Another problem, or danger, with free verse, is that it depends almost entirely on the image, so you get people using what I call "hysterical images," images which are too powerful because you've got to hit the reader over the head with something big . . . like talking about love in terms of the Crucifixion. Or the Holocaust. A tremendously strong image to say something which doesn't deserve that intensity and only shocks the reader, but in a rather superficial way.

INTERVIEWER: What poets have had the most influence on you?

SARTON: H. D., when I was young. It was the age of Millay. Millay was the great . . . well, everybody adored her. And I did too. I loved those lyrics. But I was fascinated by H. D. because of the freshness she managed to get into free verse. Then the other women lyric poets: Elinor Wylie certainly influenced me, and later on Louise Bogan, who I think was probably the most distinguished pure lyric poet of our time. There you get that marvelous economy and music and depth and also the archetypal images. And then Valéry, whom I translated with Louise Bogan.

INTERVIEWER: Because your parents were European, and you yourself were born in Belgium, has that made a difference to you as a poet?

SARTON: I think an enormous difference. Because the things that touched me most, the literary things, were mostly in French, and later on, at fourteen, I came under the influence of Jean Dominique.*

INTERVIEWER: What about those very early years?

SARTON: During the first two years of my life we lived in a small heaven of a house in Wondelgem, Belgium. Then we were driven out by the war and went to England. In 1916, when I was four, we settled for good in Cambridge, Massachusetts. Even so, every seven years, when my father had a sabbati-

Nom de plume of Marie Closset of the Institut Belge de Culture Française.

cal, we all went to Europe. It took me until I was forty-five to become an American at heart. It was in 1958, after my parents were both dead, that I bought a house in Nelson, a small village in New Hampshire, and settled in for fifteen years and made roots. I describe that in *Plant Dreaming Deep*. I planted the dreams then and became an American.

But for very long, all my youth, from nineteen on anyway, I went to Europe every year. Although we never had much money, my father gave me a hundred dollars a month allowance, and an extra three hundred dollars, which at the time covered a boat round trip, tourist class. I either stayed with friends, or, in London, in one of those dreary one-room flats which cost £2 a week with an English breakfast thrown in. I felt European partly because—I still believe this—the emotional loam is deeper in Europe. People are less afraid of feeling. The lesbian part of me came into this because in the Bloomsbury society of the thirties there was no trouble about that. I didn't feel like a pariah. I didn't feel that I had to explain myself. And among my mother's generation there were passionate friendships between women that were probably not sexually played out, but it was common for women to be a little in love with each other. It was taken for granted. It wasn't a big issue.

One of the themes in all I have written is the fear of feeling. It comes into the last novel where Anna asks, "Must it go on from generation to generation, this fear of feeling?" I want feelings to be expressed, to be open, to be natural, not to be looked on as strange. It's not weird, I mean, if you feel deeply. And, really, most Americans think it is. Sex is all right, but feeling is not. You can have five people in your bed and no one will worry much, but if you say, "I've fallen in love at seventy," people's hair is going to stand on end. They'll think, "The poor thing, there's something awfully wrong with her."

INTERVIEWER: Young people read *Halfway to Silence* and

quote the poems . . . it goes so much against our cultural norms, the idea of a woman of sixty-five writing a passionate love poem to another woman.

SARTON: Yes, I know. And I have done it more than once. The poem "Old Lovers at the Ballet" is really about this: how is the sexuality different for an older couple, old lovers watching these magnificent bodies which they don't have and the grace which they no longer have? I suggest that what they do have is something else, an ability to communicate spiritually through sex. I believe that at its deepest, sex is a communication of souls through the body. That can go on forever.

INTERVIEWER: Did you ever write poems in French?

SARTON: I wrote poems for Jean Dominique in French, but I didn't know the language well enough, the prosody, and so they have a certain charm but nothing more. I'd never publish them.

INTERVIEWER: So the European influence is in the emotional climate more than anything.

SARTON: Yes. But as I said, the seminal influences in my writing were French; Mauriac for the novels, Valéry for the poetry, and also Gide at a certain time, particularly in the journals.

INTERVIEWER: Would you talk about the poems you're writing now?

SARTON: I'm writing new poems now called "Letters from Maine." It's a new form for me. I've written so many poems in sonnet form, or in other forms, and I wish I could find something a little freer which is not free verse. These are a sort of loose iambic pentameter. They don't rhyme, and they flow. It's impossible for me to tell whether they're any good. In six months I'll look back and say, "That was a bad idea, it didn't work," or I'll say, "These are really quite good." Then I can begin to revise.

The poems come from a new Muse. A very distant one whom I probably won't see very much of. But it's opened up that mysterious door again. It's amazing, so mysterious, so extremely hard to talk about. Why should it happen that among all the people, the great many women whom I see and am fond of, suddenly somebody I meet for half an hour opens the door into poetry? Something is released. The deepest source is reached. Some of my best poems have been written for occasions which did not materialize, if you will. "In Time Like Air" is an example. "In time like air is essence stated" is the final line. Here is an example of an image which haunts for years, an archetypal image, *salt,* which I got from the French philosopher Gaston Bachelard. Bachelard has written a whole series of books analyzing images. In one of them he talks about the image of salt, and says it is a Janus material because it dissolves in water, crystallizes in air. I put that in a notebook and carried it around for years. Then I met somebody who started poetry for me again. I realized that salt was the image I needed. A metaphysical poem about love. And time. Love and time. There's only that one poem.

INTERVIEWER: You've discussed the different forms, or modes, you use to express your vision of life: poetry, novels, journals, memoirs. Were you ever tempted to write short stories?

SARTON: I did at one time write a number of stories when I was living in Cambridge and making very little money. I sold some to the then slicks, a lot of which don't exist anymore, and also to places like *Redbook* and *Ladies' Home Journal.* There are about thirty stories. I broke some taboos. For instance, I wrote about a woman dying of cancer and you weren't supposed to do that—write about it, I mean. *Ladies' Home Journal* published that. But they were not wonderful and I wouldn't like to see them reprinted. They were just . . . well, I sold one little piece for $600, which to me was a fortune, so that sort of set me off. I thought—Well! This is great! I'll write lots! And I did write quite a few but I finally had to stop because when I sat at the typewriter dollar signs were floating around in my eyes. It was the money. I somehow couldn't handle it.

INTERVIEWER: Could you write stories now?

SARTON: The form doesn't appeal to me very much. The short story is too much like a lyric, so that side goes into poetry.

INTERVIEWER: You have spoken with great admiration of Yeats, who changed his style and grew in poetic power even when he was an old man. Earlier, you mentioned the new form of your latest poems. Using that sort of comparison, how does it feel to be seventy?

SARTON: For the first time in my life I have a sense of achievement. I've written all these books and they're there! Nobody can take that from me. And the work is getting through at last. For so long I felt there were people who would like to read me but didn't know I existed. So I'm more relaxed inside now, less compulsive . . . somewhat less compulsive.

INTERVIEWER: You don't find that your past achievement acts as a brake on further achievement?

SARTON: Not at all. I feel much more creative now that I'm not carrying around that load of bitterness and despair because I was getting so little critical attention and therefore the readers weren't finding my work. Now they are finding it.

INTERVIEWER: You once wrote that to be worthy of the task, the poet moves toward a purer innocence where "the wonderful is familiar and the familiar wonderful . . ."

SARTON: That's a quote from Coleridge, of course. Where did I say that? In *Writings on Writing*, maybe. One of the good things about old age is that one often feels like a child. There is a childlike innocence, often, that has nothing to do with the childishness of senility. The moments become precious.

Ideally, one would live as if one were going to die the next day. I mean, if you were going to die the next day it would be well worth sitting and watching the sun set, or rise. It might not be worth doing a huge laundry.

INTERVIEWER: Your aspirations for yourself when you were young were quite lofty . . .

SARTON: Where did you read that?

INTERVIEWER: You told me.

SARTON: What do you mean? Of course my ambitions were lofty. I knew that I was a poet. This, like mathematical or musical gifts, you know when you are very young. My first poems were published in *Poetry* magazine when I was seventeen—five sonnets which open the first book, *Encounter in April.* Of course, I did think for a long time that I was going to be in the theater because I had fallen in love with *a* theater, the Civic Repertory Theater founded by Eva Le Gallienne in New York. She accepted me as an apprentice. I could have gone to Vassar, but I chose the theater. It was a difficult decision for my parents to accept, but in the end they backed the whole precarious plan.

INTERVIEWER: If you could be the seventeen-year-old looking at the woman of seventy, what would you think?

SARTON: I think I would be proud of myself. I've done what I set out to do and without a great deal of help. I never took permanent jobs in the academic world, which most poets have to do, not that they want to, and this has cost me something because the critical acclaim comes from the academic world, which launches a poet. But yes, I think that if at seventeen I'd known there'd be twelve books of poems (at that time I never imagined novels at all), I would feel pretty good. I'd say, "You did what was in you to do."

But I don't sit here and think, "Oh, how wonderful you are, Sarton." I think, on the contrary, "Oh, how much there is still to do!"

INTERVIEWER: You often see other poets and writers at conferences. Are you stimulated by this mixing with your peers, so to speak?

SARTON: I don't like writers. I don't like seeing writers. I'm not good at it. It upsets me. It's been too hard a struggle. I'm very competitive, and that side comes out. I'm uncomfortable with writers. I love painters and sculptors.

In relation to writers, the people whom I did love to see were the people who I felt were way ahead of me, like Louise Bogan and Elizabeth Bowen and Virginia Woolf. People from whom I had everything to learn and where my position was that of a neophyte. *That* I enjoyed. I have one very good new friend, a poet, Bill Heyen. He's a marvelously good poet, I think. But I really like to see what I call "real people"—who are not writers!

INTERVIEWER: One theme I wanted to ask you about is the phoenix.

SARTON: The phoenix, yes. The mythical bird that is consumed by fire and rises again from its ashes. That was D. H. Lawrence's symbol. I've appropriated it. I think I have died and been reborn quite a few times. One renewal from the ashes, to stick to the symbol, is recorded in my latest journal, *Recovering*, which describes a combination of the end of a love affair, a mastectomy, and a third very hard blow: an attack on my novel *A Reckoning*. I knew this novel was going to have value for people who were dying, and for their children and friends and so on, and it was more or less damned in the *New York Times* as a lesbian novel. This hurt. So I was getting over a lot of things. Again, as with *Journal of a Solitude*, I used the journal as a way of coming to terms with depression, and that journal is helping a lot of people. I get many letters about it.

INTERVIEWER: Have you been reborn recently?

SARTON: Yes. Yes, I have. I had gotten to a very sterile place because I was seeing so many people this summer and making so many public appearances, and yet at the center there was a kind of emptiness. I began to feel like a well that had gone dry. And then I did meet a woman who started the poems again, and has centered everything again for me. It's quite miraculous.

INTERVIEWER: Would you talk about the theme of the creative woman as a monster?

SARTON: Ruth Pitter, the poet, said in a letter to me once, "We are all monsters," meaning women poets. *Le monstre sacré.* As I say in the poem "My Sisters, Oh My Sisters," I think that was to some extent true. It isn't now. Now it's possible for women to have much more complete lives, and that's what we're working towards, really.

But let me go back for a minute to the phoenix. You see, at twenty-six I had been in the theater for six or seven years, first as an apprentice to Le Gallienne and then, when her theater failed, I kept the apprentices together and founded something called the Apprentice Theater. We did a season at the New School for Social Research in New York—rehearsal performances of Modern European plays in translation that had never been seen on Broadway. We got quite a lot of notice. It was a kind of first off-Broadway theater. But then we had to go into production in order to be a theater. I was offered a small theater in Hartford and we did a season there which was not a great success. I was looking all the time for new American plays and didn't find one. Finally we opened in Boston the following year and failed immediately, having spent $5,000 that I had managed to raise. So at twenty-six I faced failure, the complete failure of my dream of making a studio theater a little bit like the Moscow Art Theatre Studio. This was one of the times when the phoenix died and had to be reborn again and I was reborn as a writer. I was very ill after the theater failed. I guess I had what used to be called a nervous breakdown. My mother announced, "May has to rest," and took over. I rested for three months, just lay out on a chaise longue. I was exhausted. Emptied out. But one has extraordinary powers of remaking oneself. I learned it physically with the mastectomy. I was amazed at the power of the body to come back after such a shock. For that reason, the mastectomy was a thrilling experience, odd as it sounds. The body has this power, and so does the mind and the soul, to remake itself. That is the phoenix.

INTERVIEWER: Given your experience in the theater, might you not have been reborn as a playwright? Especially since you have such a strong sense of dialogue.

SARTON: I've written two full-length plays.

INTERVIEWER: Should I know that?

SARTON: No, you shouldn't. They were never produced, although Archibald MacLeish thought one of them had real possibilities and tried to get Robert Brustein at Yale to do it. The other one won a prize but I can't even remember what sort of contest it was. I wrote them quite fast, in about three weeks each, which is probably why they weren't better! But I wrote them long after the theater failed. Ten years, at least. Maybe twenty years.

It was like a fever, the theater, for me, but it was so closely connected with the Civic Repertory and Eva Le Gallienne and that marvelous theater which was so pure. The theater is heartbreak. I admire people who have the guts to take it.

INTERVIEWER: Apart from the informal teaching arrangements, you've earned your living entirely by your writing, isn't that true?

SARTON: Yes. I've never had a bonanza, but my books have been consistently read and now many of them are in paperback. It's been tough at times, but my writing has kept me afloat financially.

INTERVIEWER: Everyone wants to know about a writer's work habits . . .

SARTON: I do all my work before eleven in the morning. That's why I get up so early. Around five.

INTERVIEWER: Have you pretty much stuck to the same kind of discipline over the years?

SARTON: Yes, I have. That I got from my father. I think the great thing he gave me was an example of what steady work, disciplined work, can finally produce. In not waiting for "the moment," you know, but saying: "I'm going to write every day for two or three hours." The trouble, for me, is the letters. They interrupt, and I give much too much energy to that. It's an insoluble problem.

INTERVIEWER: Would it be helpful, say, if you were stuck in your work, to switch over to the letters?

SARTON: I sometimes start the day with the letters. Just to get the oil into the machine.

INTERVIEWER: Do you have other ways of getting oil into the machine?

SARTON: Music. I play records, mostly eighteenth-century music. I find that the Romantics—Beethoven—don't work for me. I love them to listen to, but not to work with, alongside of, whereas Mozart, Bach, Albinoni . . . Haydn, I love. I feel the tremendous masculine joy of Haydn. That gets me going.

INTERVIEWER: It gets you going, but do you keep it going?

SARTON: Yes. It's probably a terrible thing to do to the music but it does a lot for me.

INTERVIEWER: You have mentioned that you are writing a journal, and there are the new poems . . .

SARTON: And a novel. I'm hoping now to get back to a novel that went dead on me before I wrote *Anger,* called *The Magnificent Spinster.* I'm looking forward to doing it because it will be rather rich and poetic in a way that *Anger* was not. *Anger* was a novel like a blow, trying to get at things almost brutally.

This brings up an interesting point, I think. Here I have this novel, which I set aside for a long time and which I am going back to. In other words, you can plan for a novel. You can say, "I'm going to write a novel next year" and then go ahead and do it. Except that it might not work out, but still you can plan for it. You simply cannot do this with poems, they come out of a seizure of feeling. You can't plan for a seizure of feeling, and for this reason I put everything else aside when I'm inspired, because, as I've said, you can't summon a poem. You can try, but it won't be much good if it's written on command.

INTERVIEWER: You've written movingly about your parents in *A World of Light.*

SARTON: That is a memoir recapturing twelve different people, a celebration of great friendships. All of the people were dead, or "gone into the world of light"—the Henry Vaughan quote—at the time I wrote it, except one. I included my parents because their friendship has weighed on me all my life. Their influence was the most difficult to deal with, and the most inspiring. I've spoken about the value of memoirs as the past considered, as essences. In "The Fervent Years," the chapters in *I Knew a Phoenix,* I talk about my parents' youth. It taught me an awful lot about them, and about a whole period. They were tremendously idealistic people. They had the nineteenth-century vision of life, the perfectability of man. Ever since the Holocaust, something has happened to people, to all of us. We've had to face certain things which make it impossible for us to foresee a much better future. We're faced with a whole lot of choices that are pretty depressing. Whereas my parents still had that well of idealism and faith in humanity which runs through all of my father's work.

INTERVIEWER: What about your phrase "usable truth . . ."?

SARTON: This is the function of poetry. To make people experience. That's where it's completely different from philosophy, where you think something out but don't have to experience it in your whole being so that you are changed. It's perfectly stated by Rilke in the sonnet "To the Archaic Torso of Apollo." One must visualize this ideally beautiful sculpture with no head and no eyes. The poem ends, "Here there is nothing that does not see you. You must change your life." That is what art is all about.

KAREN SAUM
Fall 1982

5. Eugene Ionesco

Born in Slatina, Romania, on November 26, 1912, Eugene Ionesco has been called the "Shakespeare of the Absurd." While attending the University of Bucharest he received a grant to study in France. He completed his education at the Sorbonne and returned to Bucharest in 1936 to teach French until 1939.

His first published writing was *Hugoliades,* a satirical portrait of Victor Hugo, which he wrote at the age of twenty while still a student at the University of Bucharest. Ionesco's early plays *The Bald Soprano* (1953) and *The Lesson* (1953) received tremendous critical acclaim and launched a career that would greatly affect the course of both European and American theater; both works have been playing nightly in Paris since 1960. Ionesco has written over thirty plays, including *Rhinoceros, The Chairs, Jack, or The Submission, The Future Is in Eggs, Exit the King, Macbett, Story Number Four,* and *Man with Bags.* His most recent publication is *Journey Among the Dead,* a collage of Ionesco's dreams, autobiographical writings, and extracts from earlier works.

Eugene Ionesco is a member of the Académie Française and lives in Paris with his wife, Rodika.

bornée à ce conflit simple, — il n'y aurait rien en
de nouveau, de vrai, de profond, — mais une
réalité grossière et schématique. Nous nous apercevons
que tout est bien plus complexe. Et dans cette
prison, un homme doit mourir être exécuté. On
ne voit pas ce condamné sur la scène. Il est pourtant
présent à notre conscience, infiniment obsédant. C'est
le héros de la pièce. Ou plutôt : c'est la mort
qui est ce héros. Gardiens et prisonniers ressentent
cette mort, la ressen ensemble, vivent cette mort, —
sauf le bourreau et le vieux prisonnier : il n'y a
que ces derniers qui soit déshumanisés. A part eux,
l'humanité profonde de cette œuvre réside dans la
communion vraie, aux terrible de cette hantise,
cette angoisse qui est celle de tous. Une union,
au-delà de la désunion ; une fraternité, presque
inconsciente mais dont l'auteur nous fait prendre
conscience, s'é se crée ou se révèle. Il est
évident que cette angoisse est propre à nous tous.
Les gardiens, les prisonniers sont les uns et les
autres, des mortels que hantent le fait essentiel
qu'ils sont des mortels, — et la pièce touche
aux problèmes essentiels des hommes qui fait que
les hommes soient des hommes. Voilà un théâtre
populaire, — celui de la communion dans la
même angoisse. Impopulaire, aussi, — car
à Paris, du moins, le Oblient du matin n'a pas eu

A Eugene Ionesco manuscript page.

Eugene Ionesco's passport photograph.

Eugene Ionesco

The last few years have been exceptionally busy for Eugene Ionesco. His seventieth birthday was celebrated in 1982 with a series of events, publications, and productions of his work, not only in France but worldwide. Hugoliades, *Ionesco's satirical portrait of Victor Hugo, which he wrote at the age of twenty, was newly published by Gallimard. In Lyons, Roger Planchon, the director of the Théâtre Nationale Populaire, staged* Journey Among the Dead, *a collage of Ionesco's dreams, autobiographical writings, and extracts from his latest play,* The Man with Suitcases. *The show, which toured France to both critical and popular acclaim, was due to be staged at the Comédie Française in Paris. Recently, the cast of Ionesco's two early plays* The Bald Soprano *and* The Lesson *gave a birthday party for the playwright which also celebrated both plays' twenty-fifth year of uninterrupted runs at the Théâtre de la Huchette in Paris.*

*Over the past thirty years, Ionesco has been called a "tragic
clown," the "Shakespeare of the Absurd," the "Enfant Terrible
of the Avant-Garde," and the "Inventor of the Metaphysical
Farce"—epithets that point to his evolution from a young playwright at a tiny Left Bank theater to an esteemed member of the
Académie Française. For the past forty-five years, Ionesco has
been married to Rodika, his Romanian wife. They live in an
exotic top-floor apartment on the Boulevard Montparnasse
above La Coupole, surrounded by a collection of books and
pictures by some of Ionesco's oldest friends and colleagues,
including Hemingway, Picasso, Sartre, and Henry Miller. Our
interview took place in the drawing room, where Miro's por-
traits, Max Ernst's drawing of Ionesco's* Rhinoceros, *and a
selection of Romanian and Greek icons adorn the walls.*

*Ionesco, a small, bald man with sad, gentle eyes, seems quite
fragile at first glance—an impression which is immediately be-
lied by his mischievous sense of humor and his passionate
speech. Beside him Rodika, also slight, with dark slanted eyes
and an ivory complexion, looks like a placid Oriental doll.
During the course of the interview she brought us tea and
frequently asked how we were getting on. The Ionescos' steady
exchange of endearments and their courtesy with one another
reminded me of some of the wonderful old couples portrayed by
Ionesco in many of his plays.*

INTERVIEWER: You once wrote, "The story of my life is the
story of a wandering." Where and when did the wandering
start?

IONESCO: At the age of one. I was born near Bucharest, but
my parents came to France a year later. We moved back to
Romania when I was thirteen, and my world was shattered. I
hated Bucharest, its society, and its mores—its anti-Semitism
for example. I was not Jewish, but I pronounced my *r*'s as the
French do and was often taken for a Jew, for which I was
ruthlessly bullied. I worked hard to change my *r*'s and to sound

Bourguignon! It was the time of the rise of Nazism and every-one was becoming pro-Nazi—writers, teachers, biologists, his-torians. . . . Everyone read Chamberlain's *The Origins of the Twentieth Century* and books by rightists like Charles Maurras and Léon Daudet. It was a plague! They despised France and England because they were *yiddified* and racially impure. On top of everything, my father remarried and his new wife's family was very right-wing. I remember one day there was a military parade. A lieutenant was marching in front of the palace guards. I can still see him carrying the flag. I was stand-ing beside a peasant with a big fur hat who was watching the parade, absolutely wide-eyed. Suddenly the lieutenant broke rank, rushed toward us, and slapped the peasant, saying, "Take off your hat when you see the flag!" I was horrified. My thoughts were not yet organized or coherent at that age, but I had feelings, a certain nascent humanism, and I found these things inadmissible. The worst thing of all, for an adolescent, was to be different from everyone else. Could I be right and the whole country wrong? Perhaps there were people like that in France—at the time of the Dreyfus trials, when Paul Dérou-lède, the chief of the anti-Dreyfussards, wrote "En Avant Sol-dat!"—but I had never known it. The France I knew was my childhood paradise. I had lost it, and I was inconsolable. So I planned to go back as soon as I could. But first, I had to get through school and university, and then get a grant.

INTERVIEWER: When did you become aware of your vocation as a writer?

IONESCO: I always had been. When I was nine, the teacher asked us to write a piece about our village *fête*. He read mine in class. I was encouraged and continued. I even wanted to write my memoirs at the age of ten. At twelve I wrote poetry, mostly about friendship—"Ode to Friendship." Then my class wanted to make a film and one little boy suggested that I write the script. It was a story about some children who invite some other children to a party, and they end up throwing all the furniture and the parents out of the window. Then I wrote a patriotic play, *Pro Patria.* You see how I went for the grand titles!

INTERVIEWER: After these valiant childhood efforts you began to write in earnest. You wrote *Hugoliades* while you were still at university. What made you take on poor Hugo?

IONESCO: It was quite fashionable to poke fun at Hugo. You remember Gide's "Victor Hugo is the greatest French poet, alas!" or Cocteau's "Victor Hugo was a madman who thought he was Victor Hugo." Anyway, I hated rhetoric and eloquence. I agreed with Verlaine, who said, "You have to get hold of eloquence and twist its neck off!" Nonetheless, it took some courage. Nowadays it is common to debunk great men, but it wasn't then.

INTERVIEWER: French poetry is rhetorical, except for a few exceptions like Villon, Louise Labé, and Baudelaire.

IONESCO: Ronsard isn't. Nor are Gérard de Nerval and Rimbaud. But even Baudelaire sinks into rhetoric: "Je suis belle, Ô Mortelle . . . ," and then when you see the actual statue he's referring to, it's a pompous one! Or:

> Mon enfant, ma soeur,
> songe à la douceur,
> d'aller là-bas vivre ensemble . . .

It could be used for a brochure on exotic cruises for American millionaires.

INTERVIEWER: Come on! There were no *American* millionaires in those days.

IONESCO: Ah, but there *were!* I agree with Albert Béguin, a famous critic in the thirties [author of *Dreams and the Romantics*], who said that Hugo, Lamartine, Musset, etc. . . . were *not* Romantics, and that French Romantic poetry really started with Nerval and Rimbaud. You see, the former produced versified rhetoric; they talked about death, even monologued on death. But from Nerval on, death became visceral and poetic. They didn't speak of death, they *died* of death. That's the difference.

INTERVIEWER: Baudelaire died of death, did he not?

IONESCO: All right then, you can have your Baudelaire. In the theater, the same thing happened with us—Beckett, Adamov, and myself. We were not far from Sartre and Camus—the Sartre of *La Nausée*, the Camus of *L'Étranger*—but they were thinkers who demonstrated their ideas, whereas with us, especially Beckett, death becomes a living evidence, like Giacometti, whose sculptures are walking skeletons. Beckett shows death; his people are in dustbins or waiting for God. (Beckett will be cross with me for mentioning God, but never mind.) Similarly, in my play *The New Tenant*, there is no speech, or rather, the speeches are given to the Janitor. The Tenant just suffocates beneath proliferating furniture and objects—which is a symbol of death. There were no longer words being spoken, but images being visualized. We achieved it above all by the dislocation of language. Do you remember the monologue in *Waiting for Godot* and the dialogue in *The Bald Soprano?* Beckett destroys language with silence. I do it with too much language, with characters talking at random, and by inventing words.

INTERVIEWER: Apart from the central theme of death and the black humor which you share with the other two dramatists, there is an important oneiric, or dreamlike, element in your work. Does this suggest the influence of Surrealism and psychoanalysis?

IONESCO: None of us would have written as we do without Surrealism and Dadaism. By liberating the language, those movements paved the way for us. But Beckett's work, especially his prose, was influenced above all by Joyce and the Irish Circus people. Whereas my theater was born in Bucharest. We had a French teacher who read us a poem by Tristan Tzara one day which started, "Sur une ride du soleil," to demonstrate how ridiculous it was and what rubbish modern French poets were writing. It had the opposite effect. I was bowled over and immediately went and bought the book. Then I read all the other Surrealists—André Breton, Robert Desnos . . . I loved the black humor. I met Tzara at the very end of his life. He, who had refused to speak Romanian all his life, suddenly started talking to me in that language, reminiscing about his childhood, his youth, and his loves. But you see, the most implacable enemies of culture—Rimbaud, Lautréamont, Dadaism, Surrealism—end up being assimilated and absorbed by it. They all wanted to destroy culture, at least organized culture, and now they're part of our heritage. It's culture and not the bourgeoisie, as has been alleged, that is capable of absorbing everything for its own nourishment. As for the oneiric element, that is due partly to Surrealism, but to a larger extent due to personal taste and to Romanian folklore—werewolves and magical practices. For example, when someone is dying, women surround him and chant, "Be careful! Don't tarry on the way! Don't be afraid of the wolf; it is not a real wolf!"— exactly as in *Exit the King*. They do that so the dead man won't stay in infernal regions. The same thing can be found in the *Tibetan Book of the Dead*, which had a great impact on me too. However, my deepest anxieties were awakened, or reactivated, through Kafka.

INTERVIEWER: Especially the Kafka of *Metamorphosis?*

IONESCO: Yes, and of *Amerika*. Remember how his character, Karl Rossmann, goes from cabin to cabin and can't find his way? It is very oneiric. And Dostoyevsky interested me because of the way he deals with the conflict between good and evil. But all this already had happened by the time I left Bucharest.

INTERVIEWER: How did you manage to return to Paris—I believe at the age of twenty-six—and stay for good?

IONESCO: I had a degree in French literature and the French government gave me a grant to come and do a doctorate. In the meantime, I had married and was working as a teacher. My wife, Rodika, was one of the few people who thought the same as I did. Perhaps it's because she comes from that part of Romania which is very Asiatic—the people are small and have slit eyes. Now I'm becoming a racialist! Anyway, I was going to write a thesis on "The Theme of Death and Sin in French Poetry." There's the grand title again.

INTERVIEWER: Did you write it?

IONESCO: Oh no! As I researched, I noticed that the French —Pascal, Péguy, etc.—had problems of faith, but they had no feeling for death and they *certainly* never felt guilty. What they had plenty of was the feeling of age, of physical deterioration and decay. From Ronsard's famous sonnet about aging, "Quand tu seras vieille . . . ," to Baudelaire's *La Charogne (The Carrion)*, to Zola's *Thérèse Raquin* and *Nana*—it's all degradation, decomposition, and rot. But not death. Never. The feeling of death is more metaphysical. So I didn't write it.

INTERVIEWER: Is that why you also gave up dramatizing Proust, because his preoccupation with time is different from yours?

IONESCO: Precisely. Also, *Remembrance of Things Past* is too long and difficult, and what is interesting is the seventh volume, *Time Regained*. Otherwise, Proust's work is concerned with irony, social criticism, worldliness, and the passage of time, which are not my preoccupations.

INTERVIEWER: When you settled in Paris, did you try to meet the authors whose works you had read, and get into the literary world?

IONESCO: I did research at the National Library and met other students. Later, I met Breton, who came to see my play *Amédee* in 1954. I continued seeing him until his death in 1966. But he had been dropped by the literary establishment because, unlike Aragon, Éluard, and Picasso, he refused to join the Communist Party, and so he wasn't fashionable anymore.

INTERVIEWER: You also got involved with the Collège de Pataphysique. Could you tell me about it?

IONESCO: Quite by chance, I met a man named Sainmont,

who was a professor of philosophy and the founder, or *Le Providateur Général,* of the Collège de Pataphysique. Later I met Raymond Queneau and Boris Vian, who were the most important and active members. The Collège was an enterprise dedicated to nihilism and irony, which in my view corresponded to Zen. Its chief occupation was to devise commissions, whose job it was to create subcommissions, which in turn did nothing. There was one commission which was preparing a thesis on the history of latrines from the beginning of civilization to our time. The members were students of Dr. Faustrol, who was an invented character and the prophet of Alfred Jarry. So the purpose of the Collège was the demolition of culture, even of Surrealism, which they considered too organized. But make no mistake, these people were graduates of the École Normale Supérieure and highly cultured. Their method was based on puns and practical jokes—*le canular.* There is a great tradition of puns in Anglo-Saxon literature—Shakespeare, *Alice in Wonderland*—but not in French. So they adopted it. They believed that the science of sciences is the *pataphysique* and its dogma, *le canular.*

INTERVIEWER: How was the Collège organized, and how did one join it?

IONESCO: It was organized with great precision: there was a hierarchy, grades, a pastiche of Freemasonry. Anybody could join, and the first grade was that of *Auditeur Amphitéote.* After that, you became a *Regent,* and finally a *Satrap.* The satrap was entitled to be addressed as *Votre Transcendence,* and when you left his presence you had to walk backwards. Our principal activity was to write pamphlets and to make absurd statements, such as "Jean Paulhan does not exist!" Our meetings took place in a little café-restaurant in the Latin Quarter, and we discussed nothing, because we believed—and I still do—that there is no reason for anything, that everything is meaningless.

INTERVIEWER: Is that not contradictory to your religious conversion?

IONESCO: No, because we exist on several different planes, and when we said nothing had any reason we were referring to the psychological and social plane. Our God was Alfred Jarry, and, apart from our meetings, we made pilgrimages to his grave near Paris. As you know, Jarry had written *Ubu Roi,* which was a parody of *Macbeth.* Much later I wrote a play based on *Macbeth* too. Anyway, the Collège gave decorations, the most important of which was *La Gidouille,* which was a large turd to be pinned on your lapel.

INTERVIEWER: How did you acquire the honor of becoming a satrap?

IONESCO: By writing *The Bald Soprano* and *The Lesson,* since the plays made fun of everything. They both had a conventional format—scenes, dialogue, characters—but no psychology.

INTERVIEWER: Did those at the Collège ever play a practical joke on you?

IONESCO: Yes. At the premiere of *The Bald Soprano,* twenty to thirty of them turned up wearing their *gidouilles* on their lapels. The audience was shocked at the sight of so many big turds, and thought they were members of a secret cult. I didn't produce many puns, but I did contribute to the *Cahiers de Pataphysique,* the Collège's quarterly magazine, with letters in Italian, Spanish, and German—all the languages I don't speak. The letters just sounded Italian, Spanish, and German. I wish I had kept some but I haven't. The chief makers of puns and *canulars* were Sainmont and Queneau. They invented a poet named Julien Torma, who of course never existed, and they published his works in the *Cahiers.* They even invented a biography for him, complete with a tragic death in the mountains.

INTERVIEWER: When did the Collège cease to exist?

IONESCO: When the founders and guiding spirits—Vian, Sainmont, and finally Queneau—began to die. There was an honorary president, a certain Baron Mollet, who was not a baron at all, but a madman who had once been Guillaume Apollinaire's valet. But the Pataphysique is not dead. It lives on in the minds of certain men, even if they are not aware of it. It has gone into "occultation," as we say, and will come back again one day.

INTERVIEWER: To get back to your work: After you dropped your thesis in favor of your own writing, why did you choose the theater and not another literary form?

IONESCO: The theater chose me. As I said, I started with poetry, and I also wrote criticism and dialogue. But I realized that I was most successful at dialogue. Perhaps I abandoned criticism because I am full of contradictions, and when you write an essay you are not supposed to contradict yourself. But in the theater, by inventing various characters, you can. My characters are contradictory not only in their language, but in their behavior as well.

INTERVIEWER: So in 1950 you appeared, or should I say erupted, on the French stage with *The Bald Soprano*. Adamov's plays were staged almost simultaneously, and two years later there was Beckett's *Waiting for Godot*—three avant-garde playwrights who, though very different in personality and output, had a great deal in common thematically and formally, and who later became known as the chief exponents of the "theater of the absurd." Do you agree with this appellation?

IONESCO: Yes and no. I think it was Martin Esslin who wrote a book with that title about us. At first I rejected it, because I thought that everything was absurd, and that the notion of the absurd had become prominent only because of existentialism, because of Sartre and Camus. But then I found ancestors, like Shakespeare, who said, in *Macbeth,* that the world is full of sound and fury, a tale told by an idiot, *signifying nothing.* Macbeth is a victim of fate. So is Oedipus. But what happens to them is not absurd in the eyes of destiny, because destiny, or fate, has its own norms, its own morality, its own laws, which cannot be flouted with impunity. Oedipus sleeps with his Mummy, kills his Daddy, and breaks the laws of fate. He must pay for it by suffering. It is tragic and absurd, but at the same time it's reassuring and comforting, since the idea is that if we don't break destiny's laws, we should be all right. Not so with our characters. They have no metaphysics, no order, no law. They are miserable and they don't know why. They are puppets, undone. In short, they represent modern man. Their situation is not tragic, since it has no relation to a higher order. Instead, it's ridiculous, laughable, and derisory.

INTERVIEWER: After the success of *The Bald Soprano* and *The Lesson* you became suddenly and controversially famous. Were you lionized? Did you start frequenting literary salons and gatherings?

IONESCO: Yes, I did. Literary salons don't exist any longer in Paris, but in those days there were two. The first was the salon of Madame Dézenas—a rich lady who liked literature and the arts. All sorts of celebrities came there: Stravinsky, Etiemble, young Michel Butor, Henri Michaux. . . . The second salon was La Vicomtesse de Noailles's. I went there once and met Jean-Louis Barrault. I remember how a ripple of excitement, a *frisson,* ran through the gathering when Aragon and Elsa Triolet were announced. "Here come the Communists!" they all said. Aragon was in a dinner jacket and Elsa was covered in jewelry. But *I* went there to drink whiskey and to meet friends, not out of worldliness.

INTERVIEWER: Do you think worldly distractions, social life and parties, dissipate a writer's concentration and damage his work?

IONESCO: Yes, to a certain extent. But there have been great writers who have been great partygoers at the same time, such as Valéry, Claudel, and Henry James. Valéry used to get up at five in the morning, work until nine, then spend the rest of the day having fun in one way or another.

INTERVIEWER: Do you think success can be damaging for a writer, not only as a distraction but because it could make him seek out easy options and compromises?

IONESCO: It depends on how you use it. I detest and despise success, yet I cannot do without it. I am like a drug addict—if nobody talks about me for a couple of months I have withdrawal symptoms. It is stupid to be hooked on fame, because it is like being hooked on corpses. After all, the people who come to see my plays, who create my fame, are going to die. But you can stay in society and be alone, as long as you can be detached from the world. This is why I don't think I have ever gone for the easy option or done things that were expected of me. I have the vanity to think that every play I have written is different from the previous ones. Yet, even though they are written in a different way, they all deal with the same themes, the same preoccupations. *Exit the King* is also *The Bald Soprano.*

INTERVIEWER: You also wrote a play called *Macbett,* which is very different from Shakespeare's *Macbeth.* What made you go for a remake of the Bard?

IONESCO: My Macbett is not a victim of fate, but of politics. I agree with Jan Kott, the Polish author of *Shakespeare, Our Contemporary,* who gives the following explanation: A bad king is on the throne, a noble prince kills him to free the country of tyranny, but ipso facto he becomes a criminal and has to be killed in turn by someone else—and on it goes. The same thing has happened in recent history: The French Revolution liberated people from the power of the aristocrats. But the bourgeoisie that took over represented the exploitation of man by man, and had to be destroyed—as in the Russian Revolution, which then degenerated into totalitarianism, Stalinism, and genocide. The more you make revolutions, the worse it gets. Man is driven by evil instincts that are often stronger than moral laws.

INTERVIEWER: This sounds very pessimistic and hopeless and

seems at variance with your mystical and religious tendencies.

IONESCO: Well, there is a higher order, but man can separate himself from it because he is free—which is what we have done. We have lost the sense of this higher order, and things will get worse and worse, culminating perhaps in a nuclear holocaust—the destruction predicted in the Apocalyptic texts. Only our apocalypse will be absurd and ridiculous because it will not be related to any transcendence. Modern man is a puppet, a jumping jack. You know, the Cathars [a Christian sect of the later Middle Ages] believed that the world was not created by God but by a demon who had stolen a few technological secrets from Him and made this world—which is why it doesn't work. I don't share this heresy. I'm too afraid! But I put it in a play called *This Extraordinary Brothel,* in which the protagonist doesn't talk at all. There is a revolution, everybody kills everybody else, and he doesn't understand. But at the very end, he speaks for the first time. He points his finger towards the sky and shakes it at God, saying, "You rogue! You little rogue!" and he bursts out laughing. He understands that the world is an enormous farce, a *canular* played by God against man, and that he has to play God's game and laugh about it. That is why I prefer the phrase "theater of derision," which Emmanuel Jacquart used for the title of his book on Beckett, Adamov, and myself, to "theater of the absurd."

INTERVIEWER: I think Esslin was dealing with the first period of your work—*The Bald Soprano, The Lesson, Jacques,* and *The Chairs.* With the introduction of your central character, Béranger, the plays seem to change somewhat. The dislocation of language, the black humor, and the element of farce are all still there, but not to the same degree. Instead, you develop new elements of both plot and character. How did you come to choose the name Béranger, and did the creation of this character help with the transition?

IONESCO: I wanted a very common name. Several came to my mind and I finally chose Béranger. I don't think the name means anything, but it is very ordinary and innocuous. In the first plays the characters were puppets and spoke in the third person as *one*, not as *I* or as *you*. The impersonal *one*, as in "one should take an umbrella when it is raining." They lived in what Heidegger calls "the world of one." Afterwards, the characters acquired a certain volume, or weight. They have become more individualized, psychologized. Béranger represents the modern man. He is a victim of totalitarianism—of both kinds of totalitarianism, of the Right and of the Left. When *Rhinoceros* was produced in Germany, it had fifty curtain calls. The next day the papers wrote, "Ionesco shows us how we became Nazis." But in Moscow, they wanted me to rewrite it and make sure that it dealt with Nazism and not with their kind of totalitarianism. In Buenos Aires, the military government thought it was an attack on Perónism. And in England they accused me of being a petit bourgeois. Even in the new *Encyclopaedia Britannica* they call me a reactionary. You see, when it comes to misunderstanding, I have had my full share. Yet I have never been to the Right, nor have I been a Communist, because I have experienced, personally, both forms of totalitarianism. It is those who have never lived under tyranny who call me petit bourgeois.

INTERVIEWER: The misunderstanding of your work in England and the fact that your plays have not been widely produced there or in America dates back to your quarrel with the late critic Kenneth Tynan in the early sixties.

IONESCO: That's right. I didn't much care for the Angry Young Men whose work Tynan was backing. I thought *them* very petit bourgeois and insignificant. I found their revolutionary zeal unconvincing, their anger small and personal, and their work of little interest.

INTERVIEWER: Also, Brecht was enjoying a vogue at the time, and you were definitely not Brechtian.

IONESCO: I think that Brecht was a good producer, but not really a poet or a dramatist, except in his early plays, *Three-*

penny Opera, Baal, and a couple of others. But his committed plays don't work. I believe that, as Nabokov said, an author should not have to deliver a message, because he is not a postman.

INTERVIEWER: Sam Goldwyn said the same thing about films, "Leave the messages to Western Union."

IONESCO: Did he say that? I quite agree. In France everybody was Brechtian—Bernard Dort, Roland Barthes—and they wanted to rule the theater. Later, Tynan asked me to write something for his erotic revue, *Oh! Calcutta!,* which I did. Then he said: "You have so much talent, you could be Europe's first dramatist." So I said, "What should I do?" and he said, "Become Brechtian." I said, "But then I would be the second, not the first."

INTERVIEWER: Now we seem to have come full circle. A Brechtian, Roger Planchon, has just produced *Journey Among the Dead,* your autobiographical play, and you are considered one of the greatest dramatists of our time. You have been sitting in the French Academy since 1970, next to some of the people who rejected your plays at first. I understand that the process of election to the Academy involves writing letters and calling on each member personally, pleading your case and asking to be elected. There are many famous rejections, like Baudelaire's heartbreaking letters to the members of the Academy, begging them to vote for him. And Zola. It seems a humiliating process. Yet you, a rebel, why did you go through with it?

IONESCO: I didn't. There were people who wanted me there, like René Clair, Jean Delay, and others; and I said I would apply on the condition that I would not have to call on people and write letters. I simply presented my letter of candidacy and I was elected by seventeen votes against sixteen.

INTERVIEWER: How do the meetings of the Academy compare with those of the Collège de Pataphysique in the old days?

IONESCO: All the members of the Academy are pataphysicians, whether consciously, like the late René Clair, or unconsciously. Anyway, I don't go there that often, only a couple of times a year for the elections of new members, and I always vote against them!

INTERVIEWER: Against whom?

IONESCO: Against everybody! Unfortunately, I'm such a poor intriguer that I have not succeeded in keeping out certain undesirable persons, and there are people I would like to see as members who have not yet been elected. But the elections are fun. Claudel used to say that they were so amusing that there should be one every week. You see, the French Academy is an association of solitaries: Jean Delay, the inventor of modern postpsychoanalytic psychiatry; Lévi-Strauss, the creator of modern anthropology and structuralism; Louis de Broglie, one of the founders of modern physics; and George Dumézil, a great specialist in religions. These are the most cultured men in France, truly liberated minds and free spirits. I assure you, only third-rate journalists denigrate the French Academy, the petit bourgeois who think they are intellectuals and who would not dream of mocking the Soviet Academy—where the members must accept all manner of indignity, pay allegiance to the Communist Party, and be censured constantly.

INTERVIEWER: You said that you didn't care much for the Angry Young Men of the theater. What about those, like Pinter and Albee, whose works were clearly influenced by yours and Beckett's?

IONESCO: Pinter's first play, *The Caretaker*, was derived from Beckett and was very good. Since then, he seems to be doing what I call *du boulevard intelligent*—which is to say, he is writing clever, well-made commercial plays. In truth, these playwrights were influenced only by our language, not really by our spirit. Stoppard's play *Rosencrantz and Guildenstern Are Dead* was admirable. I also liked Albee's *The Zoo Story*, but I haven't read anything in the same vein since. Several French playwrights, Dubillard and a few others, tried their hands, but it didn't really go anywhere. What we tried to do was to put man on the stage to face himself. That is why our theater was called metaphysical. In England, where people like Edward Bond write plays in which terrible things happen, it is still on the political level. The sacred and the ritual are missing. Did I tell you that I recently went to Taiwan? It is a nice American place, and everybody speaks English. But they seem to have lost touch completely with their own traditions, their own sages, and I, not a particularly erudite amateur, had to tell them about Confucius, Buddha, Zen. In the West, also, people have lost the feeling for the sacred, *le sentiment du sacré.* We tried to bring it back by going to our sources, to the theater of antiquity. In Racine, adultery is considered a very important crime, punishable by death. In the theater of the nineteenth century, adultery is a *divertissement,* an entertainment—the *only* entertainment! So although we are considered modern, too modern, even avant-garde, *we* are the real classicists, not the writers of the nineteenth century.

INTERVIEWER: After four plays—*Amédée, The Killer, Exit the King,* and *Rhinoceros*—you dropped Béranger. Did you think you had said enough about him?

IONESCO: I changed his name because I thought people might get bored. I called him Jean, or The Character.

INTERVIEWER: In your new play, which is a kind of oneiric biography, he is called Jean again. In the opening scene, there are two coffins, Sartre's and Adamov's, and you are standing behind them. Why did you choose those two from among all the people you have known?

IONESCO: Adamov was a great friend of mine for years, until my plays really caught on; then he turned against me. I resented him for giving in to pressure and becoming "committed," Brechtian, and pro-Communist, although he never actually joined the party. We finally broke up over some silly literary dispute. I think I accused him of stealing my dreams! With Sartre it was different. It was a case of a missed appoint-

ment, *un rendez-vous manqué,* as one journalist put it. I had
loved *La Nausée,* which had influenced my only novel, *Le
Solitaire (The Hermit),* but he annoyed me with his constant
ideological changes. He was given solid proof of concentration
camps in Russia, yet he did not publicize it because he feared
it would disillusion the workers and strengthen the bourgeoisie.
Towards the end, when the New Philosophers arrived on the
scene, people like Foucault and Glucksmann, he told them
that he was no longer a Marxist. He always had to be aligned
with *le dernier cri,* the latest ideological fashion. I would have
preferred him to be more obdurate, even if in error. He was
called "The Conscience of Our Time;" I feel he was rather the
*Un*conscience of our time—*L'inconscience.*

But he was always nice and courteous to me, and my plays
were the only ones he allowed to be put on a double bill with
his, so I am sad that I didn't get close to him. I had a dream
about him recently: I am on a stage in front of a huge, empty
auditorium, and I say, "That's it, nobody comes to see my plays
any more." Then a little man walks on stage, and I recognize
him as Sartre. He says, "Not true, look there, up in the gallery,
it's full of young people." And I say to him, "Ah, Monsieur
Sartre, how I would like to talk to you, at last." And he replies,
"Too late . . . too late." So you see, it was a missed appointment.

INTERVIEWER: This play, *Journey Among the Dead,* has been
a great success with the public as well as with the critics. It's
coming to the Comédie Française in the spring. With that out
of the way, have you started work on something else?

IONESCO: It's a play about the life and martyrdom of a modern saint, who has just been canonized by the Church—or is
it beatified? Which comes first? I'm not sure. Anyway, his
name was Father Maximilian Kolbe, a Pole, and he died in
Auschwitz. They were going to send some prisoners to a mine,
where they would die of hunger and thirst. Father Kolbe offered to go instead of a man who had a wife and children and

didn't want to die. That man is still alive.

INTERVIEWER: Does it matter to you if the Church canonizes him or not? And what about the recent allegations of anti-Semitism regarding him?

IONESCO: Oh dear! It won't matter to me at all whether the Church canonizes him or not. The important thing is that such a man existed. As for his anti-Semitism, I have not heard anything. People always try to find base motives behind every good action. We are afraid of pure goodness and of pure evil. I very much doubt that such a man could have been remotely anti-Semitic.

INTERVIEWER: For this play, you already had a clear idea of the character and the plot. Do you always start with an idea?

IONESCO: It depends. Some plays start with a plan. For example, *Macbett* was a conscious parody of Shakespeare. I already had the idea for *Rhinoceros*. But I had no idea at all where plays like *The Chairs, The Lesson,* and *The Bald Soprano* would lead. I had the idea of the corpse for *Amédée,* but the rest came bit by bit.

INTERVIEWER: How do you work?

IONESCO: I work in the morning. I sit comfortably in an armchair, opposite my secretary. Luckily, although she's intelligent, she knows nothing about literature and can't judge whether what I write is good or worthless. I speak slowly, as I'm talking to you, and she takes it down. I let characters and symbols emerge from me, as if I were dreaming. I always use what remains of my dreams of the night before. Dreams are reality at its most profound, and what you invent is truth because invention, by its nature, can't be a lie. Writers who try to prove something are unattractive to me, because there is nothing to prove and everything to imagine. So I let words and images emerge from within. If you do that, you might prove something in the process. As for dictating the text to my secretary, for twenty-five years I wrote by hand. But now it is impossible for me; my hands shake and I am too nervous.

Indeed, I am so nervous that I kill my characters immediately. By dictating, I give them the chance to live and grow.

INTERVIEWER: Do you correct what she has written afterward?

IONESCO: Hardly. But to get back to my new play, I tried to change the incoherent language of the previous plays into the language of dreams. I think it works, more or less.

INTERVIEWER: Do you have a favorite among your plays?

IONESCO: Until recently it was *The Chairs,* because the old man remembers a scene from his childhood, but very vaguely, like the light of a dying candle, and he remembers a garden whose gate is closed. For me that is paradise—the lost paradise. This scene is far more important to me than the end, which is more spectacular.

INTERVIEWER: We have talked about the metaphysical and ritualistic aspects of your work, but there is a comic element as well, which has greatly contributed to your popularity.

IONESCO: Georges Duhamel used to say that "humor is the courtesy of despair." Humor is therefore very important. At the same time, I can understand people who can't laugh any more. How can you, with the carnage that is going on in the world—in the Middle East, in Africa, in South America, everywhere? There is awfully little that is conducive to mirth.

INTERVIEWER: Whatever happens in the future, your place in the literary history of our time is secure. What is your own assessment of your work?

IONESCO: I'll tell you about a dream I had recently. When I was a schoolboy in Bucharest, my father used to come into my room in the evening and check my homework. He would open my drawers and find nothing but bits of poetry, drawings, and papers. He would get very angry and say that I was a lazybones, a good-for-nothing. In my dream, he comes into my room and says, "I hear you have done things in the world, you have written books. Show me what you have done." And I open my drawers and find only singed papers, dust and ashes.

He gets very angry and I try to appease him, saying, "You are right, Daddy, I've done nothing, nothing."

INTERVIEWER: Yet you go on writing.

IONESCO: Because I can't do anything else. I have always regretted having gotten involved with literature up to my neck. I would have preferred to have been a monk; but, as I said, I was torn between wanting fame and wishing to renounce the world. The basic problem is that if God exists, what is the point of literature? And if He *doesn't* exist, what is the point of literature? Either way, my writing, the only thing I have ever succeeded in doing, is invalidated.

INTERVIEWER: Can literature have any justification?

IONESCO: Oh yes, to entertain people. But that is not important. Yet, to introduce people to a different world, to encounter the miracle of being, that is important. When I write "The train arrives at the station," it is banal, but at the same time sensational, because it is invented. Literature can also help people. Two of my translators, a Romanian and a German, were dying of cancer when they were translating *Exit the King.* They told me that they knew they were going to die, and the play helped them. Alas, it does not help me, since I am not reconciled to the idea of death, of man's mortality. So you see, I am contradicting myself a little by saying that literature can be significant. People who don't read are brutes. It is better to write than to make war, isn't it?

INTERVIEWER: So, perhaps writing has been a way of exorcising your basic anxiety about death? Or at least learning to live with it?

IONESCO: Perhaps. But my work has been essentially a dialogue with death, asking him, "Why? Why?" So only death can silence me. Only death can close my lips.

SHUSHA GUPPY
Fall 1983

6. Elizabeth Hardwick

Elizabeth Hardwick was born in Lexington, Kentucky, in 1916. She came to New York to attend graduate school at Columbia University in the 1940s, and has for the most part lived there ever since. For many years she was married to the American poet Robert Lowell. In addition to her long association with *Partisan Review,* she is a founder and advisory editor of *The New York Review of Books,* the editor of *The Selected Letters of William James* (1961), and the author of three novels—*The Ghostly Lover* (1945), *The Simple Truth* (1955), and *Sleepless Nights* (1979)—and three collections of essays—*Seduction and Betrayal: Women and Literature* (1974), *A View of My Own: Essays in Literature and Society* (1980), and *Bartleby in Manhattan and Other Essays* (1983).

Winner of a Guggenheim Fellowship and many other prizes, Hardwick was the first woman recipient of the George Jean Nathan Award for dramatic criticism in 1967. She is a member of the American Academy of Arts & Letters.

4.

The beginning of June was hot. I took a journey and, of course, everything was ~~different and strange~~ new. When you travel your first discovery is that ~~somehow~~ you ~~no longer~~ do not exist. The phlox bloomed in its faded purples; on the hillside, phallic pines. Foreigners in the arcades, in the ~~little~~ basket shops. A steamy haze blurred the lines of the hills. A dirty, exhausting sky. Already, ~~it seemed,~~ the summer was passing away. Soon the boats would be gathered in, ferries roped to the dock.

I ~~was~~ am looking for the fosselized, for something-- persons and places thick and encrusted with final shape; instead there are many, many minnows, wildly swimming, trembling, vigilant to escape the net.

Kentucky-- that ~~was~~ is certainly ~~always~~ part of it. My mother lived as a girl in so many North Carolina towns they are confused in my mind. Raleigh and Charlotte. ~~Those two I remember~~ She hardly knew her own parents; they died quickly as people did then of whatever was in the air-- pneumonia, diphtheria, tuberculosis. I never knew a person so indifferent to the past. It was as if she didn't know who she was, ~~in some sense~~ She had brothers and sisters and was raised by them, passing their names down to us. I met one of her sisters when I was a child. She ran a hotel in asheville, north carolina,

Her face, my mother's, is not quite clear to me. A boneless, soft prettiness, with small brown eyes and the scarcest of eyebrows, darkened with a lead pencil. Not ~~a face easy to describe~~

1962

Dearest M: Here I am back in New York, on 67th Street in a high steep place with long, dirty windows. ~~It is quite nice, but~~ In the late

A manuscript page from Elizabeth Hardwick's novel *Sleepless Nights*.

© Jeffrey Allen

Elizabeth Hardwick

Elizabeth Hardwick lives on the West Side of Manhattan, on a quiet street near enough to Central Park to have heard the crowds and speakers at the great political demonstrations in Sheep's Meadow. Her apartment is light and spacious. "Like modern architecture," she says, "it looks much better in photographs." The building was designed for artists, and the living room is dominated by a large window. Behind the enormous plants and the freestanding tiles, one can see a comforting fixture of urban life: a fire escape.

Her home is clearly that of a writer constantly at work, and strewn throughout is a lifetime's accumulation of furniture, objects, paintings, posters, photographs, records, heirlooms, and countless books. On either side of the living room are more books: ceiling-high shelves of histories, fiction, and poetry. It is a working library, accumulated with her late hus-

band, the poet Robert Lowell. The daily effort to keep a large
library in order has made Hardwick favor paperbacks, preferably those lightweight and storable ones that can be whipped
out on a bus or an airplane—nonsmoking section—without
too much fuss.

Just as there are books everywhere that indicate the life of the
mind, so one frequently comes upon notebooks and notepads on
the coffee table, on the dining room table, things in which she
has jotted down lines, questions, ideas. The typewriter goes from
room to room, one day upstairs in her study, the next morning
downstairs. And then there are the manuscripts from former as
well as current students from her various writing classes, which
she will read and comment on extensively.

This interview took place in her home, where she occasionally
puttered, setting stray books in their places as we talked.

INTERVIEWER: I have the feeling you don't like to talk about
yourself, at least not in a formal way.

HARDWICK: Well, I do a lot of talking and the "I" is not often
absent. In general I'd rather talk about other people. Gossip,
or as we gossips like to say, character analysis.

INTERVIEWER: *Sleepless Nights* is reticent, perhaps, but it
certainly has the tone of lived experience, of a kind of autobiography.

HARDWICK: I guess so. After all, I wrote it in the first person
and used my own name, Elizabeth. Not very confessional,
however. And not entirely taken from life, rather less than the
reader might think.

INTERVIEWER: Many of the essays in *Seduction and Betrayal*
have an oddly personal tone. The stress on certain parts of the
texts shows that you have dug things out in an unusual, somehow urgent manner, as if you had lived them. I'm thinking of
the Jane Carlyle essay and your way of looking at Ibsen's
Rosmersholm.

HARDWICK: Jane Carlyle was real, but of course I didn't *really* know her, as the saying goes. The people in *Rosmersholm* are figures of Ibsen's imagination.

INTERVIEWER: What is the reason for your deep attraction to Ibsen?

HARDWICK: I don't know that I have a deep attraction for Ibsen. Sometimes I think he's an awful dolt . . . wooden, and in certain plays stolidly grandiose like the mountains that are such an unfortunate apotheosis in *Little Eyolf* and *When We Dead Awaken.* I don't like the poetic Ibsen, but I have found myself deeply engaged by the beauty, you might call it, of the old Ibsen domestic misery.

INTERVIEWER: Someone once said to me that he was fascinated by your essay on *Rosmersholm,* about the triangle between the man and the two women. But when he went to the play he couldn't always find your ideas there on the page. What do you make of that?

HARDWICK: I certainly hope what I said is on Ibsen's pages and of course I think it is. Still, you're not writing an essay to give a résumé of the plots. You choose to write because you think you have something fresh to say on a topic. That is, if you're writing from choice and not just as a journeyman doing a job. Perhaps it's true that in reading certain works, not all works, I do sometimes enter a sort of hallucinatory state and I think I see undercurrents and light in dark places about the imagined emotions and actions. This often stimulates me to write, particularly about novels. Of course the text is the object, the given, and the period is not often one's own and if there is anything detestable it is the looking at fictional characters as if they were your friends. I have found that horrible inclination among students, more and more so. They don't know the difference between calling a character "silly" and realizing that they are reading a masterpiece of created, located, visionary "silliness." I think every reader and critic falls into a hallucinatory state and that is as true of the technocrats, the deconstructionists, as of any others.

INTERVIEWER: When you say "hallucinatory state," are you trying to describe how the creative process works for you?

HARDWICK: Perhaps "hallucinatory" is too strong or too mysterious a word. What I meant was that in reading books and planning to write about them, or maybe just in reading certain books, you begin to see all sorts of not quite expressed things, to make connections, sometimes to feel you have discovered or felt certain things the author may not have been entirely conscious of. It's a sort of creative or "possessed" reading and that is why I think even the most technical of critics do the same thing, by their means making quite mysterious discoveries. But as I said, the text is always the first thing. It has the real claim on you, of course.

INTERVIEWER: Do you fall into this state when you write fiction?

HARDWICK: I don't fall into a state at all. I just meant to describe something happening in the brain when it is stimulated by reading imaginative works. As for writing fiction, well, you don't have any primary text, of course. You have to create that, and yet the struggle seems to be to uncover things by language, to find out what you mean and feel by the sheer effort of writing it down. By expression you discover what you wish to express or what can be expressed, by you. Things that are vague in the beginning have to be made concrete. Often, what you thought was the creative idea ahead of you vanishes or becomes something else.

INTERVIEWER: What comes first in sitting down to write—I guess we're talking about fiction. Is it a concept? Is it a character? Is it a scene?

HARDWICK: It takes many things to make a work of fiction, but I suppose it is true that there is a kind of starting point in the mind, a point that may be different for each piece of work. Sometimes I have had the impulse to begin fiction from a single line I had in my head.

INTERVIEWER: Can you give an example?

HARDWICK: I remember that I started writing *Sleepless Nights* because of a single line. The line was: "Now I will start my novel, but I don't know whether to call myself I or she."

INTERVIEWER: Was this a first line, a beginning line?

HARDWICK: No, it was to be the last line of the opening scene. I published the first chapter in *The New York Review of Books* and the line was the ending of the scene. But as I went on to write the book, I did call the narrator "I" and so I deleted the line from the final text. Some readers noticed the omission and asked me about it. I think now that I could have retained the line and just gone on with the narrative "I," as if to say I had made the decision.

INTERVIEWER: What did the line mean to you? That you knew it was going to be an autobiographical novel?

HARDWICK: Of course that line is not a theme. It is a wondering aloud about structure and also meant to indicate that sometimes in novels the use of the third person is really a disguise for the first person. I mean certain fictions have the strong feeling of autobiography even if they are written in the third person. It's something a sensitive reader can feel.

INTERVIEWER: When you started *Sleepless Nights* did you know anything more than that it would be an autobiographical novel?

HARDWICK: I wrote the first scene, starting with a description of a place and then going on to the writing of an imaginary letter to "Dearest M." The opening scene dominated the book, set the tone, and then, of course, as I worked on it I had to write the book—that is, create scenes, encounters, and so on.

INTERVIEWER: Has the impulse for writing ever started from a last line?

HARDWICK: Maybe not a last line, but a notion of the ending can be a useful stimulus.

INTERVIEWER: Does the opening paragraph mostly concern mood? Or plot? Or character?

HARDWICK: I don't have many plots and perhaps as a justification I sometimes think: if I want a plot I'll watch *Dallas*. I think it's mood. No, I mean tone. Tone arrived at by language. I can't write a story or an essay until I can, by revision after revision, get the opening tone right. Sometimes it seems to take forever, but when I have it I can usually go on. It's a matter of the voice, how you are going to approach the task at hand. It's all language and rhythm and the establishment of the relation to the material, of who's speaking, not speaking as a person exactly, but as a mind, a sensibility.

INTERVIEWER: Can you always arrive at the tone you want?

HARDWICK: No, I can't, and when that happens I put the work aside. But I've noticed that the effort is always useful. I mostly use the things, sometime, somewhere, that I've abandoned. They've been worked on, exist, if only in a few pages —and the old yellow pages flaking away in a drawer turn out to be useful. I don't know what I'm thinking about a particular thing until I have some kind of draft. It's the actual execution that tells me what I want to say, what I always wanted to say when I started.

INTERVIEWER: What do you mean when you say that you don't know what is in your mind until you've written it?

HARDWICK: I'm not sure I understand the process of writing. There is, I'm sure, something strange about imaginative concentration. The brain slowly begins to function in a different way, to make mysterious connections. Say, it is Monday, and you write a very bad draft, but if you keep trying, on Friday, words, phrases, appear almost unexpectedly. I don't know why you can't do it on Monday, or why I can't. I'm the same person, no smarter, I have nothing more at hand.

INTERVIEWER: Do you find that unique with yourself?

HARDWICK: I think it's true of a lot of writers. It's one of the things writing students don't understand. They write a first draft and are quite disappointed, or often *should* be disappointed. They don't understand that they have merely begun, and that they may be merely beginning even in the second or third draft. For the great expansive prose writers, obviously this isn't the case. Somehow everything is available to them all the time. That's the real prose gift.

INTERVIEWER: What writers have had this gift?

HARDWICK: Tolstoy, Dickens, Henry James. All the greatly productive geniuses. I am very struck by the revisions of Henry James. They seem to me always interesting, but in the end quite minor—changes in a few words, shiftings. The powers of concentration the great writers show are extraordinarily moving.

INTERVIEWER: Are there any tricks or devices that seem to help?

HARDWICK: For me, writing has not become easier after all these years. It is harder—perhaps because of the standards you set for your work. I suppose you have, by effort, a greater command than you imagine. The fact that writing remains so difficult is what puzzles.

INTERVIEWER: What is it about the writing process that gives you the most pleasure?

HARDWICK: The revision. That's what I like, working on a page or a scene.

INTERVIEWER: What about help with revision? Did Cal [Robert Lowell] ever help you with the books or essays?

HARDWICK: Not really. His suggestions were always wonderful, but so general I couldn't make much use of them. And he was always revising his own work and showing it to me and to his friends. He was revising something from the moment he got up until the moment he went to sleep, if only in his head, and so much of the time with him when you were alone was spent reading and talking to him about what he had done during the day. And that was very pleasant to me, it was always very interesting reading it, and it wasn't just to me that he read his work in progress. I have noticed the same method with other poets. I can remember having dear old I. A. Richards to dinner, and we weren't sitting there very long before the sheaf came out of the pocket of his coat, and he read his new poems, and that was wonderful.

INTERVIEWER: You didn't offer your own work in progress in that way?

HARDWICK: Well, it was a little bit different, you know, prose being longer, and it's not quite the same as seeing a quatrain at the end of the day. Cal did read my work, of course, and he was very encouraging and nice about it, and all of that, but it wasn't the same as going over each little part.

INTERVIEWER: How about the intellectual content of the essays?

HARDWICK: I must say he often looked discomfited on that score. Sometimes he thought I was too snippy.

INTERVIEWER: Really? He'd ask you to de-snip?

HARDWICK: I remember in one of the first issues of *The New York Review* I wrote a piece about a biographical book on Robert Frost. It was more or less mild, but Cal was quite annoyed—annoyed for a short time. I noticed in Randall Jarrell's letters that he gave a bit of approval to my Frost essay and so I said to myself, "O.K., Cal?" On the whole, Cal was encouraging. He liked women writers and I don't think he ever had a true interest in a woman who wasn't a writer—an odd turn-on indeed and one I've noticed not greatly shared. Women writers don't tend to be passive vessels or wives, saying, "Oh, that's good, dear."

INTERVIEWER: Was it stimulating to your own work to be involved in that sort of tremendously volatile writers' atmosphere?

HARDWICK: What do you mean "involved"? That would have been my atmosphere no matter what. Literature was always my passion. I do remember however that I was once asked if I had felt overpowered by Lowell's work, meaning, I guess, if it overpowered my own. I said, "Well, I should hope so." I had great regard and admiration for it. Learned from him and from it, got pleasure from it.

INTERVIEWER: If you could say what was particularly enriching about your life with Lowell, what would it be? The spirit of it, or technical literary matters?

HARDWICK: The quality of his mind—quite the most thrilling I've known. Once at dinner something came up about what people you have known whom you considered to be geniuses. Mary McCarthy was there. We all thought for a while and Mary and I came up with the same two names. Cal and Hannah Arendt.

INTERVIEWER: What do you think is the essential piece of equipment a writer must have?

HARDWICK: Well, you know, there is such a thing as talent, a bit of talent. I'll leave it at that.

INTERVIEWER: Given the talent, should writers be concerned with the issues of the times . . . things like that?

HARDWICK: Not necessarily. Of course they usually *are* concerned with the issues of the times in some way. The variety and strangeness of literary works is amazing. You wake up one morning and someone's done something a little bit new, something fresh and genuine, a new accent, quality of experience, way of composing and structuring. That's very beautiful to me. I am very happy when I see an interesting, gifted struggle with fictional form. I know as well as the next person that many fine things use traditional methods of narration and there will be, naturally,much that is traditional in those who experiment. Here I am not talking about a great innovator like Joyce, but about lesser struggles. When I open a new work of fiction I like to notice the way it is constructed, to learn something from it. Like Milan Kundera's latest novel, *The Unbearable Lightness of Being.* The narrator comes in and out and yet the form shifts to stories, to feelings, actions the narrator could not have known. I think it is done successfully there. There is always the problem of who is seeing, who is thinking. I am excited when I feel the author is trying to cope with this dilemma—and it is often a compositional dilemma.

INTERVIEWER: Can talent be taught?

HARDWICK: Perhaps not. I try to uncover what talent may be hiding by teaching creative reading. That turns out to be rather difficult—to read as a writer reads. I guess that is what I meant by reading in a "hallucinatory state." Not the perfect phrase.

INTERVIEWER: What state of mind are you in when the writing seems to be moving along?

HARDWICK: I don't know. I don't know why I am so helplessly led to condensation in both my fiction and my essays. Some people find it hard to follow my meaning because I don't spell it out, not entirely. My writing is simple but I like to be sort of emphatic and then let it go. I remember when I was writing exams in school I'd be the first one finished. All these people writing away. As I look back on it I think I didn't want to tell the teacher what he already knew, but to try to get at things from an angle—nothing very grand, just a little twist. That little twist always got me an *A minus.*

INTERVIEWER: In your first novel, *The Ghostly Lover,* and in your early short stories that appeared in various magazines, you seemed to be a Southern writer. And then you became much more identified with New York. Why is that?

HARDWICK: I don't like to quote myself, but since one doesn't have many ideas—or perhaps just *I* don't have many ideas—I will have to quote what I said in a Southern literature discussion. That is, that being a Southern writer is a decision, not a fate. Naturally, I love the best Southern writing and spent my youth, up through the university, in Lexington, Kentucky, a very beautiful and interesting place. But I think a critical, defining moment came into my life one summer. I had received a fellowship to LSU, a magical place then, with the *Southern Review* and all sorts of brilliant writers around. And then in August I suddenly didn't want to go and instead I went to Columbia . . . and without a fellowship. I'm amazed I was accepted.

INTERVIEWER: And then what happened?

HARDWICK: Well, ever trendy, I decided I had to specialize in the seventeenth century because that was the time of the Metaphysical poets, John Donne and so on. That was the hot period. After the first seminar I woke up and thought, I don't even know when the seventeenth century was! Of course I rushed out and read some books fast, filling in my literary knowledge, which began in 1920. It was all rather fun. It was New York and even back home I had been reading *Partisan Review* and had already been a Communist and an ex-Communist, Left variety, before I got here.

INTERVIEWER: Is that true?

HARDWICK: Yes, I wouldn't say it otherwise.

INTERVIEWER: I remember you once said that your dream when you were young was to be a Jewish intellectual.

HARDWICK: I said that as a joke, but it was more or less true. What I meant was the enlightenment, a certain deracination which I value, an angular vision, love of learning, cosmopolitanism, a word that practically means Jewish in Soviet lexicography. Right now, I'd say my remark depended upon which Jewish intellectual. I am not sympathetic with the political attitudes of certain members of the New Right who happen to be Jewish intellectuals, and less sympathetic to the Christian Right, most of whom are scarcely to be called intellectuals at all. I don't like the chauvinism, the militarism, the smugness, and the Social Darwinism, that jargon term, the support of Ronald Reagan . . . and all the rest.

INTERVIEWER: How do you feel about the religiosity of the New Right, the fundamentalists, and Reagan's courting of them?

HARDWICK: I think the fundamentalists' and Reagan's use of religion is an appalling blasphemy. The idea that God wants a strong America. Many Americans will naturally want a strong

America, but I don't know that God is in agreement. I hadn't thought of Him as being a patriot . . . I hadn't thought of Him as in a state of desire except against idolaters, and as we know from the Old Testament it is very easy to sink into idolatry, which a good deal of the flag-waving is just now. As for evangelizing Christians, their vulgarization of the Scriptures surpasses belief, their incredible assumption of Jesus as a pal in the cheering stand.

INTERVIEWER: Are you interested in religion?

HARDWICK: Of course, even though I'm a nonbeliever. I was brought up a Presbyterian. I still feel an attachment to the Presbyterian Church, where I know all the hymns and where I first felt the beauty and resonance of the Scriptures. Actually, when I lived in New England I was surprised to find that the denomination hardly existed there—not that if it had I was ready to put on my pumps and trot off every Sunday. The Scotch and the Scotch-Irish, which my mother's family were, mostly migrated to the upper South, especially to North Carolina, where she grew up. In New England you're supposed to think that the Presbyterians and the Congregationalists are more or less the same, but my seventeenth-century studies told me otherwise.

INTERVIEWER: What are you trying to say about religion . . . as a nonbeliever?

HARDWICK: I don't know. It may sound glib but I suppose for me religion is a vast, valuable museum . . . and, yes, I know the treasures of it are not the same as going to the Louvre . . . although now that I think of it, there's a good deal of overlapping, isn't there?

INTERVIEWER: Do you see any literary influence of the New Right, of the neoconservatives?

HARDWICK: I don't know about influence, but I do see that, as always, cultural and political attitudes swim along in the same bloodstream. Defense of American values, as these notions are called, can have a wide swing, picking up all sorts of things like homosexuals or fast women who are not doing their bit for the preservation of the American family. . . . For myself, I like many homosexuals and many self-absorbed, childless women, and I can't see them as a menace to the republic, or even to Republicans. Some of my best friends . . . and so on.

INTERVIEWER: Do you find any conservative attitudes specifically literary?

HARDWICK: I notice the creeping development of what I would call the Conservative Realism, because it brings to mind the intellectual follies of Social Realism. You get the idea that disaffected, even laid-back, attitudes in fiction, certain choices of despairing subject matter, are contemptible in a writer residing in the fullness of the United States. Certain tones of reflection are seen as a snide assault on the Free World.

INTERVIEWER: For instance?

HARDWICK: It's a rich field but I happen to remember a particular review of Ann Beattie's stories which said, "They seem treacherous to the energy and heroic idealism that are her country's saving grace." Now, I ask you! That appeared in *Partisan Review,* which is not a neo-con magazine, but "bore from within," as we used to say. Also, there is Norman Podhoretz's consignment of Henry Adams and all his works to the ash heap of history.

INTERVIEWER: You have taught a great deal. Why do you think many writers resent teaching? Do you agree with them that it interferes in subtle ways with their own writing?

HARDWICK: Nothing interferes with my own writing except my often irresolute character and of course the limitations of my talent.

INTERVIEWER: You seem rather accommodating and modest and yet you can be aggressive in your writing.

HARDWICK: And not only in my writing, alas. I don't like aggressiveness and I detest anger, a quality some feminists and many psychiatrists think one should cultivate in order to express the self. I was astonished by the number of obituaries of

Lillian Hellman that spoke with reverence of her anger. I don't see anger as an emotion to be cultivated and, in any case, it is not in short supply.

INTERVIEWER: Can you talk a bit about your background—school, childhood.

HARDWICK: Childhood? I came from a large family and many of my brothers and sisters were older than I, and I learned from them since they were, most of them, going to college when I was growing up. It was not an intellectual atmosphere, but a stimulating one. Like all writers I know of, the early days were dominated by a love of reading, just reading, like eating, anything around. It was not until I got to the University of Kentucky that the range of books was quite suddenly and very excitingly extended. I had some extraordinary teachers, some of the refugees from Europe, and very smart friends, some clever and "know-it-all" from New York, which appealed to me, and some very bright and lovable from just down home. I was not aware of any intellectual deprivation and there was none in the general sense. But aren't we all self-educated, and of course our self-education never includes all of the things we would like to know or need to know.

INTERVIEWER: And your career?

HARDWICK: Is it a career? I mean is that the right word for being a writer? It's a strange life. . . . The most peculiar thing about it is that when you write you are required to think and having once noticed that, you observe how little the rest of life makes such a demand. It demands something else, many things of course, but not sitting and thinking the way you must when you write, when you revise, when you abandon, start over, refine, all of that. About my own efforts, I sometimes feel I can say, well, I'm doing my best, or have done my best. That is not the supreme thrill for one who has spent her life reading superb writings of all kinds. But I am happy to do what I can.

INTERVIEWER: Some young women I know think of you as

very fortunate to have your place in things, your work and so forth.

HARDWICK: As I have grown older I see myself as fortunate in many ways. It is fortunate to have had all my life this passion for studying and enjoying literature and for trying to add a bit to it as interestingly as I can. This passion has given me much joy, it has given me friends who care for the same things, it has given me employment, escape from boredom, everything. The greatest gift is the passion for reading. It is cheap, it consoles, it distracts, it excites, it gives you knowledge of the world and experience of a wide kind. It is a moral illumination.

INTERVIEWER: Do you think there are special difficulties in being a woman writer?

HARDWICK: Woman writer? A bit of a crunch trying to get those two words together . . . I guess I would say no special difficulty, just the usual difficulties of the arts.

INTERVIEWER: So you feel it's the same for men and women?

HARDWICK: Nothing is the same for men and women.

INTERVIEWER: Not the same and . . . what else?

HARDWICK: Actually I have noticed lately a good deal of bitchiness with regard to certain women writers. Susan Sontag, for instance. The public scourging she was subjected to from all sides seemed to me disgusting and unworthy.

INTERVIEWER: What "public scourging" are you referring to?

HARDWICK: A sort of extended flap about a speech she made at a public gathering in which she spoke of communism as "fascism with a human face" and other matters. This was followed by attacks from the Left and the Right that seemed to go on for months. She was also scorned for writing so much about Europeans, the French particularly. I think her being a woman, a learned one, a *femme savante*, had something to do with it. As an intellectual with very special gifts and attitudes, it was somehow felt that this made her a proper object for ridicule of a coarse kind. I believe the tone was different because she was seen as a very smart, intellectually ambitious woman.

INTERVIEWER: Intellectual woman? Aren't you yourself one of them?

HARDWICK: Let me quote from *The Land of Ulro,* the latest book by the poet Czeslaw Milosz. "The history of my stupidity would fill many volumes."

INTERVIEWER: But, these days, women writers fare about as well as men, don't they?

HARDWICK: In general, of course. Just as many atrocious women writers are laughing all the way to the bank as men. But I do feel there is an inclination to punish women of what you might call presumption of one kind or another.

INTERVIEWER: Which women?

HARDWICK: For instance, Joan Didion and Renata Adler. I haven't found two books recently that have seemed to me more imaginative, intelligent, and original than *Democracy* and *Pitch Dark.* In the reviews, at least in many of them, I felt a note of contempt and superiority, often expressed in a lame, inept effort to parody. . . . And when you think of what the big guys have been turning out! And the ponderous, quaking reviews they receive!

INTERVIEWER: You mean they're getting away with something? What big guys?

HARDWICK: Never mind, never mind.

INTERVIEWER: What about reviewers today?

HARDWICK: I notice that many of them in very important places haven't written anything except their reviews, their quick, short reviews, composed with an air of easy authority. For the most part, I think the authority should be in some way earned. Well, they pass the night perhaps. . . . When a real writer discusses literature and culture you will notice a difference in style, in carefulness, and you will actually find ideas, illuminations, oddities and not merely yes-or-no opinions.

INTERVIEWER: Are you saying it's not entirely fair for a critic to do nothing but practice criticism?

HARDWICK: No. Let me say that criticism, analysis, reflection is a natural response to the existence in the world of works of art. It is an honorable and even an exalted endeavor. Without it, works of art would appear in a vacuum, as if they had no relation to the minds experiencing them. It would be a dismal, unthinkable world with these shooting stars arousing no comment, leaving no trace. But it is the mind of the critic, somehow, the establishment of his own thought and values, that counts; and that establishment is the authority of the voice, whether it comes from creative work in the arts or creative work in criticism. When I read a review, a mere short review, I am more interested at first in who is doing the reviewing than in the work under discussion. The name, what is attached to it by previous work, by serious thought, tells me whether it is likely to have any meaning or value for me. It is not a question of right or wrong specific opinions, but of the quality of the mind.

INTERVIEWER: You have been criticized for your review of Simone de Beauvoir's *The Second Sex* in *A View of My Own.* Would you still stand on that?

HARDWICK: No, I wouldn't. It's a wonderful, remarkable book. Nothing that has come since on the matter of women compares to it. When I wrote my comments I was thinking of existentialism and the idea that one can choose and not be dominated by the given . . . something like that. And of course thinking back on my remarks I see how much has changed since the 1950s, especially in the manner of life for women. You are still weaker than men in muscular force, but can sleep in the streets if you like, even, alas, if that is the only place you have to sleep, and go to Arabia in your jeans and knapsack . . . and much, much more.

INTERVIEWER: I was present a few years ago at a panel discussion where you were asked who was the greatest American female novelist, and you said Henry James. I had the feeling you meant something serious about that.

HARDWICK: Such remarks don't bear scrutiny. Did I actually say that? I do remember saying once that maybe the greatest female novelist in English was Constance Garnett. Sometimes I try to lighten the gloom of discussions but I notice that no one laughs. Instead you see a few people writing down the name.

INTERVIEWER: I have the impression that in your most recent stories about New York—"The Bookseller," "Back Issues," and "On the Eve"—you are using the city almost as a text and the characters you have chosen are instruments of decoding. Or is that too mechanistic for the way you place these people, catch the start and stop of their lives?

HARDWICK: I don't know about decoding New York. It's a large place, oh yes. And it's a place, isn't it? Still very much a place, or so I think. There's not much good feeling about New York, in spite of the T-shirts and the "Big Apple" and so on.

INTERVIEWER: You seem to be faithful to it.

HARDWICK: I like cities, big cities and even medium-sized cities. If I were traveling about America, I'd always want to spend the night downtown. If I could still find downtown. Yes, I'm faithful to New York, one might say. It's ours, our country's, our great metropolis. Many people no longer like the melting pot notion and seem to feel there are too many poor trying to be melted in the great vat. Of course everybody hates poor people. They're a damned nuisance. Always wanting something. Perhaps they used to be a part of the scheme of things, a part of nature, always with us and so on. But you might say they don't fit in anymore, or so I think many people see it.

INTERVIEWER: In a talk at the Columbia School of Architecture, you spoke of the increasing "Bombayism" of New York. What did you mean?

HARDWICK: Well, Bombay is called the New York of India, and I guess New York is becoming the Bombay of the U.S. What I had in mind was the increasing separation of the classes, the gap, as of another species. The streets filled with Untouchables. Just look the other way and move on. The intractable, milling others for whom you have no solution. Roll up the window of the limo. Step aside and into a cab. . . . New York is a city of the rich and the poor. It's a terrible place for the middle classes, and for what you would call the workers who run the elevators, build the buildings, clerk in the stores, cook in the restaurants. Manhattan is not for them. They get on the subway and go to the other boroughs at night. So the culture of the city, the vitality, the promise is more and more restricted. There's not a foot of living space and what there is is so overpriced as to raise the dead. That is a violation of the contract of the city as we knew it. When you think of old New York, I, at least, don't think of the patricians, but of the Lower East Side and Harlem—both are gone, wiped out as images of promise, change, relief from the old country or from the South or whatever, as places that created styles like the jazziness of Harlem that captivated Europe and the experience of generations of immigrants.

INTERVIEWER: Are you trying to express this in the fiction you're working on?

HARDWICK: I know that I can't. I realize how narrow my knowledge of the city is. I can't take it in as a whole. I feel I know less about it than when I first came here, but I very much like to think about it and care about it. I am using it as the landscape of my fiction just now, but whether I can make an image of the city itself I don't know. Everything in the stories I have done recently is imaginary. I even had to go to the Public Library and look around.

INTERVIEWER: You mean in "Back Issues" where you met the Greek?

HARDWICK: I've never met a Greek in my life.

INTERVIEWER: The shop in "The Bookseller" reminded me of every secondhand shop I've seen in Manhattan.

HARDWICK: I hardly ever go into a bookstore because, instead of buying, I would like to give away about five thousand of my seven thousand books, which are weighing on me like some suffocating plague.

INTERVIEWER: I'll take them.

HARDWICK: They're yours. Bring your van. I can't find those I want, thousands have not been dusted in years. I miss the time when I used to go into the old secondhand shops, looking for the modern classics. What a pleasure that was, not having them and finding them. And then to get volumes of history, all the odd tomes.

INTERVIEWER: What do you think of the state of publishing just now?

HARDWICK: Insofar as making money is concerned it is better now not to be an *author* when you write a book. Being a writer just mucks it up. I see that when I look at the best-seller list of books by movie stars and doctors, although some *literateurs* make money, fortunately. But of course the best-seller list, poor old thrashed dog, is not what things are about. Otherwise I don't think publishing changes much. It's still sort of a running faucet and words and pages pour out. I doubt that many worthwhile books don't make it to the printing presses. I like sometimes to think otherwise.

INTERVIEWER: Why do you like to think otherwise?

HARDWICK: Just the idea that something brilliant and unacceptable, something too quirky and original is being created. In general I guess I feel that what we have is what is there.

INTERVIEWER: Do you feel that the European novel, the Latin American novel, the African novel, the dissident writings are superior to what is being done here?

HARDWICK: Superior, who knows? In some ways, I suppose we are left behind in the great themes that arrive from the feeling of displacement and loss. V. S. Naipaul said something about English fiction—it's all tea parties or something like that. We seem to have divorce and adultery and being young with your parents and being a bit gay here and there, or quite gay —can I still say queer?—and drinking beer at the truck stop instead of getting ahead. But we live in a world of displaced, agonized talents who have lost country and language and family and whose condition represents so much of this century. The survival of those talents, the imaginative rendering of their experience is extraordinarily moving and large. Of course it's all in the telling. We are a protected country even though so many of us are whipped to a frenzy about the dangers around us and feel the best thing we can do for our citizens is to push them into a siege mentality. But meanwhile . . . meanwhile, you can be quite happy and make quite a good living crying havoc and getting out the siege vote. Let me say that I would not want our country overrun in order to create fiction and poetry. All I'm saying is that the introversion of our literature just now makes it narrower than the exile writing. But everyone knows that.

INTERVIEWER: Who are the readers?

HARDWICK: I don't know. It is thought that the present young generation doesn't know much about literature, hasn't read much . . . and yet a lot of the writing of the last decades is full of parodies, mimicry, learned references of a sort and readers seem to get it. I always wonder who buys the books. "100,000 in print," the ads say. Fifty thousand may have come from knowing that the first fifty thousand bought the book. That's okay. Especially if it's something of value. I don't think it's a good idea for writers to think too much about the publishing world. I sense in a good many books, even in books by the best writers, an anxiety about how it will do in the marketplace. You can feel it on the page, a sort of sweat of calculation. As if to say, well, it will be a few years before the next one and I had better be sure I don't let this chance to make some money pass by. But no more about publishing.

INTERVIEWER: Okay, no more about publishing. May I ask you how you feel about growing older?

HARDWICK: You can always ask. Or perhaps no one need ask. Just another piece of rotten luck. No, I haven't found anything good to say about it. Not a condition that can be recommended. Its only value is that it spares you the opposite, not growing older. People do cling to consciousness, and under the most dreadful circumstances. It shows you that it is all we have, doesn't it? Waking up, the first and the last privilege, waking up once more.

INTERVIEWER: Do you think it is more painful for women than for men?

HARDWICK: More about women and men? About something so burdensome it doesn't seem valuable to make distinctions. Oh, the dear grave. I like what Gottfried Benn wrote, something like, "May I die in the spring when the ground is soft and easy to plough."

INTERVIEWER: I notice that you quote poets a lot.

HARDWICK: Well, you don't exactly quote prose I guess, although I often remember prose lines and sayings.

INTERVIEWER: Has the reading of poetry and the knowing of poets influenced your own style? Some have thought so.

HARDWICK: I don't know. Certainly Cal had a great influence on every aspect of my life. In literary matters, his immense learning and love of literature were a constant magic for me. As an influence on my own writing, that is more difficult to figure out. . . . Let me shift the subject a little. Maybe I was led to this by Cal's library, led to the prose written by poets. The poet's prose is one of my passions. I like the offhand flashes, the absence of the lumber in the usual prose . . . the quickness, the deftness, confidence, and even the relief from spelling everything out, plank by plank.

INTERVIEWER: Can you give an example?

HARDWICK: Well, here is a beautiful sentence, just right, inspired, a bit of prose I've memorized. It is by Pasternak. It goes: "The beginning of April surprised Moscow in the white stupor of returning winter. On the seventh, it began to thaw for the second time, and on the fourteenth when Mayakovsky shot himself, not everyone had yet become accustomed to the novelty of spring." I love the rhythm of "the beginning of April . . . on the seventh . . . on the fourteenth" and the way the subject, Mayakovsky's suicide, is honored by the beauty of this introduction to the account. It's in *Safe Conduct,* Pasternak's autobiographical writing.

INTERVIEWER: Perhaps this leads to the subject of biography. You had a review in *The New York Times* of a biography of Katherine Anne Porter. There you had some rough things to say about the present practice.

HARDWICK: Last summer I had a striking experience. On the same day I received two letters, written by different people, each saying she was writing a biography of an author recently dead, an author not at all a household word. Two letters on the same day. I didn't know the author, but perhaps I'll merit a footnote in the book saying I did not know her. Or be thanked in the preface. Biography is a scrofulous cottage industry, done mostly by academics who get grants and have a good time going all over the place interviewing. How seldom it is that one has ever heard of the person writing the biography. What are the models, what are the qualifications? And it is not only the full-scale computer printout that these things are, but the books brought forth by lovers, friends from youth, cousins, whatever. I remember how horrified Dickens was when he met, in later life, the model for Dora in *David Copperfield.* Now Dora would hire a hack and write about Dickens. I have just read *Auden in Love* by Dorothy Farnan, the stepmother of Chester Kallman. I quite disapprove of the impertinence and the celestial glow around herself and her intimacy. Both Auden and Chester would be *mute, motionless, aghast.* Such books diminish the celebrated object and aggrandize the biographer or memoirist. I understand from the reviews of a new book about Agee that the swarm and smarm of little "facts" degrade the memory most of us have of Agee. Think how sweet Trelawny now appears; and De Quincey's beautiful memories of the Lake Poets, candid indeed, are almost a valentine because there is some equity between the subject and the author. And serious, incomparable reflection.

INTERVIEWER: How do you feel about Ian Hamilton's biography of Lowell?

HARDWICK: Hamilton is very intelligent and a very fine writer. Still the book is composed along contemporary lines and there is too little of Hamilton in it since most of the stage is given to raw documentation. When I finished it, I was reminded of Sir Walter Raleigh's executioner, who said, "There is not another such head to be chopped off!"

INTERVIEWER: Are you working on any fiction now? A future novel?

HARDWICK: Oh, yes. What are you working on? When one writer asks another that, he immediately apologizes, as if for a *gaffe.* . . . I might say I'm working on working on a novel. . . . I do hope I'll be writing a novel. I have some of it, but it is slow, of course, the writing. I hope not the work. Yes, I am writing fiction.

DARRYL PINCKNEY
Spring 1984

7. Philip Larkin

Philip Larkin was born in Coventry, Warwickshire, on August 9, 1922. He was educated at King Henry VIII School, Coventry, and St. John's College, Oxford, where he took both a B.A. and an M.A. The atmosphere at Oxford at the time could be inferred from his novel *Jill* (1946). A second novel, *A Girl in Winter*, was published the following year. While an undergraduate, he knew both Kingsley Amis and John Wain, part of a group that came to be identified in 1954 as "The Movement."

After holding posts in various British libraries from 1943 until 1955, Larkin became librarian of the Brynmor Jones Library, University of Hull, in Yorkshire, a post he held until his death. When asked why he chose his profession, he replied, "A librarian is what you are when you have failed to do all the things you do want to do and have succeeded in avoiding all the things you don't want to do."

Larkin's reputation rests largely on his work as a poet. His collections of poetry include *The North Ship* (1945; revised 1966), *XX Poems* (1951), *The Less Deceived* (1955), *The Whitsun Weddings* (1964), and *High Windows* (1974).

Larkin also held a lifelong interest in jazz. For ten years he was jazz feature writer for the *London Daily Telegraph*. His jazz columns are collected in the volume *All What Jazz: A Record Diary 1961–68*. He also edited *The Oxford Book of Twentieth-Century English Verse* (1973), and was an honorary member of the American Academy of Arts & Sciences. He died on December 2, 1985.

But much less quickly noticed was the noise
The weddings made
Each station that we stopped at, sun destroys
Your interest for what's happening in the shade,
And down the long cool platform whoops and skirls
Might have been porters larking with the mails,

Or pan-hung climbers; Once we started, though,
We passed them, grinning and pomaded, girls
In paradise of fashion, heels and veils, —
All irresolutely, watching us go,

But much less quickly noticed was the noise
The weddings made
Each station that we stopped at: sun destroys
Your interest for what's happening in shade,
And down the long cool platform whoops and skirls
porters larking with the mails,
And went on reading. Once we started, though,
We passed them, grinning and pomaded, girls
In paradise of fashion, heels and veils —
All posed irresolutely, watching us go,

A manuscript page from Philip Larkin's *The Whitsun Weddings*.

Philip Larkin

"Temperamentally and geographically remote," the Times Literary Supplement *wrote of Philip Larkin, "he has refused almost all invitations to judge, recite, review, lecture, pontificate, or to be interviewed."*

When the notion of securing a Paris Review *interview with Larkin arose, the staff was not sanguine. Much to the staff's delight, Larkin consented warily, stating that he wasn't crazy about the idea, but that "the* Paris Review *series is, of course, known to me, and I can see I should be in good company." In the case of this interview, Larkin did not let down his guard sufficiently to be interviewed in person. He stipulated that the interview be conducted entirely by mail: "You will get much better answers that way." He took nearly five months to answer the initial set of questions sent to him at his home in Hull, England, stating, "It has taken rather a long time because, to my surprise, I found writing it suffocatingly boring."*

His letterhead, P. A. Larkin, C.B.E., C.Lit., M.A., D.Lit., D.Litt., F.R.S.L., F.L.A., is indicative of the measure of worldly recognition his relatively small output has received. Indeed, he has been called the other *English poet laureate ("even more loved and needed than the official one, John Betjeman," according to Calvin Bedient in the* New York Times Book Review*). But Larkin transcends his Englishness, and is widely read on the Continent and in the United States.*

He has said his aim in writing a poem is "to construct a verbal device that would preserve an experience indefinitely by reproducing it in whoever read the poem."

INTERVIEWER: Can you describe your life at Hull? Do you live in a flat or own a house?

LARKIN: I came to Hull in 1955. After eighteen months (during which I wrote "Mr. Bleaney"), I took a University flat and lived there for nearly eighteen years. It was the top flat in a house that was reputedly the American Consulate during the war, and though it might not have suited everybody, it suited me. I wrote most of *The Whitsun Weddings* and all of *High Windows* there. Probably I should never have moved if the University hadn't decided to sell the house, but as it was I had to get out and find somewhere else. It was a dreadful experience, as at that time houses were hard to find. In the end friends reported a small house near the University, and I bought that in 1974. I haven't decided yet whether or not I like it.

INTERVIEWER: How many days a week do you work at the library, and for how many hours a day?

LARKIN: My job as University librarian is a full-time one, five days a week, forty-five weeks a year. When I came to Hull, I had eleven staff; now there are over a hundred of one sort and another. We built one new library in 1960 and another in 1970, so that my first fifteen years were busy. Of course, this was a period of university expansion in England, and Hull grew as much as if not more than the rest. Luckily the vice-chancellor during most of this time was keen on the library, which is why it is called after him. Looking back, I think that if the Brynmor Jones Library *is* a good library—and I think it is—the credit should go to him and to the library staff. And to the University as a whole, of course. But you wouldn't be interested in all that.

INTERVIEWER: What is your daily routine?

LARKIN: My life is as simple as I can make it. Work all day, cook, eat, wash up, telephone, hack writing, drink, television in the evenings. I almost never go out. I suppose everyone tries to ignore the passing of time: some people by doing a lot, being in California one year and Japan the next; or there's my way —making every day and every year exactly the same. Probably neither works.

INTERVIEWER: You didn't mention a schedule for writing . . .

LARKIN: Yes, I was afraid you'd ask about writing. Anything I say about writing poems is bound to be retrospective, because in fact I've written very little since moving into this house, or since *High Windows,* or since 1974, whichever way you like to put it. But when I did write them, well, it was in the evenings, after work, after washing up (I'm sorry: you would call this "doing the dishes"). It was a routine like any other. And really it worked very well: I don't think you can write a poem for more than two hours. After that you're going round in circles, and it's much better to leave it for twenty-four hours, by which time your subconscious or whatever has solved the block and you're ready to go on.

The best writing conditions I ever had were in Belfast, when I was working at the University there. Another top-floor flat, by the way. I wrote between eight and ten in the evenings, then went to the University bar till eleven, then played cards or talked with friends till one or two. The first part of the evening had the second part to look forward to, and I could enjoy the second part with a clear conscience because I'd done my two hours. I can't seem to organize that now.

INTERVIEWER: Does, or did, writing come easily for you? Does a poem get completed slowly or rapidly?

LARKIN: I've no standards of comparison. I wrote short poems quite quickly. Longer ones would take weeks or even months. I used to find that I was never sure I was going to finish a poem until I had thought of the last line. Of course, the last line was sometimes the first one you thought of! But usually the last line would come when I'd done about two-thirds of the poem, and then it was just a matter of closing the gap.

INTERVIEWER: Why do you write, and for whom?

LARKIN: You've been reading Auden: "To ask the hard question is simple." The short answer is that you write because you have to. If you rationalize it, it seems as if you've seen this sight, felt this feeling, had this vision, and have got to find a combination of words that will preserve it by setting it off in other people. The duty is to the original experience. It doesn't feel like self-expression, though it may look like it. As for *whom* you write, well, you write for everybody. Or anybody who will listen.

INTERVIEWER: Do you share your manuscripts with anyone before publishing them? Are there any friends whose advice you would follow in revising a poem?

LARKIN: I shouldn't normally show what I'd written to anyone: what would be the point? You remember Tennyson reading an unpublished poem to Jowett; when he had finished, Jowett said, "I shouldn't publish that if I were you, Tennyson." Tennyson replied, "If it comes to that, Master, the sherry you gave us at lunch was downright filthy." That's about all that can happen.

But when we were young, Kingsley Amis and I used to exchange unpublished poems, largely because we never thought they could be published, I suppose. He encouraged me, I encouraged him. Encouragement is very necessary to a young writer. But it's hard to find anyone worth encouraging: there aren't many Kingsleys about.

INTERVIEWER: In his *Paris Review* interview, Kingsley Amis states you helped him with the manuscript of *Lucky Jim.* What was the nature of that working relationship? Is part of that novel based upon your own experiences on staff at Leicester University?

LARKIN: Well, it's all so long ago, it's hard to remember. My general conviction was that Kingsley was quite the funniest writer I had ever met—in letters and so on—and I wanted everyone else to think so too. I know he says he got the idea of *Lucky Jim* from visiting me when I was working at University College Leicester. This has always seemed rather tenuous to me: after all, he was working at University College Swansea when he was writing it, and the theme—boy meets apparently nasty girl, but turns her into a nice girl by getting her away from nasty environment—is one I think has always meant a lot to Kingsley. He used it again in *I Want It Now.* When I read the first draft I said, Cut this, cut that, let's have more of the other. I remember I said, Let's have more "faces"—you know, his Edith Sitwell face, and so on. The wonderful thing was that Kingsley could "do" all those faces himself—"Sex Life in Ancient Rome" and so on. Someone once took photographs of them all. I wish I had a set.

INTERVIEWER: How did you come to be a librarian? Had you no interest in teaching? What was your father's profession?

LARKIN: Oh dear, this means a lot of autobiography. My father was a city treasurer, a finance officer. I never had the least desire to "be" anything when I was at school, and by the time I went to Oxford the war was on and there wasn't anything to "be" except a serviceman or a teacher or a civil servant. In 1943 when I graduated I knew I couldn't be the first, because I'd been graded unfit (I suppose through eyesight), nor the second because I stammered, and then the Civil Service turned me down twice, and I thought, Well, that lets me out, and I sat at home writing *Jill*. But of course in those days the government had powers to send you into the mines or onto the land or into industry, and they wrote quite politely to ask what in fact I was doing. I looked at the daily paper (the *Birmingham Post:* we were living at Warwick then) and saw that a small town in Shropshire was advertising for a librarian, applied for it, and got it, and told the government so, which seemed to satisfy them.

Of course, I wasn't a real librarian, more a sort of caretaker —it was a one-man library—and I can't pretend I enjoyed it much. The previous librarian had been there about forty years, and I was afraid I should be there all my life too. This made me start qualifying myself professionally, just in order to get away, which I did in 1946. By then I'd written *Jill*, and *The North Ship*, and *A Girl in Winter*. It was probably the "intensest" time of my life.

INTERVIEWER: Is Jorge Luis Borges the only other contemporary poet of note who is also a librarian, by the way? Are you aware of any others?

LARKIN: Who is Jorge Luis Borges? The writer-librarian *I* like is Archibald MacLeish. You know, he was made Librarian of Congress in 1939, and on his first day they brought him some papers to sign, and he wouldn't sign them until he understood what they were all about. When he did understand, he started making objections and countersuggestions. The upshot was that he reorganized the whole Library of Congress in five years simply by saying, I don't understand and I don't agree, and in wartime, too. Splendid man.

INTERVIEWER: What do you think of the academic world as a *milieu* for the working creative writer—teaching specifically?

LARKIN: The academic world has worked all right for me, but then, I'm not a teacher. I couldn't be. I should think that chewing over other people's work, writing I mean, must be terribly stultifying. Quite sickens you with the whole business of literature. But then, I haven't got that kind of mind, conceptual or ratiocinative or whatever it is. It would be death to me to have to think about literature as such, to say why one poem was "better" than another, and so on.

INTERVIEWER: We've heard that you don't give readings from your own work. In America, this has become a business for poets. Do you enjoy attending the readings of others?

LARKIN: I don't give readings, no, although I have recorded three of my collections, just to show how *I* should read them. Hearing a poem, as opposed to reading it on the page, means you miss so much—the shape, the punctuation, the italics, even knowing how far you are from the end. Reading it on the page means you can go your own pace, taking it in properly; hearing it means you're dragged along at the speaker's own rate, missing things, not taking it in, confusing "there" and "their" and things like that. And the speaker may interpose his own personality between you and the poem, for better or worse. For that matter, so may the audience. I don't like hearing things in public, even music. In fact, I think poetry readings grew up on a false analogy with music: the text is the "score" that doesn't "come to life" until it's "performed." It's false because people can read words, whereas they can't read music. When you write a poem, you put everything into it that's needed: the reader should "hear" it just as clearly as if you were in the room saying it to him. And of course this fashion for poetry readings has led to a kind of poetry that you *can* understand first go: easy rhythms, easy emotions, easy syntax. I don't think it stands up on the page.

INTERVIEWER: Do you think economic security an advantage to the writer?

LARKIN: The whole of British postwar society is based on the assumption that economic security is an advantage to everyone. Certainly *I* like to be economically secure. But aren't you, really, asking about *work?* This whole question of how a writer actually gets his money—especially a poet—is one to which there are probably as many answers as there are writers, and the next man's answer always seems better than your own.

On the one hand, you can't live today by being a "man of letters" as easily as a hundred or seventy-five years ago, when there were so many magazines and newspapers all having to be filled. Writers' incomes, as writers, have sunk almost below the subsistence line. On the other hand, you *can* live by "being a writer," or "being a poet," if you're prepared to join the cultural entertainment industry, and take handouts from the Arts Council (not that there are as many of them as there used to be) and be a "poet in residence" and all that. I suppose I could have said—it's a bit late now—I could have had an agent, and said, Look, I will do anything for six months of the year as long as I can be free to write for the other six months. Some people do this, and I suppose it works for them. But I was brought up to think you had to have a job, and write in your spare time, like Trollope. Then, when you started earning enough money by writing, you phase the job out. But in fact I was over fifty before I could have "lived by my writing"—and then only because I had edited a big anthology—and by that time you think, Well, I might as well get my pension, since I've gone so far.

INTERVIEWER: Any regrets?

LARKIN: Sometimes I think, Everything I've written has been done after a day's work, in the evening: what would it have been like if I'd written it in the morning, after a night's sleep? Was I wrong? Some time ago a writer said to me—and he was a full-time writer, and a good one—"I wish I had your life. Dealing with people, having colleagues. Being a writer is so lonely." Everyone envies everyone else.

All I can say is, having a job hasn't been a hard price to pay for economic security. Some people, I know, would sooner have the economic insecurity because they have to "feel free" before they can write. But it's worked for me. The only thing that does strike me as odd, looking back, is that what society has been willing to *pay* me for is being a librarian. You get medals and prizes and honorary-this-and-thats—and flattering interviews —but if you turned round and said, Right, if I'm so good, give me an index-linked permanent income equal to what I can get for being an undistinguished university administrator—well, reason would remount its throne pretty quickly.

INTERVIEWER: How did you come to write poems? Was time a factor in choosing poetry over the novel form?

LARKIN: What questions you ask. I wrote prose and poems equally from the age of, say, fifteen. I didn't choose poetry: poetry chose me.

INTERVIEWER: Nicely put. Your last novel, *A Girl in Winter* —which is a small masterpiece—was published twenty-five years ago. Do you think you will ever write another?

LARKIN: I don't know: I shouldn't think so. I tried very hard to write a third novel for about five years. The ability to do so had just vanished. I can't say any more than that. . . .

INTERVIEWER: *Jill* was written when you were about twenty-one, and your second novel only a year or so later. Was it your intention, then, to be a novelist only?

LARKIN: I wanted to "be a novelist" in a way I never wanted to "be a poet," yes. Novels seem to me to be richer, broader, deeper, more enjoyable than poems. When I was young, *Scrutiny* ran a series of articles under the general heading of "The Novel as Dramatic Poem." That was a stimulating, an exciting conception. Something that was both a poem and novel. Of course, thinking about my own two stories means going back nearly forty years, and at this distance I can't remember what their genesis was.

I seem to recall that *Jill* was based on the idea that running away from life, John's fantasy about an imaginary sister, might lead you straight into it—meeting the real Jill, I mean. With disastrous results.

A Girl in Winter, which I always think of as *The Kingdom of Winter,* which was its first title, or *Winterreich,* as Bruce Montgomery used to call it—well, that was written when I was feeling pretty low, in this first library job I told you about. It's what Eliot would call an objective correlative. When I look at it today, I do think it's remarkably . . . I suppose the word is *knowing* . . . not really mature, or wise, just incredibly clever. By my standards, I mean. And considering I was only twenty-two. All the same, some people whose opinion I respect prefer *Jill*, as being more natural, more sincere, more directly emotional.

INTERVIEWER: In your preface to the reprint of *Jill*, you say it is "in essence an unambitious short story." What is your definition of a novel?

LARKIN: I think a novel should follow the fortunes of more than one character.

INTERVIEWER: At least one critic has cited *Jill* as the forerunner of the new British postwar novel—the literature of the displaced working-class hero which spawned later works by Alan Sillitoe, John Wain, Keith Waterhouse, Amis, and others. Do you feel a part of any of this?

LARKIN: I don't think so, no. Because *Jill* has none of the political overtones of that *genre*. John's being working-class was a kind of equivalent of my stammer, a built-in handicap to put him one down.

I'm glad you mention Keith Waterhouse. I think *Billy Liar* and *Jubb* are remarkably original novels, the first very funny, the second harrowing. Much better than my two.

INTERVIEWER: You're extremely modest. Wouldn't you say that an open assumption of the British sense of class is important to your work—*Jill, A Girl in Winter,* a poem like "The Whitsun Weddings"?

LARKIN: Are you suggesting there's no sense of class in America? That's not the impression I get from the works of Mr. John O'Hara.

INTERVIEWER: O'Hara overstated. Did you prefigure a shape to your two novels, or did they evolve? You've stated your mentors in poetry, especially Hardy. But whom in fiction early on did you frequently read and admire?

LARKIN: Hard to say. Of course I had read a great many novels, and knew the mannerisms of most modern writers, but looking back I can't say I ever imitated anyone. Now don't think I mind imitation, in a young writer. It's just a way of learning the job. Really, my novels were more original than my poems, at the time. My favorite novelists were Lawrence, Isherwood, Maugham, Waugh—oh, and George Moore. I was on a great Moore kick at that time: probably he was at the bottom of my style, then.

INTERVIEWER: *A Girl in Winter* reminds me stylistically of Elizabeth Bowen's fiction, particularly *The Death of the Heart* and *The House in Paris.* Is Bowen a writer you've also admired?

LARKIN: No, I hadn't read Elizabeth Bowen. In fact, someone lent me *The Death of the Heart* when *A Girl in Winter* came out—two years after it was finished. I quite liked it, but it was never one of my personal favorites.

INTERVIEWER: Let's talk about the structure of *A Girl in Winter* for a moment: did you write it chronologically? That is, did you write "Part Two" first, then shuffle the pack for effect and counterpoint? Or did you actually conceive the novel as present-to-past-to-present?

LARKIN: The second way.

INTERVIEWER: Letters are an important and integral part of both novels, as plot and as texture. Are you a voluminous letter writer?

LARKIN: I suppose I used to write many more letters than I do now, but so did everyone. Nowadays I keep up with one or two people, in the sense of writing when there isn't anything special to say. I love *getting* letters, which means you have to answer them, and there isn't always time. I had a very amusing and undemanding correspondence with the novelist Barbara Pym, who died in 1980, that arose simply out of a fan letter I wrote her and went on for over ten years before we actually met. I hope she liked getting my letters: I certainly liked hers.

I talk about our correspondence in a foreword I provided for the U.K. edition of her posthumous novel, *An Unsuitable Attachment*.

INTERVIEWER: Can you describe your relationship with the contemporary literary community?

LARKIN: I'm somewhat withdrawn from what you call "the contemporary literary community," for two reasons: in the first place, I don't write for a living, and so don't have to keep in touch with literary editors and publishers and television people in order to earn money; and in the second, I don't live in London. Given that, my relations with it are quite amicable.

INTERVIEWER: Is Hull a place where you are likely to stay put? If so, have you as a person changed since the writing of the poem "Places, Loved Ones"—or is the speaker of that poem a *persona?*

LARKIN: Hull is a place where I *have* stayed. On my twenty-fifth anniversary, I held a little luncheon party for the members of my staff who'd been there as long as I had, or almost as long, and they made me a presentation with a card bearing the very lines you mean. *Touché,* as the French say.

INTERVIEWER: As a bachelor, have you sometimes felt an outsider? Or, like the speaker of your poems "Reasons for Attendance," "Dockery & Son," and "Self's the Man," have you enjoyed being single and remained so because you liked and preferred living that way?

LARKIN: Hard to say. Yes, I've remained single by choice, and shouldn't have liked anything else, but of course most people do get married, and divorced too, and so I suppose I am an outsider in the sense you mean. Of course it worries me from time to time, but it would take too long to explain why. Samuel Butler said, Life is an affair of being spoilt in one way or another.

INTERVIEWER: Is the character John Kemp in any way based upon your own youth? Were you *that* shy?

LARKIN: I would say, yes, I was and am extremely shy. Anyone who has stammered will know what agony it is, especially at school. It means you never take the lead in anything or do anything but try to efface yourself. I often wonder if I was shy because I stammered, or vice versa.

INTERVIEWER: Was your childhood unhappy?

LARKIN: My childhood was all right, comfortable and stable and loving, but I wasn't a happy child, or so they say. On the other hand, I've never been a recluse, contrary to reports: I've had friends, and enjoyed their company. In comparison with some people I know I'm extremely sociable.

INTERVIEWER: Do you feel happiness is unlikely in this world?

LARKIN: Well, I think if you're in good health, and have enough money, and nothing is bothering you in the foreseeable future, that's as much as you can hope for. But "happiness," in the sense of a continuous emotional orgasm, no. If only because you know that you are going to die, and the people you love are going to die.

INTERVIEWER: After "Trouble at Willow Gables," did you write any other short stories or tales?

LARKIN: No. I think a short story should be either a poem or a novel. Unless it's just an anecdote.

INTERVIEWER: Have you ever attempted a truly long poem? I've never seen one in print. If not, why?

LARKIN: I've written none. A long poem for me would be a novel. In that sense, *A Girl in Winter* is a poem.

INTERVIEWER: What about a play or a verse play?

LARKIN: I don't like plays. They happen in public, which, as I said, I don't like, and by now I have grown rather deaf, which means I can't hear what's going on. Then again, they are rather like poetry readings: they have to get an instant response, which tends to vulgarize. And of course the intrusion of *personality*—the actor, the producer—or do you call him the director—is distracting.

All the same, I admire *Murder in the Cathedral* as much as

anything Eliot ever wrote. I read it from time to time for pleasure, which is the highest compliment I can pay.

INTERVIEWER: Did you ever meet Eliot?

LARKIN: I didn't know him. Once I was in the Faber offices —the old ones, "24, Russell Square," that magic address!— talking to Charles Monteith, and he said, "Have you ever met Eliot?" I said no, and to my astonishment he stepped out and reappeared with Eliot, who must have been in the next room. We shook hands, and he explained that he was expecting someone to tea and couldn't stay. There was a pause, and he said, "I'm glad to see you in this office." The significance of that was that I wasn't a Faber author—it must have been before 1964, when they published *The Whitsun Weddings*— and I took it as a great compliment. But it was a shattering few minutes: I hardly remember what I thought.

INTERVIEWER: What about Auden? Were you acquainted?

LARKIN: I didn't know him, either. I met Auden once at Stephen Spender's house, which was very kind of Spender, and in a sense he was more frightening than Eliot. I remember he said, Do you like living in Hull? and I said, I don't suppose I'm unhappier there than I should be anywhere else. To which he replied, Naughty, naughty. I thought that was very funny.

But this business of meeting famous writers is agonizing: I had a dreadful few minutes with Forster. My fault, not his. Dylan Thomas came to Oxford to speak to a club I belonged to, and we had a drink the following morning. *He* wasn't frightening. In fact, and I know it sounds absurd to say so, but I should say I had more in common with Dylan Thomas than with any other "famous writer," in this sort of context.

INTERVIEWER: You mention Auden, Thomas, Yeats, and Hardy as early influences in your introduction to the second edition of *The North Ship*. What in particular did you learn from your study of these four?

LARKIN: Oh, for Christ's sake, one doesn't *study* poets! You *read* them, and think, That's marvelous, how is it done, could

I do it? and that's how you learn. At the end of it you can't say, That's Yeats, that's Auden, because they've gone, they're like scaffolding that's been taken down. Thomas was a dead end. What effects? Yeats and Auden, the management of lines, the formal distancing of emotion. Hardy, well . . . not to be afraid of the obvious. All those wonderful *dicta* about poetry: "the poet should touch our hearts by showing his own," "the poet takes note of nothing that he cannot feel," "the emotion of all the ages and the thought of his own"—Hardy knew what it was all about.

INTERVIEWER: When your first book, *The North Ship*, appeared, did you feel you were going to be an important poet?

LARKIN: No, certainly not. I've never felt that anyway. You must remember *The North Ship* was published by an obscure press—The Fortune Press—that didn't even send out review copies; it was next door to a vanity press. One had none of the rewards of authorship, neither money (no agreement) nor publicity. You felt you'd cooked your goose.

INTERVIEWER: How can a young poet know if his work is any good?

LARKIN: I think a young poet, or an old poet, for that matter, should try to produce something that pleases himself personally, not only when he's written it but a couple of weeks later. Then he should see if it pleases anyone else, by sending it to the kind of magazine he likes reading. But if it doesn't, he shouldn't be discouraged. I mean, in the seventeenth century every educated man could turn a verse and play the lute. Supposing no one played tennis because they wouldn't make Wimbledon? First and foremost, writing poems should be a pleasure. So should reading them, by God.

INTERVIEWER: How do you account for the great maturity and originality which developed between your first poetry collection and your second, *The Less Deceived?*

LARKIN: You know, I really don't know. After finishing my first books, say by 1945, I thought I had come to an end. I couldn't write another novel, I published nothing. My personal life was rather harassing. Then in 1950 I went to Belfast, and things reawoke somehow. I wrote some poems, and thought, These aren't bad, and had that little pamphlet *XX Poems* printed privately. I felt for the first time I was speaking for myself. Thoughts, feelings, language cohered and jumped. They have to do that. Of course they are always lying around in you, but they have to get together.

INTERVIEWER: You once wrote that "the impulse to preserve lies at the bottom of all art." In your case, what is it you are preserving in your poems?

LARKIN: Well, as I said, the experience. The beauty.

INTERVIEWER: Auden admired your forms. But you've stated that form holds little interest for you—content is everything. Could you comment on that?

LARKIN: I'm afraid that was a rather silly remark, especially now when form is so rare. I read poems, and I think, Yes, that's quite a nice idea, but why can't he make a *poem* of it? Make it memorable? It's no good just writing it down! At any level that matters, form and content are indivisible. What I meant by content is the experience the poem preserves, what it passes on. I must have been seeing too many poems that were simply agglomerations of words when I said that.

INTERVIEWER: In one early interview you stated that you were not interested in any period but the present, or in any poetry but that written in English. Did you mean that quite literally? Has your view changed?

LARKIN: It has not. I don't see how one can ever know a foreign language well enough to make reading poems in it worthwhile. Foreigners' ideas of good English poems are dreadfully crude: Byron and Poe and so on. The Russians liking Burns. But deep down I think foreign languages irrelevant. If that glass thing over there is a window, then it isn't a fenster or a *fenêtre* or whatever. *Hautes Fenêtres,* my God! A writer can have only one language, if language is going to mean anything to him.

INTERVIEWER: In D. J. Enright's *Poets of the Nineteen-Fifties,* published in 1955, you made several provocative statements about archetypes and myth which have become well-known. Specifically: "As a guiding principle I believe that every poem must be its own sole freshly created universe, and therefore have no belief in 'tradition' or a common myth-kitty. ... To me the whole of the ancient world, the whole of classical and biblical mythology means very little, and I think that using them today not only fills poems full of dead spots, but dodges the writer's duty to be original." Does this mean you really do not respond to, say, the monstrous manifestation of the Sphinx in Yeats's "The Second Coming"? Or were you merely reacting against bookishness?

LARKIN: My objection to the use in new poems of properties or personae from older poems is not a moral one, but simply because they do not work, either because I have not read the poems in which they appear, or because I have read them and think of them as part of that poem and not a property to be dragged into a new poem as a substitute for securing the effect that is desired. I admit this argument could be pushed to absurd lengths, when a poet could not refer to anything that his readers might not have seen (such as snow, for instance), but in fact poets write for people with the same background and experiences as themselves, which might be taken as a compelling argument in support of provincialism.

INTERVIEWER: The use of archetypes can weaken rather than buttress a poem?

LARKIN: I am not going to fall on my face every time someone uses words such as Orpheus or Faust or Judas. Writers should work for the effects they want to produce, and not wheel out stale old Wardour Street lay figures.

INTERVIEWER: What do you mainly read?

LARKIN: I don't read much. Books I'm sent to review. Otherwise novels I've read before. Detective stories: Gladys Mitchell, Michael Innes, Dick Francis. I'm reading *Framley Parsonage* at the moment. Nothing difficult.

INTERVIEWER: What do you think of the current state of poetry in England today? Are things better or worse in American poetry?

LARKIN: I'm afraid I know very little about American poetry. As regards England, well, before the war, when I was growing up, we had Yeats, Eliot, Graves, Auden, Dylan Thomas, John Betjeman—could you pick a comparable team today?

INTERVIEWER: You haven't been to America, have you?

LARKIN: Oh no, I've never been to America, nor to anywhere else, for that matter. Does that sound very snubbing? It isn't meant to. I suppose I'm pretty unadventurous by nature, partly that isn't the way I earn my living—reading and lecturing and taking classes and so on. I should hate it.

And of course I'm so deaf now that I shouldn't dare. Someone would say, What about Ashbery, and I'd say, I'd prefer strawberry, that kind of thing. I suppose everyone has his own dream of America. A writer once said to me, If you ever go to America, go either to the East Coast or the West Coast: the rest is a desert full of bigots. That's what I think I'd like: where if you help a girl trim the Christmas tree you're regarded as engaged, and her brothers start oiling their shotguns if you don't call on the minister. A version of pastoral.

INTERVIEWER: How is your writing physically accomplished? At what stage does a poem go through the typewriter?

LARKIN: I write—or used to—in notebooks in pencil, trying to complete each stanza before going on to the next. Then when the poem is finished I type it out, and sometimes make small alterations.

INTERVIEWER: You use a lot of idioms and very common phrases—for irony, I'd guess, or to bear more meaning than usual, never for shock value. Do these phrases come late, to add texture or whatever, or are they integral from the beginning?

LARKIN: They occur naturally.

INTERVIEWER: How important is enjambment for you? In certain lines, you seem to isolate lives by the very line breaks . . .

LARKIN: No device is important in itself. Writing poetry is playing off the natural rhythms and word order of speech against the artificialities of rhyme and meter. One has a few private rules: Never split an adjective and its noun, for instance.

INTERVIEWER: How do you decide whether or not to rhyme?

LARKIN: Usually the idea of a poem comes with a line or two of it, and they determine the rest. Normally one does rhyme. Deciding *not* to is much harder.

INTERVIEWER: Can you drink and write? Have you tried any consciousness-expanding drugs?

LARKIN: No, though of course those of my generation are drinkers. Not druggers.

INTERVIEWER: Can you describe the genesis and working-out of a poem based upon an image that most people would simply pass by? (A clear road between neighbors, an ambulance in city traffic?)

LARKIN: If I could answer this sort of question, I'd be a professor rather than a librarian. And in any case, I shouldn't want to. It's a thing you don't want to think about. It happens, or happened, and if it's something to be grateful for, you're grateful.

I remember saying once, I can't understand these chaps who go round American universities explaining how they write poems: it's like going round explaining how you sleep with your wife. Whoever I was talking to said, They'd do that, too, if their agents could fix it.

INTERVIEWER: Do you throw away a lot of poems?

LARKIN: Some poems didn't get finished. Some didn't get published. I never throw anything away.

INTERVIEWER: You included only six of your own poems in *The Oxford Book of Twentieth-Century English Verse* (as opposed, say, to twelve by John Betjeman). Do you consider these to be your half-dozen best, or are they merely "representative"? I was surprised not to find "Church Going," arguably your single most famous poem.

LARKIN: My recollection is that I decided on six as a limit for my generation and anyone younger, to save hurt feelings. Mine were representative, as you say—one pretty one, one funny one, one long one, and so on. As editor, I couldn't give myself much space . . . could I?

INTERVIEWER: In your introduction to that anthology, you make a fine point of saying you didn't include any poems "requiring a glossary for their full understanding." Do you feel your own lucid work has helped close the gap between poetry and the public, a gap which experiment and obscurity have widened?

LARKIN: This was to explain why I hadn't included dialect poems. We have poets who write in pretty dense Lallans. Nothing to do with obscurity in the sense you mean.

INTERVIEWER: Okay, but your introduction to *All What Jazz?* takes a stance against experiment, citing the trio of Picasso, Pound, and Parker. Why do you distrust the new?

LARKIN: It seems to me undeniable that up to this century literature used language in the way we all use it, painting represented what anyone with normal vision sees, and music was an affair of nice noises rather than nasty ones. The innovation of "modernism" in the arts consisted of doing the opposite. I don't know why, I'm not a historian. You have to distinguish between things that seemed odd when they were new but are now quite familiar, such as Ibsen and Wagner, and things that seemed crazy when they were new and seem crazy now, like *Finnegans Wake* and Picasso.

INTERVIEWER: What's that got to do with jazz?

LARKIN: Everything. Jazz showed this very clearly because it is such a telescoped art, only as old as the century, if that.

Charlie Parker wrecked jazz by—or so they tell me—using the chromatic rather than the diatonic scale. The diatonic scale is what you use if you want to write a national anthem, or a love song, or a lullaby. The chromatic scale is what you use to give the effect of drinking a quinine martini and having an enema simultaneously.

If I sound heated on this, it's because I love jazz, the jazz of Armstrong and Bechet and Ellington and Bessie Smith and Beiderbecke. To have it all destroyed by a paranoiac drug addict made me furious. Anyway, it's dead now, dead as Elizabethan madrigal singing. We can only treasure the records. And I do.

INTERVIEWER: Let's return to the Oxford anthology for a moment. Some of its critics said your selections not only favored traditional poetic forms, but minor poets as well. How do you respond to that?

LARKIN: Since it was *The Oxford Book of Twentieth-Century English Verse,* I had of course to represent the principal poets of the century by their best or most typical works. I think I did this. The trouble is that if this is all you do, the result will be a worthy but boring book, since there are quite enough books doing this already, and I thought it would be diverting to put in less familiar poems that were good or typical in themselves, but by authors who didn't rank full representation. I saw them as unexpected flowers along an only-too-well-trodden path. I think they upset people in a way I hadn't intended, although it's surprising how they are now being quoted and anthologized themselves.

Most people make anthologies out of other anthologies; I spent five years reading everyone's complete works, ending with six months in the basement of the Bodleian Library handling all the twentieth-century poetry they had received. It was great fun. I don't say I made any major discoveries, but I hope I managed to suggest that there are good poems around that no one knows about. At any rate, I made a readable book. I made twentieth-century poetry sound nice. That's quite an achievement in itself.

INTERVIEWER: Not many have commented upon the humor in your poetry, like the wonderful pun on "the stuff that dreams are made on" in "Toads." Do you consciously use humor to achieve a particular effect, or to avoid an opposite emotion?

LARKIN: One uses humor to make people laugh. In my case, I don't know whether they in fact do. The trouble is, it makes them think you aren't being serious. That's the risk you take.

INTERVIEWER: Your most recent collection, *High Windows*, contains at least three poems I'd call satirical—"Posterity," "Homage to a Government," and "This Be the Verse." Do you consider yourself a satirist?

LARKIN: No, I shouldn't call myself a satirist, or any other sort of *-ist*. The poems you mention were conceived in the same way as the rest. That is to say, as poems. To be a satirist, you have to think you know better than everyone else. I've never done that.

INTERVIEWER: An American poet-critic, Peter Davison, has characterized yours as a "diminutional talent"—meaning you make things clear by making them small—England reduced to "squares of wheat," and so forth. Is this a fair comment? Is it a technique you're aware of?

LARKIN: It's difficult to answer remarks like that. The line "Its postal districts packed like squares of wheat" refers to London, not England. It doesn't seem "diminutional" to me, rather the reverse, if anything. It's meant to make the postal districts seem rich and fruitful.

INTERVIEWER: Davison also sees your favorite subjects as failure and weakness.

LARKIN: I think a poet should be judged by what he does with his subjects, not by what his subjects are. Otherwise you're getting near the totalitarian attitude of wanting poems about steel production figures rather than *"Mais où sont les neiges d'antan?"* Poetry isn't a kind of paint spray you use to cover selected objects with. A good poem about failure is a success.

INTERVIEWER: Is it intentional that the form of "Toads" is alternating uneven trimeters and dimeters, with alternating off-rhymes, whereas "Toads Revisited" is in trimeters and off-rhymed couplets? What determines the form of a poem for you? Is it the first line, with its attendant rhythms?

LARKIN: Well, yes: I think I've admitted this already. At this distance I can't recall how far the second Toad poem was planned as a companion to the first. It's more likely that I found it turning out to be a poem about work, but different from the first, and so it seemed amusing to link them.

INTERVIEWER: How did you arrive upon the image of a toad for work or labor?

LARKIN: Sheer genius.

INTERVIEWER: As a writer, what are your particular quirks? Do you feel you have any conspicuous or secret flaw as a writer?

LARKIN: I really don't know. I suppose I've used the iambic pentameter a lot: some people find this oppressive and try to get away from it. My secret flaw is just not being very good, like everyone else. I've never been didactic, never tried to make poetry *do* things, never gone out to look for it. I waited for it to come to me, in whatever shape it chose.

INTERVIEWER: Do you feel you belong to any particular tradition in English letters?

LARKIN: I seem to remember George Fraser saying that poetry was either "veeshion"—he was Scotch—or "moaral deescourse," and I was the second, and the first was better. A well-known publisher asked me how one punctuated poetry, and looked flabbergasted when I said, The same as prose. By which I mean that I write, or wrote, as everyone did till the mad lads started, using words and syntax in the normal way to describe recognizable experiences as memorably as possible.

That doesn't seem to me a tradition. The other stuff, the mad stuff, is more an aberration.

INTERVIEWER: Have you any thoughts on the office of poet laureate? Does it serve a valid function?

LARKIN: Poetry and sovereignty are very primitive things. I like to think of their being united in this way, in England. On the other hand, it's not clear what the laureate is, or does. Deliberately so, in a way: it isn't a job, there are no duties, no salary, and yet it isn't quite an honor, either, or not just an honor. I'm sure the worst thing about it, especially today, is the publicity it brings, the pressure to be involved publicly with poetry, which must be pretty inimical to any real writing.

Of course, the days when Tennyson would publish a sonnet telling Gladstone what to do about foreign policy are over. It's funny that Kipling, who is what most people think of as a poet as national spokesman, never was laureate. He should have had it when Bridges was appointed, but it's typical that he didn't —the post isn't thought of in that way. It really is a genuine attempt to honor someone. But the publicity that anything to do with the Palace gets these days is so fierce, it must be really more of an ordeal than an honor.

INTERVIEWER: Your poetry volumes have appeared at the rate of one per decade. From what you say, though, is it unlikely we'll have another around 1984? Did you really only complete about three poems in any given year?

LARKIN: It's unlikely I shall write any more poems, but when I did, yes, I did write slowly. I was looking at "The Whitsun Weddings" [the poem] just the other day, and found that I began it sometime in the summer of 1957. After three pages, I dropped it for another poem that in fact was finished but never published. I picked it up again, in March 1958, and worked on it till October, when it was finished. But when I look at the diary I was keeping at the time, I see that the kind of incident it describes happened in July 1955! So in all, it took over three years. Of course, that's an exception. But I did write slowly, partly because you're finding out what to say as well as how to say it, and that takes time.

INTERVIEWER: For someone who dislikes being interviewed, you've responded generously.

LARKIN: I'm afraid I haven't said anything very interesting. You must realize I've never had "ideas" about poetry. To me it's always been a personal, almost physical release or solution to a complex pressure of needs—wanting to create, to justify, to praise, to explain, to externalize, depending on the circumstances. And I've never been much interested in other people's poetry—one reason for writing, of course, is that no one's written what you want to read.

Probably my notion of poetry is very simple. Some time ago I agreed to help judge a poetry competition—you know, the kind where they get about 35,000 entries, and you look at the best few thousand. After a bit I said, Where are all the love poems? And nature poems? And they said, Oh, we threw all those away. I expect they were the ones I should have liked.

ROBERT PHILLIPS
Fall 1981–Spring 1982

8. John Ashbery

Born in Rochester, New York, on July 28, 1927, John Ashbery grew up on a farm near Sodus, New York. He attended Deerfield and Harvard, and later did graduate work in English at Columbia and in French at New York University. From 1955 until 1965, he lived in France, first as a Fulbright Fellow and later as art critic for the *Paris Herald Tribune*. His first book of poems, *Some Trees*, was chosen by W. H. Auden for the Yale Series of Younger Poets Award in 1956. Since 1965 he has lived in New York, working first as executive editor of *Art News*, then as professor of writing at Brooklyn College, and most recently as art critic for *Newsweek*.

In 1976 Ashbery was awarded the Pulitzer Prize, the National Book Award, and the National Book Critics Circle Award for his collection *Self-Portrait in a Convex Mirror*. In addition to a novel, *A Nest of Ninnies* (1969), written in collaboration with James Schuyler, and a collection, *Three Plays* (1978), he is the author of eleven books of poetry, the most recent of which is *Selected Poems* (1985). Twice named a Guggenheim Fellow, John Ashbery was awarded the annual Fellowship of the Academy of American Poets in 1982 and was named cowinner of the Bollingen Prize in Poetry for 1985. He received a MacArthur Award in 1985.

Forties Flick

The shadows of the venetian blinds on the *painted* opposite wall,
Shadows of the cacti, of the china animals
Focus the tragic melancholy of the bright stare
Into nowhere, a hole like the black holes in space.
In bra and panties she sidles to the window:
Zip! Up with the blind. A fragile street scene offers itself
With wafer-thin pedetstrians who know where they are going.
The blind comes down slowly, the slats are slowly tilted up.

Why must it always *end like* come to this?
A dais with woman reading, with the eddies of her hair   *To her,*
And all that is unsaid about her sucking us back with her
Into the silence that night alone doesn't explain?
Silence of the library, of the telephone with its pad
But we didn't have to reinvent these either:
They had gone away into construction of a plot,
The "art" part, or so it seemed: knowing what details to leave out
And about the development of character: things too real
To be of much concern, hence artificial, yet now all over the page
the The indoors with the outside becoming part of you
these As you realize you had never left off laughing at death,
The "background," dark vine at edge of porch.

Larry and Herman, Herman and Larry, lumber
Greasers, companions, rivals at the ENLARGED compnay
Purposely ignorant of so much that is being said
Yet conspirators too in your ambiguity:
What is it like up on the screen?
Do the faces so adroit at the end of their batons of light
Curl up once "The End" has come XXXXXXXXXX XX XXXXXXXXXXX
Or do you figure that by keeping up a front
You will be saved from your own gift of gab
As it becomes time to unravel these old notions
And whatever meant something recedes into the past?

the way character is developed

John Ashbery

The interview was conducted at John Ashbery's apartment in the section of Manhattan known as Chelsea. When I arrived, Ashbery was away, and the doorman asked me to wait outside. Soon the poet arrived and we went up by elevator to a spacious, well-lighted apartment in which a secretary was hard at work. We sat in easy chairs in the living room, Ashbery with his back to the large windows. The predominant decor was blue and white, and books lined the whole of one wall.

We talked for more than three hours with only one short break for refreshment—soda, tea, water, nothing stronger. Ashbery's answers to my questions required little editing. He did, however, throughout the conversation give the impression of distraction, as though he wasn't quite sure just what was going on or what his role in the proceedings might be. The interviewer attempted valiantly to ·extract humorous material, but—as is

often the case for readers of Ashbery's poetry—wasn't sure when
he succeeded. Since that afternoon a few additional questions
were asked and answered, and these have been incorporated into
the whole.

INTERVIEWER: I would like to start at the very beginning.
When and why did you first decide on a career as a poet?

ASHBERY: I don't think I ever decided on a career as a poet.
I began by writing a few little verses, but I never thought any
of them would be published or that I would go on to publish
books. I was in high school at the time and hadn't read any
modern poetry. Then in a contest I won a prize in which you
could choose different books; the only one which seemed appealing was Untermeyer's anthology, which cost five dollars, a
great deal of money. That's how I began reading modern
poetry, which wasn't taught in the schools then, especially in
rural schools like the one I attended. I didn't understand much
of it at first. There were people like Elinor Wylie whom I found
appealing—wonderful craftsmanship—but I couldn't get very
far with Auden and Eliot and Stevens. Later I went back to
them and started getting their books out of the library. I guess
it was just a desire to emulate that started me writing poetry.
I can't think of any other reason. I am often asked why I write,
and I don't know really—I just want to.

INTERVIEWER: When did you get more serious about it,
thinking about publishing and that sort of thing?

ASHBERY: For my last two years of high school, I went to
Deerfield Academy, and the first time I saw my work in print
was in the school paper there. I had tried painting earlier, but
I found that poetry was easier than painting. I must have been
fifteen at the time. I remember reading *Scholastic* magazine
and thinking I could write better poems than the ones they had
in there, but I was never able to get one accepted. Then a
student at Deerfield sent in some of my poems under his name
to *Poetry* magazine, and when I sent them the same poems a

few months later the editors there naturally assumed that I was the plagiarist. Very discouraging. *Poetry* was the most illustrious magazine to be published in at that time, and for a long time after they shunned my work. Then I went on to Harvard and in my second year I met Kenneth Koch. I was trying to get on the *Harvard Advocate,* and he was already one of the editors. He saw my poetry and liked it, and we started reading each other's work. He was really the first poet that I ever knew, so that was rather an important meeting. Of course I published in the *Advocate,* and then in 1949 I had a poem published in *Furioso.* That was a major event in my life because, even though it was a relatively small magazine, it did take me beyond the confines of the college. But it was hard to follow that up with other publications, and it really wasn't until my late twenties that I could submit things with some hope of them getting accepted.

INTERVIEWER: Was there ever a time when you thought you would have to make a choice between art criticism and poetry, or have the two just always worked out well together?

ASHBERY: I was never interested in doing art criticism at all —I'm not sure that I am even now. Back in the fifties, Thomas Hess, the editor of *ARTnews,* had a lot of poets writing for the magazine. One reason was that they paid almost nothing and poets are always penurious. Trained art historians would not write reviews for five dollars, which is what they were paying when I began. I needed some bread at the time—this was in 1957 when I was thirty—and my friends who were already writing for *ARTnews* suggested that I do it too. So I wrote a review of Bradley Tomlin, an Abstract Expressionist painter who had a posthumous show at the Whitney. After that I reviewed on a monthly basis for a while until I returned to France. Then in 1960 it happened that I knew the woman who was writing art criticism for the *Herald Tribune.* She was going back to live in America and asked if I knew anybody who would like to take over her job. It didn't pay very much, but it enabled me to get other jobs doing art criticism, which I didn't want to do very much, but as so often when you exhibit reluctance to do something, people think you must be very good at it. If I had set out to be an art critic, I might never have succeeded.

INTERVIEWER: Are there any aspects of your childhood that you think might have contributed to making you the poet you are?

ASHBERY: I don't know what the poet that I am is, very much. I was rather an outsider as a child—I didn't have many friends. We lived out in the country on a farm. I had a younger brother whom I didn't get along with—we were always fighting the way kids do—and he died at the age of nine. I felt guilty because I had been so nasty to him, so that was a terrible shock. These are experiences which have been important to me. I don't know quite how they may have fed into my poetry. My ambition was to be a painter, so I took weekly classes at the art museum in Rochester from the age of about eleven until fifteen or sixteen. I fell deeply in love with a girl who was in the class but who wouldn't have anything to do with me. So I went to this weekly class knowing that I would see this girl, and somehow this being involved with art may have something to do with my poetry. Also, my grandfather was a professor at the University of Rochester, and I lived with them as a small child and went to kindergarten and first grade in the city. I always loved his house; there were lots of kids around, and I missed all this terribly when I went back to live with my parents. Then going back there each week for art class was a returning to things I had thought were lost, and gave me a curious combination of satisfaction and dissatisfaction.

INTERVIEWER: These are all rather traumatic things. I think of how most critics seem to see your poetry as rather light-hearted. One critic, however, has spoken of your "rare startlements into happiness." Is happiness so rare in your work?

ASHBERY: Some people wouldn't agree that my poetry is lighthearted. Frank O'Hara once said, "I don't see why

Kenneth likes John's work so much because he thinks every-thing should be funny and John's poetry is about as funny as a wrecked train." In my life I am reasonably happy now. There are days when I think I am not, but I think there are probably more days when I think I am. I was impressed by an Ingmar Bergman movie I saw years ago—I can't remember the name of it—in which a woman tells the story of her life, which has been full of tragic experiences. She's telling the story in the dressing room of a theater where she is about to go on and perform in a ballet. At the end of it she says, "But I am happy." Then it says, "The End."

INTERVIEWER: Do you like to tease or play games with the reader?

ASHBERY: Funny you should ask—I just blew up at a critic who asked me the same question, though I shouldn't have, in a list of questions for a book she is compiling of poets' state-ments. I guess it depends on what you mean by "tease." It's all right if it's done affectionately, though how can this be with someone you don't know? I would like to please the reader, and I think that surprise has to be an element of this, and that may necessitate a certain amount of teasing. To shock the reader is something else again. That has to be handled with great care if you're not going to alienate and hurt him, and I'm firmly against that, just as I disapprove of people who dress with that in mind—dye their hair blue and stick safety pins through their noses and so on. The message here seems to be merely aggres-sion—"hey, you can't be part of my strangeness" sort of thing. At the same time I try to dress in a way that is just slightly off, so the spectator, if he notices, will feel slightly bemused but not excluded, remembering his own imperfect mode of dress.

INTERVIEWER: But you would not be above inflicting a trick or a gag on your readers?

ASHBERY: A gag that's probably gone unnoticed turns up in the last sentence of the novel I wrote with James Schuyler. Actually it's my sentence. It reads: "So it was that the cliff

dwellers, after bidding their cousins good night, moved off
towards the parking area, while the latter bent their steps
toward the partially rebuilt shopping plaza in the teeth of the
freshening foehn." *Foehn* is a kind of warm wind that blows
in Bavaria that produces a fog. I would doubt that many people
know that. I liked the idea that people, if they bothered to,
would have to open the dictionary to find out what the last
word in the novel meant. They'd be closing one book and
opening another.

INTERVIEWER: Were there older living poets whom you visited, learned from, or studied with as a young writer?

ASHBERY: I particularly admired Auden, whom I would say
was the first big influence on my work, more so than Stevens.
I wrote an honors thesis on his poetry and got a chance to meet
him at Harvard. When I was at Harvard also I studied with
Theodore Spencer, a poet who is no longer very well known.
He actually taught a poetry-writing workshop, which was very
rare in those days—especially at Harvard, where they still are
rare. It wasn't that I was particularly fond of Spencer's poetry,
but he was a "genuine" poet, a real-live poet, and the feedback
I got from him in class was very valuable to me. I also read
Elizabeth Bishop quite early and met her once. I wrote her a
letter about one of her poems that I had liked and she wrote
back, and then after I moved to New York I met her. But I
was rather shy about putting myself forward, so there weren't
very many known poets then that I did have any contact with.
I wish I could have visited older poets! But things were different then—young poets simply didn't send their poems to older
ones with requests for advice and criticism and "suggestions for
publication." At least I don't think they did—none of the ones
I knew did. Everyone is bolder now. This leads to a sad situation (and I've often discussed this with poets of my generation
like Kinnell and Merwin) of having a tremendous pile of unanswered correspondence about poetry—Kinnell calls it his "guilt
pile"—from poets who want help and should receive it; only

in this busy world of doing things to make a living and trying to find some time for oneself to write poetry, it isn't usually possible to summon the time and energy it would require to deal seriously with so many requests; at least for me it isn't. But I feel sad because I would like to help; you remember how valuable it would have been for you; and it's an honor to get these requests. People think they have gotten to know you through your poetry and can address you familiarly (I get lots of "Dear John" letters from strangers) and that in itself is a tremendous reward, a satisfaction—if only we could attend to everybody! Actually the one poet I really wanted to know when I was young was Auden. I met him briefly twice after he gave readings at Harvard, and later on in New York saw a bit of him through Chester Kallman who was a great friend of Jimmy Schuyler's, but it was very hard to talk to him since he already knew everything. I once said to Kenneth Koch, "What are you supposed to say to Auden?" And he said that about the only thing there was to say was "I'm glad you're alive."

INTERVIEWER: Why is it always Auden?

ASHBERY: It's odd to be asked today what I saw in Auden. Forty years ago when I first began to read modern poetry no one would have asked—he was *the* modern poet. Stevens was a curiosity, Pound probably a monstrosity, William Carlos Williams—who hadn't yet published his best poetry—an "imagist." Eliot and Yeats were too hallowed and anointed to count. I read him at the suggestion of Kathryn Koller, a professor of English at the University of Rochester who was a neighbor of my parents. She had been kind enough to look at my early scribblings and, probably shaking her head over them, suggested Auden as perhaps a kind of antidote. What immediately struck me was his use of colloquial speech—I didn't think you were supposed to do that in poetry. That, and his startling way of making abstractions concrete and alive—remember: "Abruptly mounting her ramshackle wheel/Fortune has pedaled furiously away./The sobbing mess is on our hands today,"

which seem to crystallize the thirties into a few battered and
quirky images. And again a kind of romantic tone which took
abandoned mines and factory chimneys into account. There is
perhaps a note of both childishness and sophistication which
struck an answering chord in me. I cannot agree, though, with
the current view that his late work is equal to if not better than
the early stuff. Except for "The Sea and the Mirror" there is
little that enchants me in the poetry he wrote after coming to
America. There are felicities, of course, but on the whole it's
too chatty and too self-congratulatory at not being "poetry
with a capital P," as he put it. Auden was of two minds about
my own work. He once said he never understood a line of it.
On the other hand he published *Some Trees* in the Yale
Younger Poets Series. You'll remember, though, that he once
said in later life that one of his early works, *The Orators,* must
have been written by a madman.

INTERVIEWER: Tell me about the New York School—were
there regular meetings, perhaps classes or seminars? Did you
plot to take over the literary world?

ASHBERY: No. This label was foisted upon us by a man
named John Bernard Meyers, who ran the Tibor de Nagy
Gallery and published some pamphlets of our poems. I found
out recently from one of my students that Meyers coined the
term in 1961 in an article he wrote for a little magazine in
California called *Nomad.* I think the idea was that, since everybody was talking about the New York School of painting, if he
created a New York School of poets then they would automatically be considered important because of the sound of the
name. But by that time I was living in France, and wasn't part
of what was happening in New York. I don't think we ever
were a school. There are vast differences between my poetry
and Koch's and O'Hara's and Schuyler's and Guest's. We were
a bunch of poets who happened to know each other; we would
get together and read our poems to each other and sometimes
we would write collaborations. It never occurred to us that it

would be possible to take over the literary world, so that was not part of the plan. Somebody wrote an article about the New York School a few years ago in the *Times Book Review,* and a woman wrote in to find out how she could enroll.

INTERVIEWER: What was your relation to Paris at the time when you were there—you used to drink Coca-Colas . . .

ASHBERY: That question probably requires a book-length essay. I did at one point in Paris develop an addiction to Coca-Cola which I've never had before or since, but I don't know whether that was due to nostalgia for America or the fact that the French like it so much. Paris is "the city," isn't it, and I am a lover of cities. It can be experienced much more pleasantly and conveniently than any other city I know. It's so easy to get around on the metro, and so interesting when you get there—each *arrondissement* is like a separate province, with its own capital and customs and even costumes. I used to pick a different section to explore and set out on a miniexpedition, often with a movie theater in mind where they were showing some movie I wanted to see, often an old Laurel and Hardy film since I love them, especially when dubbed into French with comic American accents. And then there is always a principal café in the neighborhood where you can sample some nice wine and look at the people. You get to know a lot of life this way. Sometimes I would do a Proustian excursion, looking at buildings he or his characters had lived in. Like his childhood home in the Boulevard Malesherbes or Odette's house in the rue La Pérouse.

I didn't have many friends the first years I was there—they were mainly the American writers Harry Mathews and Elliott Stein, and Pierre Martory, a French writer with whom I lived for the last nine of the ten years I spent in France, and who has remained a very close friend. He once published a novel but never anything after that, though the novel was well received and he continues to write voluminously—poems, novels, and stories which he produces constantly but never tries to publish or show to anybody, even me—the only writer of that kind I've ever met. I've translated a few of his poems but they haven't appeared in France, where they don't fit in with the cliques that prevail there. Some were published in *Locus Solus,* a small magazine Harry Mathews and I edited—the title is taken from a novel by Raymond Roussel, whom we both loved and on whom I was once going to do a dissertation. A little later I met Anne and Rodrigo Moynihan, English painters who live mostly in France, who sponsored a review called *Art and Literature,* which I helped to edit. They too have remained close friends whom I see often. I return to Pierre—most of my knowledge of France and things French comes from him. He is a sort of walking encyclopedia of French culture but at the same time views it all from a perspective that is somewhat American. He once spent six months in New York working for *Paris Match,* for which he still works, and we sailed back to France together on the S.S. *France.* When he set foot on French soil at Le Havre he said, "It is so wonderful to be back in France! *But I hate ze French!"*

INTERVIEWER: What early reading did you do, say in high school or college, that has stayed with you?

ASHBERY: Like many young people, I was attracted by long novels. My grandfather had several sets of Victorian writers in his house. The first long novel I read was *Vanity Fair,* and I liked it so much that I decided to read *Gone With the Wind,* which I liked too. I read Dickens and George Eliot then, but not very much poetry. I didn't really get a feeling for the poetry of the past until I had discovered modern poetry. Then I began to see how nineteenth-century poetry wasn't just something lifeless in an ancient museum but must have grown out of the lives of the people who wrote it. In college I majored in English and read the usual curriculum. I guess I was particularly attracted to the Metaphysical poets and to Keats, and I had a Chaucer course, which I enjoyed very much. I also had a modern poetry course from F. O. Matthiessen, which is where

I really began to read Wallace Stevens. I wrote a paper, I recall, on "Chocorua to Its Neighbor." Mostly I wasn't a very good student and just sort of got by—laziness. I read Proust for a course with Harry Levin, and that was a major shock.

INTERVIEWER: Why?

ASHBERY: I don't know. I started reading it when I was twenty (before I took Levin's course) and it took me almost a year. I read very slowly anyway, but particularly in the case of a writer whom I wanted to read every word of. It's just that I think one ends up feeling sadder and wiser in equal proportions when one is finished reading him—I can no longer look at the world in quite the same way.

INTERVIEWER: Were you attracted by the intimate, meditative voice of his work?

ASHBERY: Yes, and the way somehow everything could be included in this vast, open form that he created for himself— particularly certain almost surreal passages. There's one part where a philologist or specialist on place names goes on at great length concerning place names in Normandy. I don't know why it is so gripping, but it seizes the way life sometimes seems to have of droning on in a sort of dreamlike space. I also identified, on account of the girl in my art class, with the narrator, who had a totally impractical passion which somehow both enveloped the beloved like a cocoon and didn't have much to do with her.

INTERVIEWER: You said a minute ago that reading modern poetry enabled you to see the vitality present in older poetry. In your mind, is there a close connection between life and poetry?

ASHBERY: In my case I would say there is a very close but oblique connection. I have always been averse to talking about myself, and so I don't write about my life the way the confessional poets do. I don't want to bore people with experiences of mine that are simply versions of what everybody goes through. For me, poetry starts after that point. I write with experiences in mind, but I don't write about them, I write out of them. I know that I have exactly the opposite reputation, that I am totally self-involved, but that's not the way I see it.

INTERVIEWER: You have often been characterized as a solipsist, and I wonder if this isn't related to your reputation for obscurity. The way the details of a poem will be so clear, but the context, the surrounding situation, unclear. Perhaps this is more a matter of perspective than any desire to befuddle.

ASHBERY: This is the way that life appears to me, the way that experience happens. I can concentrate on the things in this room and our talking together, but what the context is is mysterious to me. And it's not that I want to make it more mysterious in my poems—really, I just want to make it more photographic. I often wonder if I am suffering from some mental dysfunction because of how weird and baffling my poetry seems to so many people and sometimes to me too. Let me read you a comment which appeared in a review of my most recent book, from some newspaper in Virginia. It says: "John Ashbery is emerging as a very important poet, if not by unanimous critical consent then certainly by the admiration and awe he inspires in younger poets. Oddly, no one understands Ashbery." That is a simplification, but in a sense it is true, and I wonder how things happened that way. I'm not the person who knows. When I originally started writing, I expected that probably very few people would read my poetry because in those days people didn't read poetry much anyway. But I also felt that my work was not beyond understanding. It seemed to me rather derivative of or at least in touch with contemporary poetry of the time, and I was quite surprised that nobody seemed to see this. So I live with this paradox: on the one hand, I am an important poet, read by younger writers, and on the other hand, nobody understands me. I am often asked to account for this state of affairs, but I can't.

INTERVIEWER: When you say that sometimes you think your poetry is weird, what do you mean exactly?

ASHBERY: Every once in a while I will pick up a page and it has something, but what is it? It seems so unlike what poetry "as we know it" is. But at other moments I feel very much at home with it. It's a question of a sudden feeling of unsureness at what I am doing, wondering why I am writing the way I am, and also not feeling the urge to write in another way.

INTERVIEWER: Is the issue of meaning or message something that is uppermost in your mind when you write?

ASHBERY: Meaning yes, but message no. I think my poems mean what they say, and whatever might be implicit within a particular passage, but there is no message, nothing I want to tell the world particularly except what I am thinking when I am writing. Many critics tend to want to see an allegorical meaning in every concrete statement, and if we just choose a line at random, I think we will find this isn't the way it works. . . . I can't seem to find anything that's an example of what I mean. Well, let's take this . . . no. Everything I look at does seem to mean something other than what is being said, all of a sudden. Ah, here—the beginning of "Daffy Duck in Hollywood," for instance, where all these strange objects avalanche into the poem. I meant them to be there for themselves, and not for some hidden meaning. Rumford's Baking Powder (by the way, it's actually Rumford and not Rumford's Baking Powder. I knew that, but preferred the sound of my version—I don't usually do that), a celluloid earring, Speedy Gonzales— they are just the things that I selected to be exhibited in the poem at that point. In fact, there is a line here, "The allegory comes unsnarled too soon," that might be my observation of poetry and my poetry in particular. The allegory coming unsnarled meaning that the various things that make it up are dissolving into a poetic statement, and that is something I feel is both happening and I don't want to happen. And, as so often, two opposing forces are working to cancel each other out. "Coming unsnarled" is probably a good thing, but "too soon" isn't.

INTERVIEWER: So for you a poem is an object in and of itself rather than a clue to some abstraction, to something other than itself?

ASHBERY: Yes, I would like it to be what Stevens calls a completely new set of objects. My intention is to present the reader with a pleasant surprise, not an unpleasant one, not a nonsurprise. I think this is the way pleasure happens when you are reading poetry. Years ago Kenneth Koch and I did an interview with each other, and something I said then, in 1964, is pertinent to what we are talking about. "It's rather hard to be a good artist and also be able to explain intelligently what your art is about. In fact, the worse your art is, the easier it is to talk about, at least I would like to think so. Ambiguity seems to be the same thing as happiness or pleasant surprise. I am assuming that from the moment life cannot be one continual orgasm, real happiness is impossible, and pleasant surprise is promoted to the front rank of the emotions. The idea of relief from pain has something to do with ambiguity. Ambiguity supposes eventual resolution of itself whereas certitude implies further ambiguity. I guess that is why so much 'depressing' modern art makes me feel cheerful."

INTERVIEWER: Could you explain the paradox concerning ambiguity and certitude?

ASHBERY: Things are in a continual state of motion and evolution, and if we come to a point where we say, with certitude, right here, this is the end of the universe, then of course we must deal with everything that goes on after that, whereas ambiguity seems to take further developments into account. We might realize that the present moment may be one of an eternal or sempiternal series of moments, all of which will resemble it because, in some ways, they are the present, and won't in other ways, because the present will be the past by that time.

INTERVIEWER: Is it bothersome that critics seem to have considerable trouble saying exactly what your poems are about?

ASHBERY: You have probably read David Bromwich's review of *As We Know* in the *Times*. He decided that the entire book deals with living in a silver age rather than a golden age. This is an idea that occurs only briefly, along with a great many other things, in "Litany." By making this arbitrary decision he was able to deal with the poetry. I intended, in "Litany," to write something so utterly discursive that it would be beyond criticism—not because I wanted to punish critics, but because this would somehow exemplify the fullness, or, if you wish, the emptiness, of life, or, at any rate, its dimensionless quality. And I think that any true work of art does defuse criticism; if it left anything important to be said, it wouldn't be doing its job. (This is not an idea I expect critics to sympathize with, especially at a time when criticism has set itself up as a separate branch of the arts, and, perhaps by implication, the most important one.) The poem is of an immense length, and there is a lack of coherence between the parts. Given all this, I don't really see how one could deal critically with the poem, so I suppose it is necessary for the critic to draw up certain guidelines before beginning. It was a very sympathetic review, and I admire Bromwich, but it seemed to leave a great deal out of account. I guess I am pleased that my method has given every critic something to hate or like. For me, my poems have their own form, which is the one that I want, even though other people might not agree that it is there. I feel that there is always a resolution in my poems.

INTERVIEWER: Did you see the controversy that erupted in *The New York Review* about how "Litany" should be read? Whether one should read all of voice A, then all of voice B, or intermingle them in some way . . .

ASHBERY: I don't think there is any particular way. I seem to have opened up a can of worms with my instruction, which the publisher asked me to put in, that the parts should be read simultaneously. I don't think people ever read things the way they are supposed to. I myself will skip ahead several chapters, or read a little bit of this page and a little bit of that page, and I assume that is what everybody does. I just wanted the whole thing to be, as I have said, presentable; it's not a form that has a cohesive structure, so it could be read just as one pleases. I think I consider the poem as a sort of environment, and one is not obliged to take notice of every aspect of one's environment—one can't, in fact. That is why it came out the way it did.

INTERVIEWER: One's environment at a single moment?

ASHBERY: No, it is a succession of moments. I am always impressed by how difficult and yet how easy it is to get from one moment to the next of one's life—particularly while traveling, as I just was in Poland. There is a problem every few minutes—one doesn't know whether one is going to get on the plane, or will they confiscate one's luggage. Somehow I did all this and got back, but I was aware of so much difficulty, and at the same time of the pleasure, the novelty of it all. Susan Sontag was at this writers' conference also—there were just four of us—and one night in Warsaw we were provided with tickets to a ballet. I said, "Do you think we should go? It doesn't sound like it will be too interesting." And she said, "Sure, we should go. If it is boring that will be interesting too" —which turned out to be the case.

INTERVIEWER: Given what you said about "Litany," it seems that in a way you are leaving it up to each reader to make his or her own poem out of the raw materials you have given. Do you visualize an ideal reader when you write, or do you conceive of a multitude of different apprehending sensibilities?

ASHBERY: Every writer faces the problem of the person that he is writing for, and I think nobody has ever been able to imagine satisfactorily who this *"homme moyen sensuel"* will be. I try to aim at as wide an audience as I can so that as many people as possible will read my poetry. Therefore I depersonalize it, but in the same way personalize it, so that a person who is going to be different from me but is also going to resemble

me just because he is different from me, since we are all different from each other, can see something in it. You know—I
shot an arrow into the air but I could only aim it. Often after
I have given a poetry reading, people will say, "I never really
got anything out of your work before, but now that I have
heard you read it, I can see something in it." I guess something
about my voice and my projection of myself meshes with the
poems. That is nice, but it is also rather saddening because
I can't sit down with every potential reader and read aloud
to him.

INTERVIEWER: Your poems often have a spoken quality, as
though they are monologues or dialogues. Do you try to create
characters who then speak in your poems, or is this all your own
voice? In the dialogues perhaps it is two aspects of your own
voice that are speaking.

ASHBERY: It doesn't seem to me like my voice. I have had
many arguments about this with my analyst, who is actually a
South American concert pianist, more interested in playing the
piano than in being a therapist. He says, "Yes, I know, you
always think that these poems come from somewhere else. You
refuse to realize that it is really you that is writing the poems
and not having them dictated by some spirit somewhere." It
is hard for me to realize that because I have such an imprecise
impression of what kind of a person I am. I know I appear
differently to other people because I behave differently on
different occasions. Some people think that I am very laid-back
and charming and some people think I am egotistical and
disagreeable. Or as Edward Lear put it in his great poem "How
Pleasant to Know Mr. Lear": "Some think him ill-tempered
and queer, but a few find him pleasant enough." Any of the
above, I suppose. Of course, my reason tells me that my poems
are not dictated, that I am not a voyant. I suppose they come
from a part of me that I am not in touch with very much except
when I am actually writing. The rest of the time I guess I want
to give this other person a rest, this other one of my selves that

does the talking in my poems, so that he won't get tired and stop.

INTERVIEWER: So you have a sense of several selves?

ASHBERY: No, no more than the average person, I shouldn't think. I mean, we are all different depending on who we happen to be with and what we are doing at a particular moment, but I wouldn't say that it goes any further than that.

INTERVIEWER: Some people have thought that you set up characters who converse in several poems. One could say that in "Litany" you have character A and character B, who are very similar to one another. It is possible at times to see them as lovers on the point of separating, while at other times they look like two aspects of one personality.

ASHBERY: I think I am trying to reproduce the polyphony that goes on inside me, which I don't think is radically different from that of other people. After all, one is constantly changing one's mind and thereby becoming something slightly different. But what was I doing? Perhaps the two columns are like two people whom I am in love with simultaneously. A student of mine who likes this poem says that when you read one column you start to "miss" the other one, as you would miss one beloved when you spend time with the other. I once half-jokingly said that my object was to direct the reader's attention to the white space between the columns. Maybe that's part of it. Reading is a pleasure, but to finish reading, to come to the blank space at the end, is also a pleasure.

INTERVIEWER: This notion of your poems being dictated makes me wonder whether for you composition involves something like inspiration, the poems just springing out already finished, rather than a laborious process of writing and revision.

ASHBERY: That is the way it has happened to me in more recent times. In fact, since I don't have very much free time (poets seldom do, since they must somehow make a living), I've conditioned myself to write at almost any time. Sometimes it doesn't work, but on the whole I feel that poetry is going on all the time inside, an underground stream. One can let down one's bucket and bring the poem back up. (This is very well put in a passage that occurs early on in Heimito von Doderer's novel *The Demons*, which I haven't to hand at the moment.) It will be not dissimilar to what I have produced before because it is coming from the same source, but it will be dissimilar because of the different circumstances of the particular moment.

INTERVIEWER: Many poets have spoken of poetry coming from the subconscious mind rather than the conscious mind. Would you agree with that?

ASHBERY: I think that is where it probably starts out, but I think that in my case it passes through the conscious mind on its way out and is monitored by it. I don't believe in automatic writing as the Surrealists were supposed to have practiced it, simply because it is not a reflection of the whole mind, which is partly logical and reasonable, and that part should have its say too.

INTERVIEWER: Do you compose on the typewriter or in longhand?

ASHBERY: I write on the typewriter. I didn't use to, but when I was writing "The Skaters," the lines became unmanageably long. I would forget the end of the line before I could get to it. It occurred to me that perhaps I should do this at the typewriter, because I can type faster than I can write. So I did, and that is mostly the way I have written ever since. Occasionally I write a poem in longhand to see whether I can still do it. I don't want to be forever bound to this machine.

INTERVIEWER: Do you have rituals?

ASHBERY: Well, one of them is to use this very old, circa 1930 I would say, Royal typewriter I mentioned. I hate to think what will happen when it finally gives out, though you can still find them sometimes in those used office furniture stores on West 23rd Street, which are themselves an endangered species. And then I procrastinate like everybody else, though surely more than most. On days when I want to write I will usually waste the morning and go for an afternoon walk to Greenwich Village. (I live nearby in Chelsea, which is a pleasant place to walk from though maybe not to.) Sometimes this takes too long and my preferred late afternoon moment will pass. I can't really work at night. Nor in the morning, very much, when I have more ideas but am less critical of them, it seems. I never can use the time I waste doing this for some other purpose like answering letters. It's no good for anything but wasting. I've never tried Schiller's rotten apples, but I do drink tea while I write, and that is about the only time I do drink tea. On the whole, I believe I have fewer hang-ups and rituals than I used to. I feel blocked much less often, though it still happens. It's important to try to write when you are in the wrong mood or the weather is wrong. Even if you don't succeed you'll be developing a muscle that may do it later on. And I think writing does get easier as you get older. It's a question of practice and also of realizing you don't have the oceans of time to waste you had when you were young.

INTERVIEWER: Do you revise your poems heavily?

ASHBERY: Not anymore. I used to labor over them a great deal, but because of my strong desire to avoid all unnecessary work, I have somehow trained myself not to write something that I will either have to discard or be forced to work a great deal over. In fact, just last night a friend mentioned that she has a manuscript copy of one of my early poems, "Le livre est sur la table," with a lot of corrections in it. I remember that poem as one that gave me an immense amount of difficulty—I worked over it for a week or so and never did feel really happy with it. When she mentioned that, I realized how much my way of writing has changed over the last thirty years. But, although there are poems even today that I don't find satisfactory once I have finished them, most of the corrections I make are pretty minor. I like the idea of being as close to the original thought or voice as possible and not to falsify it by editing.

Here is something I just read by Max Jacob, quoted by André Salmon in the notes to Jacob's book *La Défense de Tartufe.* He talks about composing novels or stories in a notebook while taking long walks through Paris. I'll translate: "The ideas I found in this way seemed sacred to me and I didn't change a comma. I believe that prose which comes directly from meditation is a prose which has the form of the brain and which it is forbidden to touch."

INTERVIEWER: What determines a line break for you? Is there some metrical consideration, or would you say you are writing free verse?

ASHBERY: I don't know. I just know when I feel the line should break. I used to say that my criterion for a line of poetry was that it should have at least two interesting things in it. But this is not the case in a lot of my recent poetry. In "Litany" there are lines that are a single word long. As I was writing that poem—well, actually it began with the long poem before that, the "Nut-Brown Maid"—I became almost intoxicated by the idea of the line break. It seemed as if I were writing just to get to this point, this decision. But, although the line break is very important to me, I don't really understand how I know when it is supposed to happen. I have felt very uncomfortable with iambic pentameter ever since I discovered, when I first began writing poetry, that it was not impossible to write acceptable blank verse. It somehow seems to falsify poetry for me. It has an order of its own that is foreign to nature. When I was in college, I used to write a kind of four-beat line, which seemed much more real, genuine, to me. Now I guess it is free verse, whatever that is.

INTERVIEWER: What gets you started in writing a poem? Is it an idea, an image, a rhythm, a situation or event, a phrase, something else?

ASHBERY: Again, all of the above. An idea might occur to me, something very banal—for example, isn't it strange that it is possible to both talk and think at the same time? That might be an idea for a poem. Or certain words or phrases might have come to my attention with a meaning I wasn't aware of before. Also, I often put in things that I have overheard people say, on the street for instance. Suddenly something fixes itself in the flow that is going on around one and seems to have a significance. In fact, there is an example of that in this poem, "What Is Poetry?" In a bookstore I overheard a boy saying to a girl this last line: "It might give us—what?—some flowers soon?" I have no idea what the context was, but it suddenly seemed the way to end my poem. I am a believer in fortuitous accidents. The ending of my poem "Clepsydra," the last two lines, came from a notebook that I kept a number of years before, during my first trip to Italy. I actually wrote some poems while I was traveling, which I don't usually do, but I was very excited by my first visit there. So years later, when I was trying to end "Clepsydra" and getting very nervous, I happened to open that notebook and found these two lines that I had completely forgotten about: "while morning is still and before the body / Is changed by the faces of evening." They were just what I needed at that time. But it doesn't really matter so much what the individual thing is. Many times I will jot down ideas and phrases, and then when I am ready to write I can't find them. But it doesn't make any difference, because whatever comes along at that time will have the same quality. Whatever was there is replaceable. In fact, often in revising I will remove the idea that was the original stimulus. I think I am more interested in the movement among ideas than in the ideas themselves, the way one goes from one point to another rather than the destination or the origin.

INTERVIEWER: *Three Poems* is largely prose, prose poetry, rather than verse. Some readers would object rather strenuously to calling it poetry. Within this kind of form, I am wondering where, for you, the poetry specifically is to be found? What is the indispensable element that makes poetry?

ASHBERY: That is one of those good but unanswerable questions. For a long time a very prosaic language, a language of ordinary speech, has been in my poetry. It seems to me that we are most ourselves when we are talking, and we talk in a very irregular and antiliterary way. In *Three Poems*, I wanted to see how poetic the most prosaic language could be. And I don't mean just the journalese, but also the inflated rhetoric that is trying very hard to sound poetic but not making it. One of my aims has been to put together as many different kinds of language and tone as possible, and to shift them abruptly, to overlap them all. There is a very naive, romantic tone at times, all kinds of clichés, as well as a more deliberate poetic voice. I also was in a way reacting to the minimalism of some of the poems in *The Tennis Court Oath*, such as "Europe," which is sometimes just a few scattered words. I suppose I eventually thought of covering page after page with words, with not even any break for paragraphs in many cases—could I do this and still feel that I was getting the satisfaction that poetry gives me? I don't quite understand why some people are so against prose poetry, which is certainly a respectable and pedigreed form of poetry. In fact, too much so for my taste. I had written almost none before *Three Poems* because there always seemed to be a kind of rhetorical falseness in much that had been done in the past—Baudelaire's, for instance. I wanted to see if prose poetry could be written without that self-conscious drama that seems so much a part of it. So if it is poetic, it is probably because it tries to stay close to the way we talk and think without expecting what we say to be recorded or remembered. The pathos and liveliness of ordinary human communication is poetry to me.

INTERVIEWER: You were talking once about reading younger poets and being aware that you have influenced their work. You said one of the primary benefits for you in seeing this is that it alerts you to watch out for "Ashberyisms" in your own work.

What do you mean by Ashberyisms?

ASHBERY: Well, there are certain stock words that I have found myself using a great deal. When I become aware of them, it is an alarm signal meaning I was falling back on something that had served in the past—it is a sign of not thinking at the present moment, not that there is anything intrinsically bad about certain words or phrases. The word "climate" occurs in my poetry a great deal, for instance. So I try to censor it, unless I feel that there is no alternative. I also seem to be very fond of words involving a kind of osmosis, like "absorb" and "leach," as something leaching into the soil. I don't know why these particular words attract me, unless it's because they are indicative of the slow but kinetic quality of existence and experience. Also there is a typical kind of tone, the chatty quality that my poetry tends to have, the idea behind it being that there are things more important than "all this fiddle," perhaps, and sometimes I correct this.

INTERVIEWER: I suppose there are many things we might expect from a poet who has so strong an interest in painting as you do. Various critics have suggested that you are a Mannerist in words, or an Abstract Expressionist. Are you conscious of anything like that—or perhaps of performing a Cubist experiment with words?

ASHBERY: I suppose the "Self-Portrait in a Convex Mirror" is a Mannerist work in what I hope is the good sense of the word. Later on, Mannerism became mannered, but at first it was a pure novelty—Parmigianino was an early Mannerist, coming right on the heels of Michelangelo. I have probably been influenced, more or less unconsciously I suppose, by the modern art that I have looked at. Certainly the simultaneity of Cubism is something that has rubbed off on me, as well as the Abstract Expressionist idea that the work is a sort of record of its own coming-into-existence; it has an "anti-referential sensuousness," but it is nothing like flinging a bucket of words on the page, as Pollock did with paint. It is more indirect than that. When I was fresh out of college, Abstract Expressionism was the most exciting thing in the arts. There was also experimental music and film, but poetry seemed quite conventional in comparison. I guess it still is, in a way. One can accept a Picasso woman with two noses, but an equivalent attempt in poetry baffles the same audience.

INTERVIEWER: Though it has its admirers, *The Tennis Court Oath* seems to have been a widely disliked book—for its difficulty, its obscurity, and so on. How do you feel about that volume from the perspective of today?

ASHBERY: There are a lot of poems in that book that don't interest me as much as those that came before or since. I didn't expect to have a second book published, ever. The opportunity came about very suddenly, and when it did I simply sent what I had been doing. But I never expected these poems to see the light of day. I felt at that time that I needed a change in the way I was writing, so I was kind of fooling around and trying to do something I hadn't done before. I was conscious that often what I hadn't done before was inferior to what I had done. But I like a number of the poems in the book. I hadn't realized this until recently, but there was a period, after I had begun living in Paris and decided that I wanted to write in a different way, when I achieved a kind of intermediate style, say between the poems in *Some Trees* and the poem "Europe." For instance, the poem "They Dream Only of America" or "Our Youth" or "How Much Longer Will I Be Able to Inhabit the Divine Sepulcher. . . ." Those are the earlier poems in *The Tennis Court Oath.* I don't know quite why I stopped writing that way, but I feel that those are valid poems in a new way that I might well have gone on pursuing, but didn't. In the last two or three years, I have gone back and reread some of the poems which I hadn't liked before and decided that they did have something that I could work on again. I think I did this somewhat in "Litany." There are certainly things in that poem that are as outrageous as the poems that outraged the critics of *The Tennis Court Oath.*

INTERVIEWER: How do you feel about the general critical reception of your work?

ASHBERY: I am very pleased that my poems seem to have found readers. I don't know quite how this came about. But it is disappointing to me that my poetry has become a kind of shibboleth, that people feel they have to join one side or the other. It seems to me that the poetry gets lost in all the controversy that surrounds it. I feel often that people on both sides are much more familiar with the myth that has grown up about my work than they are with the work itself. I am either an inspired seer or a charlatan who is trying to torment readers. My work has become a sort of political football and has the quality of a red flag for some people before they have even begun to pay any attention to it. I suppose that is the way reputations, some of them anyway, are created, but I hate to see people intimidated before they even have begun to read me by their preconceived notion of what my poetry is. I think it has something to offer, that it was not written not to be read.

INTERVIEWER: Have you found that your students ever taught you anything about writing?

ASHBERY: I try to avoid the well-known cliché that you learn from your students. Neither do I believe that there's something ennobling for a writer to teach, that it's narcissistic to spend time wallowing in your writing when you could be out helping in the world's work. Writers should write, and poets especially spend altogether too much time at other tasks such as teaching. However, since so many of us have to do it, there are certain things to be said for it. You are forced to bring a critical attention into play when you are reading students' work that you would not use otherwise, and that can help when you return to your own writing. And being immersed in a group of young unproven writers who are fiercely serious about what they are doing can have a chastening effect sometimes on us blasé oldsters. Besides, they may be writing great poetry, only nobody knows it because nobody has seen it yet. I sometimes think that the "greatness" my friends and I used to see in each other's poetry when we were very young had a lot to do with the fact that it was unknown. It could turn out to be anything; the possibilities were limitless, more so than when we were at last discovered and identified and pinned down in our books.

PETER STITT
June 1980

9. Milan Kundera

Milan Kundera dislikes talking about himself, so much so that journalists inevitably must go to each other rather than to him for the facts of his life. He was born in Brno, Czechoslovakia, in 1929. A student when the Communists came into power in 1948, he later worked as a laborer and a jazz musician before deciding to devote himself to literature and film. In the 1960s, he taught at the film school in Prague, where many of his students were the filmmakers of the Czech New Wave.

His first novel was *The Joke*, the publication of which was one of the central literary events of the so-called Prague Spring in 1968; it won the award of the Czech Writers Union. Later in the year came the Soviet invasion of Czechoslovakia, after which Kundera lost his teaching job, and was unable to find other work of any kind. His books were removed from the libraries. He wrote *Life Is Elsewhere* in 1974, and *The Farewell Party* (published in English in 1974 and 1976, respectively), before choosing to leave his country in 1975 to live in France, where he had been offered a post as professor of literature at the University of Rennes. With the publication, in a French translation, of *The Book of Laughter and Forgetting* in 1978, his Czech citizenship was revoked and his books banned. His latest novel is *The Unbearable Lightness of Being* (1984). He has received the Prix Medecis, the Prix Mondello, and the Jerusalem Prix. Milan Kundera lives with his wife near Montparnasse in Paris.

A jestli řekl před chvíli, že dětství je budoucnost lidstva, ~~není~~
~~to~~ ~~_____~~ ~~_____~~ budoucnosti, která bude
dětství právě věkem ~~bez minulosti~~ a není síla dětství právě v té
~~_____~~
lehkosti, s níž nezatížený letí do budoucnosti vpřed?
~~_____~~ ~~_____~~

(29)

~~Ta budoucnost, o které mluvím ;~~

"V tom ~~krásné~~ ~~_____~~ budoucnosti, o které mluvím, já sám už, děti,
nebudu."

~~_____~~
A ~~sám~~ vidí před sebou ~~#~~ andělsky krásnou tvář Gabrielovu a
cítí jak mu po tváři teče slza dojetí. Opakuje: "Ne, tam já už
nebudu."

A ~~_____~~ ~~chce tím říci,~~ ~~že~~ jestliže celý smysl jeho státnického díla
tkvěl v tom ukázat závratnou ~~budoucnost zaplněni~~ ~~_____~~, nebyl to z jeho
strany akt egoisty, který vyvyšuje vlastní památku nad památku
jiných, ale ~~moudré~~ velkorysé odhalení toho, kde sám je ochoten ~~jít do~~
první příkladem a ~~vejít~~ ~~_____~~ do velké ~~(_____, modré)~~ náruče nepaměti,
v níž se sejde ve velikém smíření a sbratření se všemi i s Hublem,
i Clementisem, kterého vymazali z fotografií, i s Kafkou, kterého
vyškrtli y učebnic literatury, i se stesedmdesáti českými historiky,
jimž zakázal bádat v historii, ~~_____~~ ~~_____~~
~~_____~~ ~~_____~~
Ve zvláštním zlzavém nadšení se usmívá ~~vztáhne sve~~ a mluví koketně
~~_____~~
o své smrti a vidí proti sobě veselé úsměvy dětského publika, ~~a~~
~~ty děti se usmívají a Husák se~~ usmívá též a po tváři mu tečou
slzy dojetí a čím víc mu tečou slzy, tím víc se usmívá a děti ~~se~~ ~~_____~~
~~před tím~~ ~~_____~~ se začínají smát nahlas, je to ~~šťastný~~ smích, a Husák se ~~_____~~
smaje ~~#~~ nahlas a nahlas pláče a do svých slz opakuje už úplně
nesrozumitelným hlasem: "Te já už na světě nebudu," a slzy mu tečou
~~_____~~
~~jeho~~ vráskami ve tváři a těch vrásek je čím dál víc, čil více se
~~smáje~~

Milan Kundera

*This interview is a product of several encounters with Milan
Kundera in Paris in the fall of 1983. Our meetings took place
in his attic apartment near Montparnasse. We worked in the
small room that Kundera uses as his office. With its shelves full
of books on philosophy and musicology, an old-fashioned typewriter and a table, it looks more like a student's room than like
the study of a world-famous author. On one of the walls, two
photographs hang side by side: one of his father, a pianist, the
other of Leoš Janáček, a Czech composer whom he greatly
admires.*

*We held several free and lengthy discussions in French;
instead of a tape recorder, we used a typewriter, scissors, and
glue. Gradually, amid discarded scraps of paper and after several
revisions, this text emerged.*

This interview was conducted soon after Kundera's most re-

cent book, The Unbearable Lightness of Being, *had become an immediate best-seller. Sudden fame makes him uncomfortable; Kundera would surely agree with Malcolm Lowry that "success is like a horrible disaster, worse than a fire in one's home. Fame consumes the home of the soul." Once, when I asked him about some of the comments on his novel that were appearing in the press, he replied, "I've had an overdose of myself!"*

Kundera's wish not to talk about himself seems to be an instinctive reaction against the tendency of most critics to study the writer, and the writer's personality, politics, and private life, instead of the writer's works. "Disgust at having to talk about oneself is what distinguishes novelistic talent from lyric talent," Kundera told Le Nouvel Observateur.

Refusing to talk about oneself is therefore a way of placing literary works and forms squarely at the center of attention, and of focusing on the novel itself. That is the purpose of this discussion on the art of composition.

INTERVIEWER: You have said that you feel closer to the Viennese novelists Robert Musil and Hermann Broch than to any other authors in modern literature. Broch thought—as you do—that the age of the psychological novel had come to an end. He believed, instead, in what he called the "polyhistorical" novel.

KUNDERA: Musil and Broch saddled the novel with enormous responsibilities. They saw it as the supreme intellectual synthesis, the last place where man could still question the world as a whole. They were convinced that the novel had tremendous synthetic power, that it could be poetry, fantasy, philosophy, aphorism, and essay all rolled into one. In his letters, Broch makes some profound observations on this issue. However, it seems to me that he obscures his own intentions by using the ill-chosen term "polyhistorical novel." It was in fact Broch's compatriot, Adalbert Stifter, a classic of Austrian prose, who created a truly polyhistorical novel in his *Der Nachsommer*

(Indian Summer), published in 1857. The novel is famous: Nietzsche considered it to be one of the four greatest works of German literature. Today, it is unreadable. It's packed with information about geology, botany, zoology, the crafts, painting, and architecture; but this gigantic, uplifting encyclopedia virtually leaves out man himself, and his situation. Precisely because it *is* polyhistorical, *Der Nachsommer* totally lacks what makes the novel special. This is not the case with Broch. On the contrary! He strove to discover "that which the novel alone can discover." The specific object of what Broch liked to call "novelistic knowledge" is existence. In my view, the word "polyhistorical" must be defined as "that which brings together every device and every form of knowledge in order to *shed light on existence.*" Yes, I do feel close to such an approach.

INTERVIEWER: A long essay you published in the magazine *Le Nouvel Observateur* caused the French to rediscover Broch. You speak highly of him, and yet you are also critical. At the end of the essay, you write: "All great works (just because they *are* great) are partly incomplete."

KUNDERA: Broch is an inspiration to us not only because of what he accomplished, but also because of all that he aimed at and could not attain. The very incompleteness of his work can help us understand the need for new art forms, including: (1) a radical stripping away of unessentials (in order to capture the complexity of existence in the modern world without a loss of architectonic clarity); (2) "novelistic counterpoint" (to unite philosophy, narrative, and dream into a single music); (3) the specifically novelistic essay (in other words, instead of claiming to convey some apodictic message, remaining hypothetical, playful, or ironic).

INTERVIEWER: These three points seem to capture your entire artistic program.

KUNDERA: In order to make the novel into a polyhistorical illumination of existence, you need to master the technique of ellipsis, the art of condensation. Otherwise, you fall into the trap of endless length. Musil's *The Man Without Qualities* is one of the two or three novels that I love most. But don't ask me to admire its gigantic unfinished expanse! Imagine a castle so huge that the eye cannot take it all in at a glance. Imagine a string quartet that lasts nine hours. There are anthropological limits—human proportions—that should not be breached, such as the limits of memory. When you have finished reading, you should still be able to remember the beginning. If not, the novel loses its shape, its "architectonic clarity" becomes murky.

INTERVIEWER: *The Book of Laughter and Forgetting* is made up of seven parts. If you had dealt with them in a less elliptical fashion, you could have written seven different full-length novels.

KUNDERA: But if I had written seven independent novels, I would have lost the most important thing: I wouldn't have been able to capture the "complexity of human existence in the modern world" in a single book. The art of ellipsis is absolutely essential. It requires that one always go directly to the heart of things. In this connection, I always think of a Czech composer I have passionately admired since childhood: Leoš Janáček. He is one of the greatest masters of modern music. His determination to strip music to its essentials was revolutionary. Of course, every musical composition involves a great deal of technique: exposition of the themes, their development, variations, polyphonic work (often very automatic), filling in the orchestration, the transitions, etc. Today one can compose music with a computer, but the computer always existed in composers' heads—if they had to, composers could write sonatas without a single original idea, just by "cybernetically" expanding on the rules of composition. Janáček's purpose was to destroy this computer! Brutal juxtaposition instead of transitions; repetition instead of variation—and always straight to the heart of things: only the note with something essential to say is entitled to exist. It is nearly the same with the novel; it too is encumbered by "technique," by rules that do the author's work for him: present a character, describe a milieu, bring the action into its historical setting, fill up the lifetime of the characters with useless episodes. Every change of scene requires new expositions, descriptions, explanations. My purpose is like Janáček's: to rid the novel of the automatism of novelistic technique, of novelistic word-spinning.

INTERVIEWER: The second art form you mentioned was "novelistic counterpoint."

KUNDERA: The idea of the novel as a great intellectual synthesis almost automatically raises the problem of "polyphony." This problem still has to be resolved. Take the third part of Broch's novel *The Sleepwalkers*; it is made up of five heterogeneous elements: (1) "novelistic" narrative based on the three main characters: Pasenow, Esch, Huguenau; (2) the personal story of Hanna Wendling; (3) factual description of life in a military hospital; (4) a narrative (partly in verse) of a Salvation Army girl; (5) a philosophical essay (written in scientific language) on the debasement of values. Each part is magnificent. Yet despite the fact that they are all dealt with simultaneously, in constant alternation (in other words, in a polyphonic manner), the five elements remain disunited—in other words, they do not constitute a *true* polyphony.

INTERVIEWER: By using the metaphor of polyphony and applying it to literature, do you not in fact make demands on the novel that it cannot possibly live up to?

KUNDERA: The novel can incorporate outside elements in two ways. In the course of his travels, Don Quixote meets various characters who tell him their tales. In this way, independent stories are inserted into the whole, fitted into the frame of the novel. This type of composition is often found in seventeenth- and eighteenth-century novels. Broch, however, instead of fitting the story of Hanna Wendling into the main story of Esch and Huguenau, lets both unfold *simultaneously*. Sartre (in *The Reprieve*), and Dos Passos before him, also used this technique of simultaneity. Their aim, however, was to bring together different novelistic stories, in other words, homogeneous rather than heterogeneous elements as in the case of Broch. Moreover, their use of this technique strikes me as too mechanical and devoid of poetry. I cannot think of better terms than "polyphony" or "counterpoint" to describe this form of composition and, furthermore, the musical analogy is a useful one. For instance, the first thing that bothers me about the third part of *The Sleepwalkers* is that the five elements are not all equal. Whereas the equality of all the voices in musical counterpoint is the basic ground rule, the *sine qua non*. In Broch's work, the first element (the novelistic narrative of Esch and Huguenau) takes up much more physical space than the other elements, and, even more important, it is privileged insofar as it is linked to the two preceding parts of the novel and therefore assumes the task of unifying it. It therefore attracts more attention and threatens to turn the other elements into mere accompaniment. The second thing that bothers me is that though a fugue by Bach cannot do without any one of its voices, the story of Hanna Wendling or the essay on the decline of values could very well stand alone as an independent work. Taken separately, they would lose nothing of their meaning or of their quality.

In my view, the basic requirements of novelistic counterpoint are: (1) the equality of the various elements; (2) the indivisibility of the whole. I remember that the day I finished "The Angels," part three of *The Book of Laughter and Forgetting*, I was terribly proud of myself. I was sure that I had discovered the key to a new way of putting together a narrative. The text was made up of the following elements: (1) an anecdote about two female students and their levitation; (2) an autobiographical narrative; (3) a critical essay on a feminist book; (4) a fable about an angel and the devil; (5) a dream-narrative of Paul Éluard flying over Prague. None of these elements could exist without the others, each one illuminates and explains the others as they all explore a single theme and ask a single question: "What is an angel?"

Part six, also entitled "The Angels," is made up of: (1) a dream-narrative of Tamina's death; (2) an autobiographical narrative of my father's death; (3) musicological reflections; (4) reflections on the epidemic of forgetting that is devastating Prague. What is the link between my father and the torturing of Tamina by children? It is "the meeting of a sewing machine and an umbrella" on the table of one theme, to borrow Lautréamont's famous image. Novelistic polyphony is poetry much more than technique. I can find no example of such polyphonic poetry elsewhere in literature, but I have been very astonished by Alain Resnais's latest films. His use of the art of counterpoint is admirable.

INTERVIEWER: Counterpoint is less apparent in *The Unbearable Lightness of Being*.

KUNDERA: That was my aim. There, I wanted dream, narrative, and reflection to flow together in an indivisible and totally natural stream. But the polyphonic character of the novel is very striking in part six: the story of Stalin's son, theological reflections, a political event in Asia, Franz's death in Bangkok, and Tomas's funeral in Bohemia are all linked by the same everlasting question: "What is kitsch?" This polyphonic passage is the pillar that supports the entire structure of the novel. It is the key to the secret of its architecture.

INTERVIEWER: By calling for "a specifically novelistic essay," you expressed several reservations about the essay on the debasement of values which appeared in *The Sleepwalkers*.

KUNDERA: It is a terrific essay!

INTERVIEWER: You have doubts about the way it is incorporated into the novel. Broch relinquishes none of his scientific language, he expresses his views in a straightforward way without hiding behind one of his characters—the way Mann or Musil would do. Isn't that Broch's real contribution, his new challenge?

KUNDERA: That is true, and he was well aware of his own courage. But there is also a risk: his essay can be read and understood as the ideological key to the novel, as its "Truth," and that could transform the rest of the novel into a mere illustration of a thought. Then the novel's equilibrium is upset; the truth of the essay becomes too heavy and the novel's subtle architecture is in danger of collapsing. A novel that had no intention of expounding a philosophical thesis (Broch loathed that type of novel!) may wind up being read in exactly that way. How does one incorporate an essay into the novel? It is important to have one basic fact in mind: the very essence of reflection changes the minute it is included in the body of a novel. Outside of the novel, one is in the realm of assertions: everyone —philosopher, politician, concierge—is sure of what he says. The novel, however, is a territory where one does not make assertions; it is a territory of play and of hypotheses. Reflection within the novel is hypothetical by its very essence.

INTERVIEWER: But why would a novelist want to deprive himself of the right to express his philosophy overtly and assertively in his novel?

KUNDERA: Because he has none! People often talk about Chekhov's philosophy, or Kafka's, or Musil's. But just try to find a coherent philosophy in their writings! Even when they express their ideas in their notebooks, the ideas amount to intellectual exercises, playing with paradoxes, or improvisations rather than to assertions of a philosophy. And philosophers who write novels are nothing but pseudonovelists who use the form of the novel in order to illustrate their ideas. Neither Voltaire nor Camus ever discovered "that which the novel alone can discover." I know of only one exception, and that is the Diderot of *Jacques le fataliste*. What a miracle! Having crossed over the boundary of the novel, the serious philosopher becomes a playful thinker. There is not one serious sentence in the novel—everything in it is play. That's why this novel is outrageously underrated in France. Indeed, *Jacques le fataliste* contains everything that France has lost and refuses to recover. In France, ideas are preferred to works. *Jacques le fataliste* cannot be translated into the language of ideas, and therefore it cannot be understood in the homeland of ideas.

INTERVIEWER: In *The Joke,* it is Jaroslav who develops a musicological theory. The hypothetical character of his thinking is thus apparent. But the musicological meditations in *The Book of Laughter and Forgetting* are the author's, your own. How am I then to understand whether they are hypothetical or assertive?

KUNDERA: It all depends on the tone. From the very first words, my intention is to give these reflections a playful, ironic, provocative, experimental, or questioning tone. All of part six of *The Unbearable Lightness of Being* ("The Grand March") is an essay on kitsch which expounds one main thesis: kitsch is the absolute denial of the existence of shit. This meditation on kitsch is of vital importance to me. It is based on a great deal of thought, experience, study, and even passion. Yet the tone is never serious; it is provocative. This essay is unthinkable outside of the novel, it is a purely novelistic meditation.

INTERVIEWER: The polyphony of your novels also includes another element, dream-narrative. It takes up the entire second part of *Life Is Elsewhere,* it is the basis of the sixth part of *The Book of Laughter and Forgetting,* and it runs through *The Unbearable Lightness of Being* by way of Tereza's dreams.

KUNDERA: These passages are also the easiest ones to misunderstand, because people want to find some symbolic message in them. There is nothing to decipher in Tereza's dreams. They are poems about death. Their meaning lies in their beauty, which hypnotizes Tereza. By the way, do you realize that people don't know how to read Kafka simply because they want to decipher him? Instead of letting themselves be carried away by his unequaled imagination, they look for allegories—and come up with nothing but clichés: life is absurd (or it is not absurd), God is beyond reach (or within reach), etc. You

can understand nothing about art, particularly modern art, if
you do not understand that imagination is a value in itself.
Novalis knew that when he praised dreams. They "protect us
against life's monotony," he said, they "liberate us from seriousness by the delight of their games." He was the first to
understand the role that dreams and a dreamlike imagination
could play in the novel. He planned to write the second volume
of his *Heinrich von Ofterdingen* as a narrative in which dream
and reality would be so intertwined that one would no longer
be able to tell them apart. Unfortunately, all that remains of
that second volume are the notes in which Novalis described
his aesthetic intention. One hundred years later, his ambition
was fulfilled by Kafka. Kafka's novels are a fusion of dream and
reality; that is, they are neither dream nor reality. More than
anything, Kafka brought about an aesthetic revolution. An
aesthetic miracle. Of course, no one can repeat what he did.
But I share with him, and with Novalis, the desire to bring
dreams, and the imagination of dreams, into the novel. My way
of doing so is by polyphonic confrontation rather than by a
fusion of dream and reality. Dream-narrative is one of the
elements of counterpoint.

INTERVIEWER: There is nothing polyphonic about the last
part of *The Book of Laughter and Forgetting,* and yet that is
probably the most interesting part of the book. It is made up
of fourteen chapters that recount erotic situations in the life
of one man—Jan.

KUNDERA: Another musical term: this narrative is a "theme
with variations." The theme is the border beyond which things
lose their meaning. Our life unfolds in the immediate vicinity
of that border, and we risk crossing it at any moment. The
fourteen chapters are fourteen variations of the same situation
—eroticism at the border between meaning and meaningless-
ness.

INTERVIEWER: You have described *The Book of Laughter*

and Forgetting as a "novel in the form of variations." But is it still a novel?

KUNDERA: There is no unity of action, which is why it does not look like a novel. People can't *imagine* a novel without that unity. Even the experiments of the *nouveau roman* were based on unity of action (or of nonaction). Sterne and Diderot had amused themselves by making the unity extremely fragile. The journey of Jacques and his master takes up the lesser part of *Jacques le fataliste;* it's nothing more than a comic pretext in which to fit anecdotes, stories, thoughts. Nevertheless, this pretext, this "frame," is necessary to make the novel feel like a novel. In *The Book of Laughter and Forgetting* there is no longer any such pretext. It's the unity of the themes and their variations that gives coherence to the whole. Is it a novel? Yes. A novel is a meditation on existence, seen through imaginary characters. The form is unlimited freedom. Throughout its history, the novel has never known how to take advantage of its endless possibilities. It missed its chance.

INTERVIEWER: But except for *The Book of Laughter and Forgetting,* your novels are also based on unity of action, although it is indeed of a much looser variety in *The Unbearable Lightness of Being.*

KUNDERA: Yes, but other more important sorts of unity complete them: the unity of the same metaphysical questions, of the same motifs and then variations (the motif of paternity in *The Farewell Party,* for instance). But I would like to stress above all that the novel is primarily built on a number of fundamental words, like Schoenberg's series of notes. In *The Book of Laughter and Forgetting,* the series is the following: forgetting, laughter, angels, "litost," the border. In the course of the novel these five key words are analyzed, studied, defined, redefined, and thus transformed into categories of existence. It is built on these few categories in the same way as a house is built on its beams. The beams of *The Unbearable Lightness of*

Being are: weight, lightness, the soul, the body, the Grand
March, shit, kitsch, compassion, vertigo, strength, and weakness. Because of their categorical character, these words cannot
be replaced by synonyms. This always has to be explained over
and over again to translators, who—in their concern for "good
style"—seek to avoid repetition.

INTERVIEWER: Regarding the architectural clarity, I was
struck by the fact that all of your novels, except for one, are
divided into seven parts.

KUNDERA: When I had finished my first novel, *The Joke*,
there was no reason to be surprised that it had seven parts.
Then I wrote *Life Is Elsewhere*. The novel was almost finished
and it had six parts. I didn't feel satisfied. Suddenly I had the
idea of including a story that takes place three years after the
hero's death—in other words, outside the time frame of the
novel. This now became the sixth part of seven, entitled "The
Middle-Aged Man." Immediately, the novel's architecture had
become perfect. Later on, I realized that this sixth part was
oddly analogous to the sixth part of *The Joke* ("Kostka"),
which also introduces an outside character, and also opens a
secret window in the novel's wall. *Laughable Loves* started out
as ten short stories. Putting together the final version, I elimi-
nated three of them. The collection had become very coherent,
foreshadowing the composition of *The Book of Laughter and
Forgetting*. One character, Doctor Havel, ties the fourth and
sixth stories together. In *The Book of Laughter and Forgetting*,
the fourth and sixth parts are also linked by the same person:
Tamina. When I wrote *The Unbearable Lightness of Being*,
I was determined to break the spell of the number of seven.
I had long since decided on a six-part outline. But the first part
always struck me as shapeless. Finally, I understood that it was
really made up of two parts. Like Siamese twins, they had to
be separated by delicate surgery. The only reason I mention all
this is to show that I am not indulging in some superstitious
affectation about magic numbers, nor making a rational calcu-

lation. Rather, I am driven by a deep, unconscious, incomprehensible need, a formal archetype from which I cannot escape. All of my novels are variants of an architecture based on the number seven.

INTERVIEWER: The use of seven neatly divided parts is certainly linked to your goal of synthesizing the most heterogeneous elements into a unified whole. Each part of your novel is always a world of its own, and is distinct from the others because of its special form. But if the novel is divided into numbered parts, why must the parts themselves also be divided into numbered chapters?

KUNDERA: The chapters themselves must also create a little world of their own; they must be relatively independent. That is why I keep pestering my publishers to make sure that the numbers are clearly visible and that the chapters are well separated. The chapters are like the measures of a musical score! There are parts where the measures (chapters) are long, others where they are short, still others where they are of irregular length. Each part could have a musical tempo indication: *moderato, presto, andante,* etc. Part six of *Life Is Elsewhere* is *andante*: in a calm, melancholy manner, it tells of the brief encounter between a middle-aged man and a young girl who has just been released from prison. The last part is *prestissimo;* it is written in very short chapters, and jumps from the dying Jaromil to Rimbaud, Lermontov, and Pushkin. I first thought of *The Unbearable Lightness of Being* in a musical way. I knew that the last part had to be *pianissimo* and *lento:* it focuses on a rather short, uneventful period, in a single location, and the tone is quiet. I also knew that this part had to be preceded by a *prestissimo*: that is the part entitled "The Grand March."

INTERVIEWER: There is an exception to the rule of the number seven. There are only five parts to *The Farewell Party*.

KUNDERA: *The Farewell Party* is based on another formal archetype: it is absolutely homogeneous, deals with one subject, is told in one tempo; it is very theatrical, stylized, and derives its form from the farce. In *Laughable Loves,* the story entitled "The Symposium" is built exactly the same way—a farce in five acts.

INTERVIEWER: What do you mean by farce?

KUNDERA: I mean the emphasis on plot and on all its trappings of unexpected and incredible coincidences. Nothing has become as suspect, ridiculous, old-fashioned, trite, and tasteless in a novel as plot and its farcical exaggerations. From Flaubert on, novelists have tried to do away with the artifices of plot. And so the novel has become duller than the dullest of lives. Yet there is another way to get around the suspect and worn-out aspect of the plot, and that is to free it from the requirement of likelihood. You tell an unlikely story that *chooses* to be unlikely! That's exactly how Kafka conceived *Amerika.* The way Karl meets his uncle in the first chapter is through a series of the most unlikely coincidences. Kafka entered into his first "sur-real" universe, into his first "fusion of dream and reality," with a parody of the plot—through the door of farce.

INTERVIEWER: But why did you choose the farce form for a novel that is not at all meant to be an entertainment?

KUNDERA: But it *is* an entertainment! I don't understand the contempt that the French have for entertainment, why they are so ashamed of the word *"divertissement."* They run less risk of being entertaining than of being boring. And they also run the risk of falling for kitsch, that sweetish, lying embellishment of things, the rose-colored light that bathes even such modernist works as Éluard's poetry or Ettore Scola's recent film *Le Bal,* whose subtitle could be: "French history as kitsch." Yes, kitsch, not entertainment, is the *real* aesthetic disease! The great European novel started out as entertainment, and every true novelist is nostalgic for it. In fact, the themes of those great entertainments are terribly serious—think of Cervantes! In *The Farewell Party,* the question is, does man deserve to live on this earth? Shouldn't one "free the planet from man's clutches"? My lifetime ambition has been to unite the utmost seriousness of question with the utmost lightness of form. Nor is this purely an artistic ambition. The combination of a frivolous form and a serious subject immediately unmasks the truth about our dramas (those that occur in our beds as well as those that we play out on the great stage of History) and their awful insignificance. We experience the unbearable lightness of being.

INTERVIEWER: So you could just as well have used the title of your latest novel for *The Farewell Party*?

KUNDERA: Every one of my novels could be entitled *The Unbearable Lightness of Being* or *The Joke* or *Laughable Loves*; the titles are interchangeable, they reflect the small number of themes that obsess me, define me, and, unfortunately, restrict me. Beyond these themes, I have nothing else to say or to write.

INTERVIEWER: There are, then, two formal archetypes of composition in your novels: (1) polyphony, which unites heterogeneous elements into an architecture based on the number seven; (2) farce, which is homogeneous, theatrical, and skirts the unlikely. Could there be a Kundera outside of these two archetypes?

KUNDERA: I always dream of some great unexpected infidelity. But I have not yet been able to escape my bigamous state.

CHRISTIAN SALMON
Fall 1983

10. John Barth

John Barth was born in Maryland in 1930, the son of a candy-store owner. He originally hoped to become a jazz orchestrator, but abandoned his studies at Juilliard to major in journalism at Johns Hopkins University. He received his B.A. in 1951 and an M.A. the following year.

In 1956 he published his first novel, *The Floating Opera.* His other publications are *The End of the Road* (1958), *The Sot-Weed Factor* (1960), *Giles Goat-Boy* (1966), a collection of short stories entitled *Lost in the Funhouse,* which includes the famous "Night-Sea Journey" narrated by a sperm (1968), *Chimera* (1973), *Letters* (1979), *Sabbatical* (1982), and *The Friday Book* (1984), a collection of essays. He has taught at Pennsylvania State University, the State University of New York at Buffalo, and, since 1973, in the Johns Hopkins Writing Seminars. He has won the National Book Award (for *Chimera*) and the Brandeis University Creative Arts Award.

Barth lives in Baltimore, Maryland.

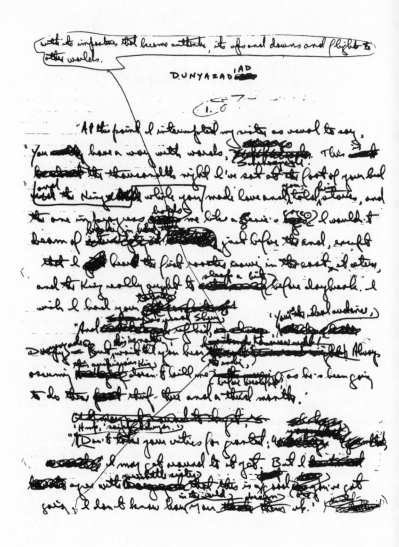

A John Barth manuscript page, page one of a novella from the *Chimera* series.

John Barth

This interview with John Barth was conducted in the studios of KUHT in Houston, Texas, for a series entitled "The Writer in Society." The stage set was made up to resemble a writer's den —the decor including a small globe of the world, bronze Remington-like animal statuary, a stand-up bookshelf with glass shelves on which were placed some potted plants and a haphazard collection of books, a few volumes of the Reader's Digest condensed novel series among them. Large pots of plants were set about. Barth sat amongst them in a cane chair. He is a tall man with a domed forehead; a pair of very large-rimmed spectacles give him a professorial, owlish look. He is a caricaturist's delight. He sports a very wide and straight mustache. Recently he had grown a beard. In manner, Barth has been described as a combination of British officer and Southern gentleman.

"*We'll have to stick to the channel,*" he wrote in his first novel, The Floating Opera, "*and let the creeks and coves go by.*" Every novel since then has been a refutation of this dictum of sticking to the main topic. He is especially influenced by the classical cyclical tales such as Burton's Thousand and One Nights and the Gesta Romanorum, and by the complexities of such modern masters as Nabokov, Borges, and Beckett. For novels distinguished by a wide range of erudition, invention, wit, historical references, whimsy, bawdiness, and a great richness of image and style, Barth has been described as an "*ecologist of information.*"

Of his working habits Barth has said that he rises at six in the morning and puts an electric percolator in the kitchen so that during the course of sitting for six hours at his desk he has an excuse for the exercise of walking back and forth from his study to the kitchen for a cup of coffee. He speaks of measuring his work not by the day (as Hemingway did) but by the month and the year. "*That way you don't feel so terrible if you put in three days straight without turning up much of anything. You don't feel blocked.*"

This interview, being restricted to a half-hour's conversation for a television audience, was thought to be a bit short by the usual standards of the magazine. It was assumed that Barth, being such a master of the prolix, would surely make some additions. Extra questions were sent him. The interview was returned to these offices with the questions unanswered, and the text of the interview edited and shortened. Perhaps Barth had not noticed the additional questions. This interview was sent back, this time with a small emolument attached for taking the trouble. The interview was returned once again, along with the uncashed check, with the following statement: "*It doesn't displease me to hear that our interview will be perhaps the shortest one you've run. In fact, it's a bit shorter now than it was before (enclosed). Better not run it by me again!*"

INTERVIEWER: When were the first stirrings? When did you actually understand that writing was going to be your profession? Was there a moment?

BARTH: It seems to happen later in the lives of American writers than Europeans. American boys and girls don't grow up thinking, "I'm going to be a writer," the way we're told Flaubert did; at about age twelve he decided he would be a great French writer and, by George, he turned out to *be* one. Writers in this country, particularly novelists, are likely to come to the medium through some back door. Nearly every writer I know was going to be something else, and then found himself writing by a kind of *passionate default.* In my case, I was going to be a musician. Then I found out that while I had an amateur's flair, I did not have preprofessional talent. So I went on to Johns Hopkins University to find something else to do. There I found myself writing stories—making all the mistakes that new writers usually make. After I had written about a novel's worth of bad pages, I understood that while I was not doing it well, *that* was the thing I was going to do. I don't remember that realization coming as a swoop of insight, or as an exhilarating experience, but as a kind of absolute recognition that for well or for ill, that was the way I was going to spend my life. I had the advantage at Johns Hopkins of a splendid old Spanish poet-teacher, with whom I read *Don Quixote.* I can't remember a thing he said about *Don Quixote,* but old Pedro Salinas, now dead, a refugee from Franco's Spain, embodied to my innocent, ingenuous eyes, the possibility that a life devoted to the making of sentences and the telling of stories can be dignified and noble. Whether the works have turned out to be dignified and noble is another question, but I think that my experience is not uncommon: you decide to be a violinist, you decide to be a sculptor or a painter, but you find yourself being a novelist.

INTERVIEWER: What was the musical instrument you started out with?

BARTH: I played drums. What I hoped to be eventually was an orchestrator—what in those days was called an arranger. An arranger is a chap who takes someone else's melody and turns it to his purpose. For better or worse, my career as a novelist has been that of an arranger. My imagination is most at ease with an old literary convention like the epistolary novel, or a classical myth—received melody lines, so to speak, which I then reorchestrate to my purpose.

INTERVIEWER: What's first when you sit down to begin a novel? Is it the form, as in the epistolary novel, or character, or plot?

BARTH: Different books start in different ways. I sometimes wish that I were the kind of writer who begins with a passionate interest in a character and then, as I've heard other writers say, just gives that character elbowroom and sees what he or she wants to do. I'm not that kind of writer. Much more often I start with a shape or form, maybe an image. The floating showboat, for example, which became the central image in *The Floating Opera,* was a photograph of an actual showboat I remember seeing as a child. It happened to be named *Captain Adams' Original Unparalleled Floating Opera,* and when nature, in her heavy-handed way, gives you an image like that, the only honorable thing to do is to make a novel out of it. This may not be the most elevated of approaches. Aleksandr Solzhenitsyn, for example, comes to the medium of fiction with a high moral purpose; he wants, literally, to try to change the world through the medium of the novel. I honor and admire that intention, but just as often a great writer will come to his novel with a much less elevated purpose than wanting to undermine the Soviet government. Henry James wanted to write a book in the shape of an hourglass. Flaubert wanted to write a novel about *nothing.* What I've learned is that the muses' decision to sing or not to sing is not based on the elevation of your moral purpose—they will sing or not regardless.

INTERVIEWER: What was in your way that you had to get out of your way?

BARTH: What was in my way? Chekhov makes a remark to his brother, the brother he was always hectoring in letters, "What the aristocrats take for granted, we pay for with our youth." I had to pay my tuition in literature that way. I came from a fairly unsophisticated family from the rural southern Eastern Shore of Maryland—which is very "deep South" in its ethos. I went to a mediocre public high school (which I enjoyed), fell into a good university on a scholarship, and then had to learn, from scratch, that civilization existed, that literature had been going on. That kind of innocence is the reverse of the exquisite sophistication with which a writer like Vladimir Nabokov comes to the medium—knowing it already, as if he's been in on the conversation since it began. Yet the innocence that writers like myself have to overcome, if it doesn't ruin us altogether, can become a sort of strength. You're not intimidated by your distinguished predecessors, the great literary dead. You have a chutzpah in your approach to the medium which may carry you through those apprentice days when nobody's telling you you're any good because you aren't yet. Everything is a discovery. I read Mark Twain's *Huckleberry Finn* when I was about twenty-five. If I had read it when I was nineteen, I might have been intimidated; the same with Dickens and other great novelists. In my position I remained armed with a kind of "invincible innocence"—I think that's what the Catholics call it—that with the best of fortune can survive even later experience and sophistication and carry you right to the end of the story.

INTERVIEWER: What were the particular guides that helped you?

BARTH: The great guides were the books I discovered in the Johns Hopkins library, where my student job was to file books away. One was more or less encouraged to take a cart of books and go back into the stacks and not come out for seven or eight hours. So I read what I was filing. My great teachers (the best thing that can happen to a writer) were Scheherazade, Homer, Virgil, and Boccaccio; also the great Sanskrit tale-tellers. I was impressed forever with the width as well as the depth of literature—just what a kid from the sticks, from the swamp, in my case, needed. As an undergraduate I had a couple of tutors in writing who were not themselves writers. They were simply good coaches. I've thought of that in a chastened way since. Dealing with my own students, many of whom are very skillful, advanced apprentice writers, I often wonder whether it's a good idea for them to have, at the other end of the table, somebody who's already working at a certain level of success and notoriety. Is that not perhaps intimidating? I just don't know, but I suspect the trade-off is fair enough. I might have learned some things faster had I been working with an established writer rather than a very sympathetic coach.

INTERVIEWER: In browsing through the libraries, was it the concept of simply telling stories that fascinated you, or was it the characters that came through the works you read? What was it that struck the spark?

BARTH: It was not the characters. Perhaps I would be a better novelist in the realm of characterization had it been. No, it was the mere mass of the narrative. My apprenticeship was a kind of Baptist total immersion in "the ocean of rivers of stories" —that's the name of one of those old Sanskrit jobs that I read in my filing days . . . one volume at a time up to volume seventeen. I think the sweetest kind of apprenticeship that a narrative artist can serve is that sort of immersion in the waters of narrative, where by a kind of osmosis you pick up early what a talented writer usually learns last: the management of narrative pace, keeping the story going.

INTERVIEWER: I noticed you call it coaching rather than teaching. I don't think I've ever heard that phrase used to describe that relationship.

BARTH: Coaching is more accurate. God knows whether we should be doing it in the universities at all. I happen to think there's some justification for having courses in so-called creative writing. I know from happy experience with young writers that the muses make no distinction between undergraduates and graduate students. The muses know only expert writers and less expert writers. A beginner—such as I was when, with the swamp still on my shoes, I came into Johns Hopkins as an undergraduate—needs to be taught that literature is there; here are some examples of it, and here's how the great writers do it. That's teaching. In time, a writer, or any artist, stops making mistakes on a crude, first level, and begins making mistakes on the next, more elevated level. And then finally you begin to make your mistakes on the highest level—let's say the upper slopes of slippery Parnassus—and it's at that point you need coaching. Now sometimes coaching means advising the skier to come down off the advanced slope and back to the bunny hill for a while, back to the snowplow. One must be gentle about it. To shift metaphors violently, one must understand that the house of fiction has many windows; you don't want to defenestrate your young apprentices. But sometimes such a simple thing as suggesting to a student that perhaps realism instead of fantasy may be a more sympathetic genre, or humor instead of the opposite, or the novel rather than the short story—sometimes a simple suggestion like that can be the one that makes things click. It doesn't always.

INTERVIEWER: How confident are you in the house of fiction, or on the upper slopes, as you were putting it?

BARTH: About my own position on the giant slalom of the muses?

INTERVIEWER: I don't mean in the eyes of others, but in your own sense of what you're up to.

BARTH: It's a combination of an almost obscene self-confidence and an ongoing terror. You remember the old story of how Hemingway would always record the number of words he wrote each day. When I learned that detail about Hemingway I understood why the poor chap went bonkers and did himself in at the end. The average professional, whether he's good or mediocre, learns enough confidence in himself so that he no longer fears the blank page. About my own fiction: my friend John Hawkes once said of it that it seems spun out against nothingness, simply so that there should not be silence. I understand that. It's Scheherazade's terror: the terror that comes from the literal or metaphorical equating of telling stories with living, with life itself. I understand that metaphor to the marrow of my bones. For me there is always a sense that when this story ends maybe the whole world will end; I wonder whether the world's really there when I'm not narrating it. Well, at this stage of my life I have enough confidence in myself to know that the page will fill up. Indeed, because I'm not a very consistent fiction writer (my books don't resemble one another very much), I have an ongoing curiosity about what will happen next. Stendhal said that once when he wanted to commit suicide, he couldn't abide to do it because he wanted to find out what would happen next in French politics. I have a similar curiosity . . . when this long project is over, what will fill the page next? I've never been able to think that far ahead; I can't do it until the project in hand is out of the shop and going through the publisher's presses. Then I begin to think about what will be next. I'm just as curious as the next chap. Maybe more so.

INTERVIEWER: How about in the middle of a book? Do you know in that case what's going to be on the next page?

BARTH: There are writers who have the good fortune to be thinking three novels down the line or even to have two or three going at the same time. Not me.

INTERVIEWER: No, I mean within the same book. Do you know what the last line of the book might be when you start?

BARTH: I have a pretty good sense of where the book is going to go. By temperament I am an incorrigible formalist, not inclined to embark on a project without knowing where I'm going. It takes me about four years to write a novel. To embark on such a project without some idea of what the landfall and the estimated time of arrival were would be rather alarming. But I have learned from experience that there are certain barriers that you cannot cross until you get to them; in a thing as long and complicated as a novel you may not even know the real shape of the obstacle until you heave in sight of it, much less how you're going to get around it. I can see in my plans that there will be this enormous pothole to cross somewhere around the third chapter from the end; I'll get out my little pocket calculator and estimate that the pothole will be reached about the second of July, 1986, let's say, and then just trust to God and the muses that by the time I get there I'll know how to get around it.

INTERVIEWER: These are climactic moments that you know you're going to have to deal with?

BARTH: Yes, important moments that I know from my sense of dramaturgy will have to be dealt with: rifles that will have to be fired.

INTERVIEWER: Like the Marabar Caves in *A Passage to India*?

BARTH: Exactly. That's a suspense in the process of writing which I've learned to be both charmed and—faintly, decently —terrified by.

INTERVIEWER: Can you work around and then come back to deal with these climactic moments later?

BARTH: You come to it. Then it's there. Early in the planning of *Sabbatical*, I knew that in the next-to-last chapter, when the characters sail their boat around a certain point, something extraordinary had to happen, something literally marvelous, but I had no idea what that ought to be until they actually did turn that corner. By then the metaphor was clear enough so that the sea monster, which had to surface at that moment, surfaced in my imagination just when it surfaced in the novel.

INTERVIEWER: When you start on a day's work, do you reread

for a while, up to where you stopped the day before?

BARTH: Sure. It's to get the rhythm partly, and partly it's a kind of magic: it *feels* like you're writing, though you're not. The processes get going; the wheels start spinning. I write in longhand. My Baltimore neighbor Anne Tyler and I are maybe the only two writers left who actually write with a fountain pen. She made the remark that there's something about the muscular movement of putting down script on the paper that gets her imagination back in the track where it was. I feel that too, very much so. My sentences in print, as in conversation, tend to go on a while before they stop: I trace that to the cursiveness of the pen. The idea of typing out first drafts, where each letter is physically separated by a little space from the next letter, I find a paralyzing notion. Good old script, which connects this letter to that, and this line to that—well, that's how good plots work, right? When this loops around and connects to that . . .

INTERVIEWER: Do you think word processors will change the style of writers to come?

BARTH: They may very well. But I remember a colleague of mine at Johns Hopkins, Professor Hugh Kenner, remarking that literature changed when writers began to compose on the typewriter. I raised my hand and said, "Professor Kenner, I still write with a fountain pen." And he said, "Never mind. You are *breathing* the air of literature that's been written on the typewriter." So I suppose that my fiction will be word-processed by association, though I myself will not become a green-screener.

INTERVIEWER: Somewhere in *Lost in the Funhouse,* you berate the reader for reading . . .

BARTH: A dangerous thing to do.

INTERVIEWER: . . . and say that he should be staring at the wall or whatever. Is that something you believe or were you simply having fun?

BARTH: That was the mood of the character in that story,

"Life-Story," which also, in my mind, corresponded to an apocalyptic mood in our country at that time: the height of the sixties, when our republic enjoyed a more than usually apocalyptic ambience. A similar sort of apocalyptic feeling was going around about the future of print generally, and the novel in particular. I don't feel strongly about the matter myself. The point of a couple of essays I've written, and some of the stories, is that the death of a genre is not the death of storytelling; storytelling is older than the form of the novel. I must say, though, that my sense of priorities about these matters has changed. In *The Floating Opera*, that first, very youthful novel of mine, the hero, who's a man my present age (he's in his early fifties), has a particular heart condition that has led him to lead his life wondering, as he moves from sentence to sentence, whether he'll get from the subject to the verb, the verb to the object. The characters in the novel I'm working on now—a little like the characters in the last novel, *Sabbatical*—are much more concerned about whether the *world* will last, never mind the novel. Joyce Carol Oates once said she doesn't like "Pop Apocalypses." Though I like that phrase, I find the question of the literal persistence of civilization, in this powder keg we're living in, a much more considerable question than the very trifling matter of whether a particular literary form is kaput, or dies for another two hundred years as happily as it's been dying for the last two hundred.

INTERVIEWER: Do you think that the novelist can have any effect on this portentous thing you're talking about?

BARTH: I don't think that as a group we'd be any better at running the world than the people who are botching it up. Poetry makes nothing happen. Politically committed artists like Gabriel García Márquez give honest voice to their political passion at no great cost to the quality control of their art. But do they really change the world? I doubt it, I doubt it, Abraham Lincoln's remark to Harriet Beecher Stowe notwithstanding: "So you're the little woman who wrote the book that made this great war!" Well, she didn't. No: without sounding too terribly decadent about it, I much prefer the late Vladimir Nabokov's remark about what he wanted from his novels: "aesthetic bliss." Well, that *does* sound too decadent. Let me change masters for a moment and say that I prefer Henry James's remark that the first obligation of the writer—which I would also regard as his last obligation—is to be interesting, *to be interesting.* To be interesting in one beautiful sentence after another. To be interesting; not to change the world.

INTERVIEWER: I've always liked that exchange between William Gass and John Gardner in which Gardner said he wanted everyone to love his books and Gass replied that he wouldn't want everyone to love his books any more than he would want everyone to love his sister or his daughter. Which side do you come down on?

BARTH: Gass accused the late Mr. Gardner with confusing love and promiscuity, which are not the same thing. Well, I am congenitally and temperamentally a novelist. The novel has its roots, very honorably, in the pop culture. The art novel notwithstanding, I think most of us novelists have a sneaking wish that we could have it both ways, as Charles Dickens did and as Gabriel García Márquez sort of does—to write novels that are both shatteringly beautiful and at the same time popular. Not to make a lot of money, but so that you can reach out and touch the hearts—no, that sounds hokey, doesn't it? But it is what most novelists wish they could do—reach out a little bit beyond that audience of professional readers, those really devoted followers of contemporary fiction. That's a navigational star that I confess I steer by. But I am, in fact, an amateur sailor and therefore an amateur navigator; I don't confuse my navigational stars with my destination. No novel of mine has had that kind of popularity, and I don't expect any novel of mine ever shall. But it's a good piece of fortune when it happens. I think of the novel as being an essentially American genre in this way—I'm not talking about *American* novels, but American in a metaphorical sense: hospitable to immigrants and amateurs. My favorite literature is both of stunning literary quality and democratic of access. This is not to mean I have a secret wish to be my Chesapeake neighbor, James Michener.

INTERVIEWER: Would you ever make a compromise in your books to gain more readers?

BARTH: I would, but I can't. I start every new project saying, "This one's going to be simple, this one's going to be simple." It never turns out to be. My imagination evidently delights in complexity for its own sake. Much of life, after all, and much of what we admire is essentially complex. For a temperament such as mine, the hardest job in the world—the most *complicated* task in the world—is to become simpler. There are writers whose gift is to make terribly complicated things simple. But I know my gift is the reverse: to take relatively simple things and complicate them to the point of madness. But there you are: one learns who one is, and it is at one's peril that one attempts to become someone else.

INTERVIEWER: Do your children enjoy your books?

BARTH: I have no idea whether those rascals read them. I think they sneaked them when they were teenagers, but they've grown up to be scientists and business types. I think they're happy that their daddy writes things that have a certain heft. But do they read them? I don't know. When we finish our conversation I'll call them up one at a time and ask them.

GEORGE PLIMPTON
Spring 1984

11. Edna O'Brien

Edna O'Brien was born in the west of Ireland in a small village she describes as "enclosed, fervid and bigoted." After finishing primary school in her hometown, she was sent to convent school in Galway, and later to Dublin, where she studied at the Pharmaceutical College. She moved to London with her husband and two sons in 1960, and began to write.

Her first novel, *The Country Girls,* appeared in 1961. Her other works of fiction are *The Lonely Girl* (1962), *Girls in Their Married Bliss* (1964), *August Is a Wicked Month* (1965), *Casualties of Peace* (1966), *A Pagan Place* (1970), *Night* (1972), *Johnny I Hardly Knew You* (1977), and, most recently, *A Fanatic Heart* (1985), a selection of short stories. Her nonfiction includes *Mother Ireland* (1976), *Arabian Days* (1977), and *James and Nora: A Portrait of Joyce's Marriage* (1981). Her play *Virginia,* based on the life of Virginia Woolf, was staged at the Public Theater in New York in the spring of 1985, and her new play, *Flesh and Blood,* is to be performed in the United States in 1986. She received the Kingsley Amis Award for fiction in 1962 and the Yorkshire Post Novel Award in 1971.

O'Brien lives in the Little Venice section of London.

Memos Re Mrs. R. ①

Walking by the rough sea &
fjup to watch the telescope. the
man of course comes to her
rescue, hits it & ___ her
you are the rise ___ waves &
he says "It is what you
wanted..." ___ as he continues
to look she sees her dreams
in the ___ ___
water etc. in fact to reality
as she comes
he is still here..."

Cut to very sedate Tea-Room
Cakes.
Gâteau Basque   He is reading the
Choc.   menu out
                    Mrs R. No. No... No.

Last Lines. And what do you want new
Mrs R. I want you to make love
to me as if the first time
Mr R. which in a sense it is.
                    Their faces on the village

A page from one of Edna O'Brien's manuscripts.

Edna O'Brien

Edna O'Brien resembles one of her own heroines: beautiful in a subtle, wistful way, with reddish-blond hair, green eyes, and a savage sense of humor. She lives alone in an airy, spacious apartment in Little Venice, London, near the Canal. From her balcony, wrought-iron steps lead down to a vast tree-filled park, where O'Brien often can be found strolling during breaks from her work. The following interview took place in her writing room —a large, comfortable study cluttered with books; notebooks, records, and periodicals. The day I was there, the room was warmed by a log fire burning in the fireplace, and even more so by O'Brien's rich, softly accented Irish voice.

INTERVIEWER: You once said that as far back as you can remember you have been a writer. At what point did you actually start writing literature?

O'BRIEN: When I say I have written from the beginning, I mean that all real writers write from the beginning, that the vocation, the obsession, is already there, and that the obsession derives from an intensity of feeling which normal life cannot accommodate. I started writing snippets when I was eight or nine, but I wrote my first novel when I left Ireland and came to live in London. I had never been outside Ireland and it was November when I arrived in England. I found everything so different, so *alien.* Waterloo Station was full of people who were nameless, faceless. There were wreaths on the Cenotaph for Remembrance Sunday, and I felt bewildered and lost—an outsider. So in a sense *The Country Girls,* which I wrote in those first few weeks after my arrival, was my experience of Ireland and my farewell to it. But something happened to my style which I will tell you about. I had been trying to write short bits, and these were always flowery and overlyrical. Shortly after I arrived in London I saw an advertisement for a lecture given by Arthur Mizener [author of a book on F. Scott Fitzgerald, *The Far Side of Paradise*] on Hemingway and Fitzgerald. You must remember that I had no literary education, but a fervid religious one. So I went to the lecture and it was like a thunderbolt—Saul of Tarsus on his horse! Mizener read out the first paragraph of *A Farewell to Arms* and I couldn't believe it—this totally uncluttered, precise, true prose, which was *also* very moving and lyrical. I can say that the two things came together then: my being ready for the revelation and my urgency to write. The novel *wrote itself,* so to speak, in a few weeks. All the time I was writing it I couldn't stop crying, although it is a fairly buoyant, funny book. But it was the separation from Ireland which brought me to the point where I *had* to write, though I had always been in love with literature.

INTERVIEWER: If you had always loved literature, why did you study chemistry at university rather than English?

O'BRIEN: The usual reason, family. My family was radically opposed to anything to do with literature. Although Ireland has produced so many great writers, there is a deep suspicion about writing there. Somehow they know that writing is dangerous, seditious, as if "In the beginning was the Word and the Word was with God and the Word *was* God." I was an obedient little girl—though I hate to admit it now!—and went along with my family's wishes. I worked in a chemist's shop and then studied at the Pharmaceutical College at night.

INTERVIEWER: The protagonist of *The Country Girls* also works in a shop. Is the novel autobiographical?

O'BRIEN: The novel is autobiographical insofar as I was born and bred in the west of Ireland, educated at a convent, and was full of romantic yearnings, coupled with a sense of outrage. But any book that is any good must be, to some extent, autobiographical, because one cannot and should not fabricate emotions; and although style and narrative are crucial, the bulwark, emotion, is what finally matters. With luck, talent, and studiousness, one manages to make a little pearl, or egg, or something. . . . But what gives birth to it is what happens inside the soul and the mind, and that has almost always to do with *conflict*. And loss—an innate sense of tragedy.

INTERVIEWER: What Thomas Hardy called "the sadness of things," and Unamuno *"el sentimiento trágico de la vida"*?

O'BRIEN: Precisely. Not just subjective sadness, though you have to experience it in order to know it, but also objective. And the more I read about writers, their letters—say Flaubert's —the more I realize it. Flaubert was in a way like a *woman*. There he was, in Rouen, yearning for the bright lights of Paris and hectic affairs, yet deliberately keeping away from all that, isolating himself, in order to burn and luxuriate in the affliction of his own emotions. So writing, I think, is an interestingly perverse occupation. It is quite sick in the sense of normal human enjoyment of life, because the writer is always *removed*, the way an actor never is. An actor is with the audience, a writer is not with his readers, and by the time the work appears, he or she is again incarcerated in the next book—or in barrenness. So for both men and women writers, writing is an eminently masochistic exercise—though I wonder what Norman Mailer would say to that!

INTERVIEWER: Doesn't the theory of masochism apply to all artists, whatever the art form?

O'BRIEN: To some extent. I was reading van Gogh's letters. My God! I'm surprised he cut off only *one* ear, that he wasn't altogether shredded in pieces! But a woman writer has a double dose of masochism: the masochism of the woman and that of the artist. No way to dodge it or escape from it. Men are better at escaping their psyches and their consciences. But there is a certain dogged strength in realizing that you can make those delirious journeys and come through.

INTERVIEWER: Some don't. There is a high rate of suicide, alcoholism, madness among writers.

O'BRIEN: It is only by the grace of God, and perhaps willpower, that one comes through each time. Many wonderful writers write one or two books and then kill themselves. Sylvia Plath for instance. She was much younger than Virginia Woolf when she committed suicide, but if she had survived that terrible crisis, I feel she would have written better books. I have this theory that Woolf feared that the flame of her talent was extinguished or dwindling because her last book, *Between the Acts,* lacked the soaring genius of the others. When a writer, or an artist, has the feeling that he can't do it anymore, he descends into hell. So you must keep in mind that although it may stop, it can come back. When I was a child in Ireland, a spring would suddenly appear and yield forth buckets of beautiful clear water, then just as suddenly it would dry up. The water-diviners would come with their rods and sometimes another spring would be found. One has to be one's own water-diviner. It is hard, especially as writers are always anxious, always on the run—from the telephone, from people, from responsibilities, from the distractions of this world. The other thing that can destroy talent is too much grief. Yeats said,

"Too much sorrow can make a stone of the heart." I often wonder, if Emily Brontë had lived to be fifty, what kind of books would she have written? Her life was so penalizing—and Charlotte's too—utterly without sex. Emily was thirty when she wrote *Wuthering Heights.* I think the grinding suffering might have killed her talent later. It is not that you have to be happy—that would be asking too much—but if it gets too painful that sense of wonderment, or joy, dies, and with it the generosity so necessary to create.

INTERVIEWER: So the catalyst for your own work was that lecture on Fitzgerald and Hemingway. Before that you said that you read a great deal in Ireland, partly to escape. What sort of books did you read? And which ones influenced you most?

O'BRIEN: Looking back on it, it was not so much escape as nourishment. Of course there is an element of escape as well, that entering temporarily into a different world. But I think literature is food for the soul and the heart. There are books that are pure escapism: thrillers, detective and spy novels, but I can't read them, because they don't *deliver* to me. Whereas from one page of Dostoyevsky I feel renewed, however depressing the subject. The first book I ever *bought*—I've still got it —was called *Introducing James Joyce,* by T. S. Eliot. It contained a short story, a piece from *Portrait of the Artist,* some other pieces, and an introduction by Eliot. I read a scene from *Portrait* which is the Christmas dinner when everything begins pleasantly: a fire, largesse, the blue flame of light on the dark plum pudding, the revelry before the flare-up ensues between people who were for Parnell and those who were against him. Parnell had been dead for a long time, but the Irish, being Irish, persist with history. Reading that book made me realize that I wanted literature for the rest of my life.

INTERVIEWER: And you became a ferocious reader, first of Joyce, then of others. Who else did you read in those early days?

O'BRIEN: I am a slow reader, because I want to savor and recall what I read. The excitement and sense of discovery is not the same as in those days when I would get thoroughly wrapped up in *Vanity Fair* or *War and Peace*. Now I set myself a task of reading one great book each year. Last year I read *Bleak House*, which I think is the greatest English novel—I read a few pages a day. But one's taste changes so much. I mentioned Scott Fitzgerald, whom I read, oh, so lovingly and thoroughly! I loved *Tender Is the Night* and *The Great Gatsby*, which is a flawless novel. So I can say that he was one of my early influences. But now I know that fundamentally I respond to European literature in all its dark ramifications. I think the Russians are unsurpassable. Of course Joyce did something extraordinary: he threw out the entire heritage of English literature—language, story, structure, everything—and created a new and stupendous work. But for emotional gravity, no one can compare with the Russians. When I first read Chekhov's short stories, before I saw his plays, I knew I had heard the *voice* that I loved most in the whole world. I wrote to my sister, "Read Chekhov—he does not write, he *breathes* life off the page." And he was, and still is, my greatest influence, especially in short-story writing.

INTERVIEWER: Later on, when you tried your hand at drama, did Chekhov come to your rescue there as well?

O'BRIEN: I think so, though it is very dangerous to take Chekhov as a model. His dramatic genius is so mysterious; he does what seems to be the impossible, in that he makes dramatic something that is desultory. And of course it is not desultory—indeed, it is as tightly knit as that Persian carpet. Shakespeare is God. He knows everything and expresses it with such a density of poetry and humor and power that the mind boggles. But then he had *great* themes—*Othello, Hamlet,* the history plays. Chekhov, on the other hand, tells you, or seems to tell you, of a profligate family that is losing an orchard, or some sisters who yearn for Moscow, and inside it is a whole web of life and love and failure. I think that despite his emphasis on wanting to be funny, he was a tragic man. In a letter to his wife, actress Olga Knipper, he says, "It is nine o'clock in the evening, you are going to play act three of my play, and I am as lonely as a coffin!"

INTERVIEWER: The greatness of the Russian classics must be due in part to the vastness and variety of their country, the harshness of climate, and the cruelty and roughness of their society (which hasn't really changed) and which enhances the intensity of the emotions and the extremes of behavior.

O'BRIEN: Certainly. It makes for endurance—those long, savage winters. Also being throttled as they have always been. The more you strangle a man, the deeper he screams. Boris Pasternak put his pain to immortal use in *Dr. Zhivago.*

INTERVIEWER: Did that first book on Joyce send you to read the whole of Joyce?

O'BRIEN: Yes, but I was too young then. Later I read *Ulysses,* and at one point I thought of writing a book on Joyce, *comme tout le monde!* I read a lot of books about Joyce and wrote a monograph. Then I realized that there were already too many books on him and that the best thing you could read about Joyce was Joyce himself.

INTERVIEWER: How do you assess him now, and how is he regarded in Ireland?

O'BRIEN: He is beyond assessment—gigantic. I sometimes read bits of *Finnegans Wake* and feel my brain begin to sizzle. Joyce went mad with genius. When you read *Dubliners* and *Finnegans Wake* you feel that the man underwent a metamorphosis between twenty-five and sixty. H. G. Wells said that *Finnegans Wake* was an immense riddle, and people find it too difficult to read. I have yet to meet anyone who has read and digested the whole of it—except perhaps my friend Richard Ellmann. Joyce killed himself with exertion. He went beyond us into a labyrinth of language, and I don't know whether that was a loss or a gain.

INTERVIEWER: The generation before you in Ireland had an important literary scene: Yeats and Lady Gregory and the Abbey Theatre group, and all the people around them, which ran parallel to London's Bloomsbury group and Eliot's circle. Did you have anything similar in Ireland when you started?

O'BRIEN: Nothing on that level. There was a sort of Irish literary scene but I wasn't part of it. One reason was poverty, another that I didn't have an *entrée;* I was just a chemistry student in a bed-sit. I heard of people like Sean O'Faolain, Frank O'Connor. Samuel Beckett had left and vowed never to return, Sean O'Casey was in England. But it was good for me not to be part of any scene because it meant that I had to do my apprenticeship alone. Sweet are the uses of adversity, are they not?

INTERVIEWER: What about women writers? You haven't mentioned any as a major influence so far.

O'BRIEN: Every woman novelist has been influenced by the Brontës. *Wuthering Heights* and *Jane Eyre.* The poetry of Emily Dickinson, the early books of Elizabeth Bowen—especially the one she wrote about her home in Ireland, *Bowen's Court.* My admiration for Jane Austen came much later, and I also love the Russian poet Anna Akhmatova. Nowadays there are too many writers, and I think one of the reasons for the deterioration of language and literature in the last forty years has been the spawning of inferior novels. Everybody writes novels—journalists, broadcasters, TV announcers . . . it is a free-for-all! But writing is a vocation, like being a nun or a priest. I work at my writing as an athlete does at his training, taking it very seriously. Whether a novel is autobiographical or not does not matter. What is important is the truth in it and the way that truth is expressed. I think a casual or frivolous attitude is pernicious.

INTERVIEWER: Is there any area of fiction that you find women are better equipped to explore?

O'BRIEN: Yes. Women are better at emotions and the havoc

those emotions wreak. But it must be said that Anna Karenina is the most believable heroine. The last scene where she goes to the station and looks down at the rails and thinks of Vronski's rejection is terrible in its depiction of despair. Women, on the whole, are better at plumbing the depths. A woman artist can produce a perfect gem, as opposed to a huge piece of rock carving a man might produce. It is not a limitation of talent or intelligence, it is just a different way of looking at the world.

INTERVIEWER: So you don't believe in the feminist argument that the differences between men and women are a question of nurture and not of nature; that women look at the world differently because they have been conditioned to do so?

O'BRIEN: Not in the least! I believe that we are fundamentally, biologically, and therefore psychologically different. I am not like any man I have met, ever, and that divide is what both interests me and baffles me. A lot of things have been said by feminists about equality, about liberation, but not all of these things are gospel truth. They are opinions the way my books are opinions, nothing more. Of course I would like women to have a better time but I don't see it happening, and for a very simple and primal reason: people are pretty savage towards each other, be they men or women.

INTERVIEWER: Yet your own success is, to a certain degree, due to the fact that your writing coincided with the rise of the feminist movement, because invariably it portrayed loving, sensitive, good women, being victimized by hard, callous men, and it hit the right note at the right time. Would you agree with that?

O'BRIEN: I would think so. However, I am not the darling of the feminists. They think I am too preoccupied with old-fashioned themes like love and longing. Though one woman in *Ms.* magazine pointed out that I send bulletins from battle fronts where other women do not go. I think I do. The reason why I resent being lectured at is that my psyche is so weighed down with its own paraphernalia! No man or woman from outside could prescribe to me what to do. I have enough trouble keeping madness at bay.

INTERVIEWER: Your description of small towns and their enclosed communities reminds me of some of America's Southern writers, like Faulkner. Did they influence you?

O'BRIEN: Faulkner is an important writer though an imperfect one. I did go through a stage when I read a lot of Southern writers: Carson McCullers, Eudora Welty, Flannery O'Connor. . . . Any small, claustrophobic, ingrown community resembles another. The passion and ignorance in the Deep South of America and the west of Ireland are the same.

INTERVIEWER: This is the opposite of the high society and the aristocratic world of Proust's *Remberance of Things Past*, which has also been a major source of inspiration to you.

O'BRIEN: Proust's influence on me, along with his genius, was his preoccupation with memory and his obsession with the past. His concentration on even the simplest detail—like one petal of a flower, or the design on a dinner plate—has unique, manic intensity. Also, when I read his biography by George Painter I felt the tenderness of his soul and wished I could have met him as a human being. You see, Joyce and Proust, although very different, broke the old mold by recognizing the importance of the rambling, disjointed nature of what goes on in the head, the interior monologue. I wonder how they would fare now. These are more careless times. Literature is no longer sacred, it is a business. There is an invisible umbilical cord between the writer and his potential reader, and I fear that the time has gone when readers could sink into a book the way they did in the past, for the *pace* of life is fast and frenetic. The world is cynical: the dwelling on emotions, the perfection of style, the intensity of a Flaubert is wasted on modern sensibility. I have a feeling that there is a *dying,* if not a *death,* of great literature. Some blame the television for it. Perhaps. There is hardly any distinction between a writer and a journalist—indeed, most writers *are* journalists. Nothing wrong with journalism any more than with dentistry, but they are worlds apart! Whenever I read the English Sunday papers I notice that the standard of literacy is high—all very clever and hollow—but no dues to literature. They care about their own egos. They synopsize the book, tell the plot. Well, fuck the plot! That is for precocious schoolboys. What matters is the imaginative *truth*, and the perfection and care with which it has been rendered. After all, you don't say of a ballet dancer, "He jumped in the air, then he twirled around, etc. . . ." You are just *carried away* by his dancing. The nicest readers are—and I know by the letters I receive—youngish people who are still eager and uncontaminated, who approach a book without hostility. But when I read Anita Brookner's novel *Look at Me*, I feel I am in the grip of a most wonderful, imaginative writer. The same is true of Margaret Atwood. Also, great literature is dying because young people, although they don't talk about it much, feel and fear a holocaust.

INTERVIEWER: What about your own relationship with critics? Do you feel misunderstood and neglected by them, or have they been kind to you? Have you ever been savaged by them?

O'BRIEN: Oh yes! I have been savaged all right! I believe one reviewer lost her job on the *New Statesman* because her review of my book *A Pagan Place* was too personal. She went on and on about my illiterate background. On the whole I have had more serious consideration in the United States than in Britain or Ireland. Perhaps because I am not known there as a "personality"! I do not despair though, for the real test of writing is not in the reading but in the rereading. I am not ashamed of my books being reread. The misunderstanding may be due just to geography, and to race. The Irish and the English are poles apart in thought and disposition.

INTERVIEWER: It may also be due to a certain—and very un-British—*démesure* in your writing; I mean they find you too sentimental.

O'BRIEN: I am glad to say that Dickens was accused of sentimentality and, by God, he lives on!

INTERVIEWER: You were brought up as a devout Catholic and had a convent education. At one point you even contemplated becoming a nun. What made you give up religion?

O'BRIEN: I married a divorcé, and that was my first "Fall." Add to that the hounding nature of Irish Catholicism and you can dimly understand. We had a daily admonition which went:

> *You have but one soul to save*
> *One God to love and serve*
> *One Eternity to prepare for*
> *Death will come soon*
> *Judgment will follow, and then*
> *Heaven—or Hell—For Ever!*

INTERVIEWER: In your novel *A Pagan Place,* the heroine does become a nun. Was that a vicarious fulfillment of a subconscious wish?

O'BRIEN: Perhaps. I did think of becoming a nun when I was very young, but it went out of my mind later, chased away by sexual desire!

INTERVIEWER: Another interesting aspect of that novel is that it is written in the second person singular, like a soliloquy. It is somewhat reminiscent of Molly Bloom's soliloquy in *Ulysses;* were you conscious of the influence?

O'BRIEN: I didn't take Molly's as a model. The reason was psychological. As a child you are both your secret self and the "you" that your parents think you are. So the use of the second person was a way of combining the two identities. But I tend not to examine these things too closely—they just happen.

INTERVIEWER: Religion has played such a crucial part in your life and evolution, yet you have not dealt with it on any philosophical or moral level, as have Graham Greene or Georges Bernanos; you haven't made religion the central theme of any of your novels. Why?

O'BRIEN: That is perhaps one of the differences between men and women who go through the same experiences. I flee from my persecutors. I have not confronted religion.

INTERVIEWER: Do you think you ever will?

O'BRIEN: I hope so—when I have got rid of the terror and the anxiety. Or perhaps when I know exactly what I believe or don't believe.

INTERVIEWER: Let's talk about the subjects that are dealt with in your work, its central themes, which are romantic love and Ireland. Some people—and not only feminists!—think that your preoccupation with romance verges at times on the sentimental and the "Romantic Novel" formula. You quoted Aragon in answer: "Love is your last chance, there is really nothing else to keep you there."

O'BRIEN: Other people have said it too, even the Beatles! Emily Dickinson wrote, "And is there more than love and death, then tell me its name?" But my work is concerned with *loss* as much as with love. Loss is every child's theme because by necessity the child loses its mother and its bearings. And writers, however mature and wise and eminent, are children at heart. So my central theme is loss—loss of love, loss of self, loss of God. I have just finished a play, my third, which is about my family. In it for the first time I have allowed my father, who is always the ogre figure in my work, to weep for the loss of *his* child. Therefore, I might, if the gods are good to me, find that my understanding of love has become richer and stronger than my dread of loss. You see, my own father was what you might call the "archetypal" Irishman—a gambler, drinker, a man totally unequipped to be a husband or a father. And of course that colored my views, distorted them, and made me seek out demons.

INTERVIEWER: Is that why, in nearly all your novels, women are longing to establish a simple, loving, harmonious relationship with men, but are unable to do so?

O'BRIEN: My experience was pretty extreme, so that it is hard for me to imagine harmony, or even affinity, between men and women. I would need to be reborn.

INTERVIEWER: The other central theme of your work is Ireland. It seems to me that you have the same love-hate relationship with Ireland that most exiles have with their native country: on the one hand an incurable nostalgia and longing, and on the other the fact that one cannot go back, because the reasons that made one leave in the first place are still there. There is a constant conflict in the soul.

O'BRIEN: My relationship with Ireland is very complex. I could not live there for a variety of reasons. I felt oppressed and strangulated from an early age. That was partly to do with my parents, who were themselves products and victims of their history and culture. That is to say, alas, they were superstitious, fanatical, engulfing. At the same time they were bursting with talent—I know this from my mother's letters, as she wrote to me almost every day. So I have to thank them for a heritage that includes talent, despair, and permanent fury. When I was a student in Dublin my mother found a book of Sean O'Casey in my suitcase and wanted to *burn* it! *But without reading it!* So they hated literature without knowing it. We know that the effect of our parents is indelible, because we internalize as a child and it remains inside us forever. Even when the parents die, you dream of them as if they were still there. Everything was an occasion for fear, religion was force-fed the way they feed the geese of Strasbourg for pâté! I feel I am a cripple with a craving for wings. So much for the personal aspect. As for the country itself, it is no accident that almost all Irish writers leave the country. You know why? Ireland, as Joyce said, eats her writers the way a sow eats her farrow. He also called it a warren of "prelates and kinechites." Of course there's the beauty of the landscape, the poetry, the fairy tales, the vividness. I have shown my love and my entanglement with the place as much as I have shown my hatred. But they think that I have shown only my hatred.

INTERVIEWER: Is that why they had an auto-da-fé of your first novel in your native village?

O'BRIEN: It was a humble event, as befits a backward place. Two or three people had gone to Limerick and bought *The Country Girls*. The parish priest asked them to hand in the books, which they did, and he burnt them on the grounds of the church. Nevertheless, a lot of people read it. My mother was very harsh about it; she thought I was a disgrace. That is the sadness—it takes you half a life to get out of the pits of darkness and stupidity. It fills me with anger, and with pity.

INTERVIEWER: Do you think that after all these years and through your books you have exorcised the demon and can let it rest?

O'BRIEN: I hope not, because one needs one's demons to create.

INTERVIEWER: After that small auto-da-fé, did anything else of that kind happen?

O'BRIEN: They used to ban my books, but now when I go there, people are courteous to my face, though rather slanderous behind my back. Then again, Ireland has changed. There are a lot of young people who are irreligious, or less religious. Ironically, they wouldn't be interested in my early books—they would think them gauche. They are aping English and American mores. If I went to a dance hall in Dublin now I would feel as alien as in a disco in Oklahoma.

INTERVIEWER: You are not a political writer because, as you say, politics are concerned with the social and the external, while your preoccupations are with the inner, psychological life. Nonetheless, considering your emotional involvement with Ireland, how have you kept away from the situation in Northern Ireland—terrorism, the IRA, etc. . . . ?

O'BRIEN: I have written one long piece on Northern Ireland for the German magazine *Stern*. My feelings about it are so manifold. I think it is mad, a so-called religious war, in this day and age. At the same time, I can't bear the rhetoric of the

Unionists; I mean Ireland is *one small* island, and those six counties do not belong to Britain. Equally I abhor terrorism, whoever does it, the IRA, the Arabs, the Israelis. But when I stayed in Northern Ireland to research and write the article, I realized that the Catholics are second-class citizens. They live in terrible slums, in poverty, and know no way of improving their conditions. I have not set a novel in Northern Ireland simply because I do not know enough about it. I dislike cant —you get that from politicians. Writers have to dig deep for experience. I might go and live there for a while, in order to discover and later write about it. But so far I have refrained from bringing the topic into a book merely as a voyeur.

INTERVIEWER: Let's get back to Virginia Woolf. . . . Why and when did she become an obsession for you? After all, you are very different as writers and as people.

O'BRIEN: I first read her critical essays, *The Common Reader,* and I saw a woman who loved literature, unlike many critics who just *use* it. The essays are on Hazlitt, Wordsworth, Hardy, everyone. I was overwhelmed first by the generosity of her mind and its perspicacity. Later I read *To the Lighthouse* and my favorite, *Mrs. Dalloway,* which is very spry and sprightly. Then I was asked to write a play about her and I began to read everything she had written—diaries, letters, etc. . . . I realized that she gave of herself so utterly, so *shamelessly.* Her photographs show her as aloof, which she was in some ways. But in the diaries and letters, she tells *everything!* If she buys a pair of gloves she has to commit it to paper. So I came to know her and to love her.

INTERVIEWER: Some critics pointed to the play's neglect of her intellectual vigor and her bitchiness. Do you think her bitchiness was due to lack of sexual gratification?

O'BRIEN: She did have a bitchy side, but alongside it a child-like need for affection. She called people pet names, waited for her husband to come home, adored her sister Vanessa and wanted her approval. I saw Woolf as a troubled, *needful* creature. Her bitchiness was diminishing, certainly, and she would have been a grander figure without it. I selected those parts of her that chart her dilemma, her march towards suicide. Another writer, say an English homosexual, could write a very waspish, very witty play about her. I hope that mine was valid.

INTERVIEWER: Having been successful at novels and short stories, you tried your hand at drama—plays and screenplays. How did that come about?

O'BRIEN: I was asked to adapt my own novel *A Pagan Place* for the stage and it opened a new vista for me. Then with some experience I tackled Woolf. Now I have written a third play, which for the time being is called *Home Sweet Home*, or *Family Butchers.* I feel drama is more direct, more suitable for expressing passions. Confrontation is the stuff of drama. It happens rather than is described. The play starts in the early morning, the voice of an Irish tenor comes over the gramophone—John McCormack is singing "Bless This House, Oh Lord We Pray," then he's interrupted by a gunshot followed by another gunshot. The lights come on, a man and a woman appear, and you know that this is a play about passion and violence. You go straight for the jugular.

INTERVIEWER: When you start a play, or a novel, or a short story, do you have a basic idea? Or a sentence? Something that triggers off the process of creating the work?

O'BRIEN: I always have the first line. Even with my very first book, *The Country Girls,* I went around with this first sentence in my head long before I sat down to write it.*

INTERVIEWER: Once you have started, do you have the whole scheme in your mind or do characters and plot take their own course and lead you, as some novelists say they do? I mean, Balzac was so surprised and moved by Old Goriot's death that he opened his window and shouted, *"Le Père Goriot est mort! Le Père Goriot est mort!"*

---

*"I wakened quickly and sat up in bed abruptly."

O'BRIEN: I know more or less, but I don't discuss it with myself. It is like sleepwalking; I don't know exactly where I am going but I know I will get there. When I am writing, I am so glad to be doing it that whatever form it takes—play, novel, etc.—I am thankful to the Fates. I keep dozens of pens by me, and exercise books.

INTERVIEWER: When success came and you began to be famous and lionized, did it affect your life, work, and outlook in any way? Is success good for an artist, or does it limit his field of experience?

O'BRIEN: It depends on the degree of success and on the disposition of the artist. It was very nice for me to be published, as I had longed for it. But my success has been rather modest. It hasn't been meteoric. Nor was it financially shattering—just enough to carry me along.

INTERVIEWER: But you have had a great deal of social success: fame, publicity, so on . . .

O'BRIEN: I am not conscious of it. I go to functions more as a duty than for pleasure, and I am always *outside* looking in, not the other way round. But I am grateful to have had enough success not to feel a disaster—it has allayed my hopelessness. Undoubtedly success contributed to the breakup of my marriage. I had married very young. My husband was an attractive father figure—a Professor Higgins. When my book was published and well received, it altered things between us. The break would have come anyway, but my success sped it up. Then began a hard life; but when you are young, you have boundless energy—you run the house, mind the children, *and* write your despair. I don't know if I could do it all now. Looking back I realize that I am one of the luckiest people in the world, since no matter how down I go something brings me back. Is it God's grace or just peasant resilience?

INTERVIEWER: Perhaps it is the creative act of writing. John Updike once said that the minute he puts an unhappiness down on paper, it metamorphoses into a lump of sugar!

O'BRIEN: I think he was simplifying. The original pain that prompted the writing does not lessen, but it is gratifying to give it form and shape.

INTERVIEWER: Did money ever act as a spur? You were very prolific in the sixties, and still are.

O'BRIEN: I have never written anything in order to make money. A story comes to me, is given me, as it were, and I write it. But perhaps the need to earn a living and my need to write coincided. I know that I would still write if tomorrow I was given a huge legacy, and I will always be profligate.

INTERVIEWER: How do you organize your time? Do you write regularly, every day? Philip Roth has said that he writes eight hours a day three hundred and sixty-five days a year. Do you work as compulsively?

O'BRIEN: He is a man, you see. Women have the glorious excuse of having to shop, cook, clean! When I am working I write in a kind of trance, longhand, in these several copybooks. I meant to tidy up before you came! I write in the morning because one is nearer to the unconscious, the source of inspiration. I never work at night because by then the shackles of the day are around me, what James Stephens (author of *The Crock of Gold*) called "That flat, dull catalogue of dreary things that fasten themselves to my wings," and I don't sit down three hundred and sixty-five days a year because I'm not that kind of writer. I wish I were! Perhaps I don't take myself that seriously. Another reason why I don't write constantly is that I feel I have written all I had wanted to say about love and loss and loneliness and being a victim and all that. I have finished with that territory. And I have not yet embraced another one. It may be that I'm going towards it—I hope and pray that this is the case.

INTERVIEWER: When you are writing, are you disciplined? Do you keep regular hours, turn down invitations, and hibernate?

O'BRIEN: Yes, but discipline doesn't come into it. It is what one has to do. The impulse is stronger than anything. I don't like too much social life anyway. It is gossip and bad white wine. It's a waste. Writing is like carrying a fetus. I get up in the morning, have a cup of tea, and come into this room to work. I never go out to lunch, never, but I stop around one or two and spend the rest of the afternoon attending to mundane things. In the evening I might read or go out to a play or a film, or see my sons. Did I tell you that I spend a lot of time moping? Did Philip Roth say that he moped?

INTERVIEWER: Don't you feel restless and lonely if you have worked all day and have to spend the evening alone?

O'BRIEN: Less lonely than if I were bored at a dinner party. If I get restless I might ring up one of a handful of friends who are close enough to come to the rescue. Rilke said, "Loneliness is a very good practice for eternity." Loneliness is not intolerable—depression is.

INTERVIEWER: Before the film script on Joan of Arc that you are writing now, you wrote another two. One of them, *Zee & Co.*, starring Elizabeth Taylor, was a big-budget, Hollywood film. How did you enjoy that experience?

O'BRIEN: The film world is inhabited by gangsters. I have met many producers and very few of them could I accuse of being sensitive, or interested in writing. They are businesspeople whose material is other people's imagination, and that invariably leads to trouble. People in the clothing industry or the motor business are dealing with merchandise, but the producer's raw material is first and foremost the writer. So I can't say that I had a happy experience. But it *is* possible; low-budget films like *Gregory's Girl* or *The Country Girls* do get made. I had a marvelous time with the latter; they didn't have *four* writers all rewriting my script. It restored my faith. I do believe that cinema and the television are the media of the future, more than books, simply because people are too restive. I put as much into a film script as into anything I write—it is, I believe, an art form, and great directors like Bergman, Buñuel,

Hitchcock, and Fassbinder have made it so. What happened
with *Zee & Co.*—and what happens generally when you get
involved with Hollywood—is that you give them the script and
then the director or leading actress proceeds to write their own
stuff. They are often as capable of writing as I am of brain
surgery! So they just disembowel it. And they do it for two
reasons: one is ego and the other is ignorance. They know
nothing about writing and therefore think they can bring their
own *ideas* to it. Now, in the theater when actors want something changed they ask the author.

INTERVIEWER: If someone had time to read only one of your
books, which one would you recommend?

O'BRIEN: *A Pagan Place.*

INTERVIEWER: Do you feel that your best book, the one that
every writer aspires to, is yet to come?

O'BRIEN: It had better be! I need to develop, to enlarge my
spheres of experience.

INTERVIEWER: When you say you are changing your life, do
you also mean that the subject matter of your fiction will
change with it?

O'BRIEN: I think so. I am giving a lecture in Boston next
month about women in literature. I had to come to the forlorn
conclusion that all the great heroines have been created by
men. I had an anthology of women's writing called *Bold New
Women* in which the editor, Barbara Alson, very wisely says
that all women writers have written about sex, because sex is
their biological life, their environment, and that for a woman
a sexual encounter is not just the mechanical thing it can be
for a man but—and she uses this wonderful phrase—"a clutch
on the universe." I have written quite a lot of love stories; I
don't think I want to write those anymore. I even find them
hard to read! It doesn't mean that I am not interested in love
anymore—that goes on as long as there is breath. I mean I am
not going to *write* about it in the same way.

INTERVIEWER: Could it have something to do with age?

O'BRIEN: *Bound* to have something to do with age. The attitude toward sex changes in two ways. Sexual love becomes deeper and one realizes how fundamental it is and how rich. At the same time, one sees that it is a sort of mutual game and that attraction makes one resort to all sorts of ruses and strategies. To an outsider it is all patent, even laughable. Shakespeare saw through this glorious delusion better than anyone and *As You Like It* is the funniest play about love, yet it is steeped in love.

INTERVIEWER: What about the new cult of chastity? Germaine Greer's new book advocates restraint—a backlash against a decade or so of permissiveness. Have you been influenced by the changing mood?

O'BRIEN: I have always espoused chastity except when one can no longer resist the temptation. I know promiscuity is boring, much more than fish and chips, which is comforting.

INTERVIEWER: Do you find sex scenes difficult to write, considering your puritanical background?

O'BRIEN: Not really. When you are writing you are not conscious of the reader, so that you don't feel embarrassed. I'm sure Joyce had a most heady and wonderful time writing the last fifty pages of *Ulysses*—glorious Molly Bloom. He must have written it in one bout, thinking: I'll show the women of the world that I am omniscient!

INTERVIEWER: What do you think the future has in store for literature? You have been very pessimistic so far. For example, last year nearly three hundred novels were published in France, and few except the ones that won the big prizes were read. Will we go on endlessly writing novels with so few making a mark?

O'BRIEN: As you know the future itself is perilous. But as regards books, there is first the financial aspect of publishing. Already books are very expensive, so that a first novel of quality will have less of a chance of being picked up. Say a new Djuna Barnes, or indeed Nathalie Sarraute, might not get published. If Woolf's *The Waves* were to be published today it would have pitiful sales. Of course, "how-to" books, spy stories, thrillers, and science fiction all sell by the millions. What would be wonderful—what we *need* just now—is some astonishing fairy tale. I read somewhere the other day that the cavemen did not paint what they saw, but what they *wished* they had seen. We need that, in these lonely, lunatic times.

INTERVIEWER: So if we manage to save the planet, is there hope for literature as well?

O'BRIEN: Oh yes! At this very moment, some imagination is spawning something wonderful that might make us tremble. Let's say there will always be literature because the imagination is boundless. We just need to care more for the imagination than for the trivia and the commerce of life. Literature is the next best thing to God. Joyce would disagree. He would say literature *is,* in essence, God.

SHUSHA GUPPY
Spring 1984

12. Philip Roth

Philip Roth was born March 19, 1933, in Newark, New Jersey.
He attended Bucknell University as an undergraduate, and
received a master's degree from the University of Chicago,
where he taught from 1956 to 1958.

In 1959 he published his first book, *Goodbye, Columbus,* a
novella and five stories; it won the National Book Award that
year. His other books are *Letting Go* (1962), *When She Was
Good* (1967), *Portnoy's Complaint* (1969), *Our Gang* (1971),
The Breast (1972), *The Great American Novel* (1973), *My Life
as a Man* (1974), *Reading Myself and Others,* a collection of
essays and interviews (1975; enlarged and reissued 1985), *The
Professor of Desire* (1977), and the Zuckerman trilogy—*The
Ghost Writer, Zuckerman Unbound, The Anatomy Lesson*—
published in one volume (with a novella-length epilogue, *The
Prague Orgy*) in 1985 under the title *Zuckerman Bound.* Roth
is an active supporter of the efforts of dissident writers in other
nations, and is the General Editor of the Penguin "Writers
from the Other Europe" series. He has taught at the University
of Iowa, has been writer-in-residence at Princeton, and was
adjunct professor of English at the University of Pennsylvania
from 1966 to 1978.

Roth lives in Connecticut.

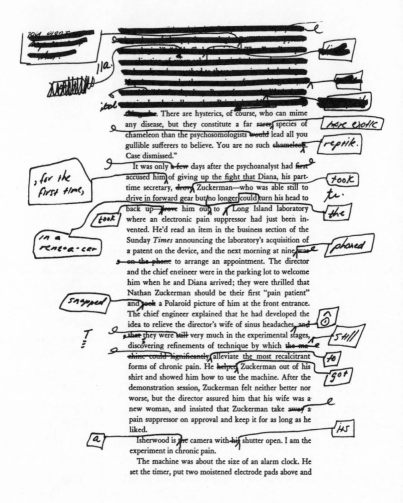

. There are hysterics, of course, who can mime any disease, but they constitute a far rarer species of chameleon than the psychosomologists would lead all you gullible sufferers to believe. You are no such chameleon. Case dismissed."

It was only a few days after the psychoanalyst had first accused him of giving up the fight that Diana, his part-time secretary, drove Zuckerman—who was able still to drive in forward gear but no longer could turn his head to back up—drove him out to a Long Island laboratory where an electronic pain suppressor had just been invented. He'd read an item in the business section of the Sunday *Times* announcing the laboratory's acquisition of a patent on the device, and the next morning at nine phoned on the phone to arrange an appointment. The director and the chief engineer were in the parking lot to welcome him when he and Diana arrived; they were thrilled that Nathan Zuckerman should be their first "pain patient" and took a Polaroid picture of him at the front entrance. The chief engineer explained that he had developed the idea to relieve the director's wife of sinus headaches, and that they were still very much in the experimental stages, discovering refinements of technique by which the machine could significantly alleviate the most recalcitrant forms of chronic pain. He helped Zuckerman out of his shirt and showed him how to use the machine. After the demonstration session, Zuckerman felt neither better nor worse, but the director assured him that his wife was a new woman, and insisted that Zuckerman take away a pain suppressor on approval and keep it for as long as he liked.

Isherwood is the camera with his shutter open. I am the experiment in chronic pain.

The machine was about the size of an alarm clock. He set the timer, put two moistened electrode pads above and

A galley proof of *The Anatomy Lesson,* with Philip Roth's corrections.

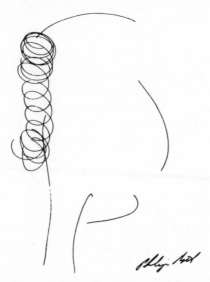

A Philip Roth self-portrait, from Burt Britton's *Self Portrait: Book People Picture Themselves* (Random House).

Philip Roth

I met Philip Roth after I had published a short book about his work for the Methuen Contemporary Writers Series. He read the book and wrote me a generous letter. After our first meeting, he sent me the fourth draft of The Anatomy Lesson, *which we later talked about, because, in the final stages of writing a novel, Roth likes to get as much criticism and response as he can from a few interested readers. Just after he finished* The Anatomy Lesson *we began the* Paris Review *interview. We met in the early summer of 1983 at the Royal Automobile Club in Pall Mall, where Roth occasionally takes a room to work in when he's visiting England. The room had been turned into a small, meticulously organized office—IBM golf-ball typewriter, alphabetical file holders, anglepoise lamps, dictionaries, aspirin, copyholder, felt-tip pens for correcting, a radio—with a few books on the mantelpiece, among them the recently published autobiography by Irving Howe,* A Margin of Hope, *Erik Erikson's* Young Man Luther: A Study in Psychoanalysis and History, *Leonard Woolf's autobiography, David Magarshaek's* Chekhov, *John Cheever's* Oh What a Paradise It Seems, *Fordyce's* Behavioral Methods for Chronic Pain and Illness *(useful for Zuckerman), Claire Bloom's autobiography,* Limelight and After, *and some* Paris Review *interviews. We talked in this businesslike cell for a day and a half, pausing only for meals. I was looked after with great thoughtfulness. Roth's manner, which matches his appearance—subdued, conventional clothes, gold-rimmed spectacles, the look of a quiet professional American visitor to London, perhaps an academic or a lawyer—is courteous, mild, and responsive. He listens carefully to everything, makes lots of quick jokes, and likes to be amused. Just underneath this benign appearance there is a ferocious concentration and mental rapacity; everything is grist for his mill, no vagueness is tolerated, differences of opinion are pounced on greedily, and nothing that might be useful is let slip. Thinking on his feet, he develops his ideas through a playful use of figurative language —as much as a way of avoiding confessional answers (though he can be very direct) as of interesting himself. The transcripts from this taped conversation were long, absorbing, funny, disorganized, and repetitive. I edited them down to a manageable size and sent my version on to him. Then there was a long pause while he went back to America and* The Anatomy Lesson *was published. Early in 1984, on his next visit to England, we resumed; he revised my version and we talked about the revision until it acquired its final form. I found this process extremely interesting. The mood of the interview had changed in the six months between his finishing a novel and starting new work; it became more combative and buoyant. And the several drafts in themselves displayed Roth's methods of work: raw chunks of talk were processed into stylish, energetic, concentrated prose, and the return to past thoughts generated new ideas. The result provides an example, as well as an account, of Philip Roth's presentation of himself.*

INTERVIEWER: How do you get started on a new book?

ROTH: Beginning a book is unpleasant. I'm entirely uncertain about the character and the predicament, and a character in his predicament is what I have to begin with. Worse than not knowing your subject is not knowing how to treat it, because that's finally everything. I type out beginnings and they're awful, more of an unconscious parody of my previous book than the breakaway from it that I want. I need something driving down the center of a book, a magnet to draw everything to it—that's what I look for during the first months of writing something new. I often have to write a hundred pages or more before there's a paragraph that's alive. Okay, I say to myself, that's your beginning, start there; that's the first paragraph of the book. I'll go over the first six months of work and underline in red a paragraph, a sentence, sometimes no more than a phrase, that has some life in it, and then I'll type all these out on one page. Usually it doesn't come to more than one page, but if I'm lucky, that's the start of page one. I look for the liveliness to set the tone. After the awful beginning come the months of freewheeling play, and after the play come the crises, turning against your material and hating the book.

INTERVIEWER: How much of a book is in your mind before you start?

ROTH: What matters most isn't there at all. I don't mean the solutions to problems, I mean the problems themselves. You're looking, as you begin, for what's going to resist you. You're looking for trouble. Sometimes in the beginning uncertainty arises not because the writing is difficult, but because it isn't difficult enough. Fluency can be a sign that nothing is happening; fluency can actually be my signal to stop, while being in the dark from sentence to sentence is what convinces me to go on.

INTERVIEWER: Must you have a beginning? Would you ever begin with an ending?

ROTH: For all I know *I am* beginning with the ending. My page one can wind up a year later as page two hundred, if it's still even around.

INTERVIEWER: What happens to those hundred or so pages that you have left over? Do you save them up?

ROTH: I generally prefer never to see them again.

INTERVIEWER: Do you work best at any particular time of the day?

ROTH: I work all day, morning and afternoon, just about every day. If I sit there like that for two or three years, at the end I have a book.

INTERVIEWER: Do you think other writers work such long hours?

ROTH: I don't ask writers about their work habits. I really don't care. Joyce Carol Oates says somewhere that when writers ask each other what time they start working and when they finish and how much time they take for lunch, they're actually trying to find out "Is he as crazy as I am?" I don't need that question answered.

INTERVIEWER: Does your reading affect what you write?

ROTH: I read all the time when I'm working, usually at night. It's a way of keeping the circuits open. It's a way of thinking about my *line* of work while getting a little rest from the work at hand. It helps inasmuch as it fuels the overall obsession.

INTERVIEWER: Do you show your work-in-progress to anyone?

ROTH: It's more useful for my mistakes to ripen and burst in their own good time. I give myself all the opposition I need while I'm writing, and praise is meaningless to me when I know something isn't even half finished. Nobody sees what I'm doing until I absolutely can't go any further and might even like to believe that I'm done.

INTERVIEWER: Do you have a Roth reader in mind when you write?

ROTH: No. I occasionally have an anti-Roth reader in mind. I think, "How he is going to hate this!" That can be just the encouragement I need.

INTERVIEWER: You spoke of the last phase of writing a novel being a "crisis" in which *you* turn against the material and hate the work. Is there always this crisis, with every book?

ROTH: Always. Months of looking at the manuscript and saying, "This is wrong—but what's wrong?" I ask myself, "If this book were a dream, it would be a dream of what?" But when I'm asking this I'm also trying to *believe* in what I've written, to forget that it's writing and to say, "This *has* taken place," even if it hasn't. The idea is to perceive your invention as a reality that can be understood as a dream. The idea is to turn flesh and blood into literary characters and literary characters into flesh and blood.

INTERVIEWER: Can you say more about these crises?

ROTH: In *The Ghost Writer* the crisis—one among many—had to do with Zuckerman, Amy Bellette, and Anne Frank. It wasn't easy to see that Amy Bellette *as* Anne Frank was Zuckerman's own creation. Only by working through numerous alternatives did I decide that not only was she his creation, but that she might possibly be her own creation too, a young woman inventing herself *within* Zuckerman's invention. To enrich his fantasy without obfuscation or muddle, to be ambiguous *and* clear—well, that was my writing problem through one whole summer and fall. In *Zuckerman Unbound* the crisis was a result of failing to see that Zuckerman's father shouldn't already be dead when the book begins. I eventually realized that the death should come at the conclusion of the book, allegedly as a consequence of the son's blasphemous best-seller. But, starting off, I'd got the thing back to front, and then I stared at it dumbly for months, seeing nothing. I knew that I wanted the book to veer away from Alvin Pepler—I like to be steamrolling along in one direction and then to spring my surprise—but I couldn't give up the premise of my earliest drafts until I saw that the novel's obsessive concern with assassinations, death threats, funerals, and funeral homes, was leading up to, rather than away from, the death of Zuckerman's father. How you juxtapose the events can tie you up in knots and rearranging the sequence can free you suddenly to streak for the finish line. In *The Anatomy Lesson* the discovery I made—having banged the typewriter with my head far too long—was that Zuckerman, in the moment that he takes flight for Chicago to try to become a doctor, should begin to impersonate a pornographer. There had to be willed extremism at either end of the moral spectrum, each of his escape-dreams of self-transformation subverting the meaning and mocking the intention of the other. If he had gone off solely to become a doctor, driven only by that high moral ardor, or, if he had just gone around impersonating a pornographer, spewing only that anarchic and alienating rage, he wouldn't have been my man. He has two dominant modes: his mode of self-abnegation, and his fuck-'em mode. You want a bad Jewish boy, that's what you're going to get. He rests from one by taking up the other; though, as we see, it's not much of a rest. The thing about Zuckerman that interests me is that everybody's split, but few so openly as this. Everybody is full of cracks and fissures, but usually we see people trying very hard to hide the places where they're split. Most people desperately want to heal their lesions, and keep trying to. Hiding them is sometimes taken for healing them (or for not having them). But Zuckerman can't successfully do either, and by the end of the trilogy has proved it even to himself. What's determined his life and his work are the lines of fracture in what is by no means a clean break. I was interested in following those lines.

INTERVIEWER: What happens to Philip Roth when he turns into Nathan Zuckerman?

ROTH: Nathan Zuckerman is an act. It's all the art of impersonation, isn't it? That's the fundamental novelistic gift. Zuckerman is a writer who wants to be a doctor impersonating a pornographer. I am a writer writing a book impersonating a writer who wants to be a doctor impersonating a pornographer —who then, to compound the impersonation, to barb the edge, pretends he's a well-known literary critic. Making fake biography, false history, concocting a half-imaginary existence out of the actual drama of my life *is* my life. There has to be some pleasure in this job, and that's it. To go around in disguise. To act a character. To pass oneself off as what one is not. To *pretend.* The sly and cunning masquerade. Think of the ventriloquist. He speaks so that his voice appears to proceed from someone at a distance from himself. But if he weren't in your line of vision you'd get no pleasure from his art at all. His art consists of being present *and* absent; he's most himself by simultaneously being someone else, neither of whom he "is" once the curtain is down. You don't necessarily, as a writer, have to abandon your biography completely to engage in an act of impersonation. It may be more intriguing when you don't. You distort it, caricature it, parody it, you torture and subvert it, you exploit it—all to give the biography that dimension that will excite your verbal life. Millions of people do this all the time, of course, and not with the justification of making literature. They *mean* it. It's amazing what lies people can sustain behind the mask of their real faces. Think of the art of the adulterer: under tremendous pressure and against enormous odds, ordinary husbands and wives, who would freeze with self-consciousness up on a stage, yet in the theater of the home, alone before the audience of the betrayed spouse, they act out roles of innocence and fidelity with flawless dramatic skill. Great, great performances, conceived with genius down to the smallest particulars, impeccably meticulous naturalistic acting, and all done by rank amateurs. People beautifully pretending to be "themselves." Make-believe can take the subtlest forms, you know. Why should a novelist, a pretender by profession, be any less deft or more reliable than a stolid, unimaginative suburban accountant cheating on his wife? Jack Benny used to pretend to be a miser, remember? Called himself by his own good name and claimed that he was stingy and mean. It excited his comic imagination to do this. He probably wasn't all that funny as just another nice fellow writing checks to the UJA and taking his friends out to dinner. Céline pretended to be a rather indifferent, even irresponsible physician, when he seems in fact to have worked hard at his practice and to have been conscientious about his patients. But that wasn't interesting.

INTERVIEWER: But it is. Being a good doctor is interesting.

ROTH: For William Carlos Williams maybe, but not for Céline. Being a devoted husband, an intelligent father, and a dedicated family physician in Rutherford, New Jersey, might have seemed as admirable to Céline as it does to you, or to me for that matter, but *his* writing drew its vigor from the demotic voice and the dramatization of his outlaw side (which was considerable), and so he created the Céline of the great novels in somewhat the way Jack Benny, also flirting with the taboo, created himself as a miser. You have to be awfully naive not to understand that a writer is a performer who puts on the act he does best—not least when he dons the mask of the first person singular. That may be the best mask of all for a second self. Some (many) pretend to be more lovable than they are and some pretend to be less. Beside the point. Literature isn't a moral beauty contest. Its power arises from the authority and audacity with which the impersonation is pulled off; the belief it inspires is what counts. The question to ask about the writer isn't "Why does he behave so badly?" but "What does he gain by wearing this mask?" I don't admire the Genet that Genet presents as himself any more than I admire the unsavory Molloy impersonated by Beckett. I admire Genet because he writes books that won't let me forget who that Genet is. When Rebecca West was writing about Augustine, she said that his *Confessions* was too subjectively true to be objectively true. I think this is so in the first-person novels of Genet and Céline, as it is in Colette, books like *The Shackle* and *The Vagabond*.

Gombrowicz has a novel called *Pornographia* in which he introduces himself as a character, using his own name—the better to implicate himself in certain highly dubious proceedings and bring the moral terror to life. Konwicki, another Pole, in his last two novels, *The Polish Complex* and *A Minor Apocalypse*, works to close the gap between the reader and the narrative by introducing "Konwicki" as the central character. He strengthens the illusion that the novel is true—and not to be discounted as "fiction"—by impersonating himself. It all goes back to Jack Benny. Need I add, however, that it's hardly a disinterested undertaking? Writing for me isn't a natural thing that I just keep doing, the way fish swim and birds fly. It's something that's done under a certain kind of provocation, a particular urgency. It's the transformation, through an elaborate impersonation, of a personal emergency into a public act (in both senses of that word). It can be a very trying spiritual exercise to siphon through your being qualities that are alien to your moral makeup—as trying for the writer as for the reader. You can wind up feeling more like a sword-swallower than a ventriloquist or impersonator. You sometimes use yourself very harshly in order to reach what is, literally speaking, beyond you. The impersonator can't afford to indulge the ordinary human instincts which direct people in what they want to present and what they want to hide.

INTERVIEWER: If the novelist is an impersonator, then what about the autobiography? What is the relationship, for example, between the deaths of the parents, which are so important in the last two Zuckerman novels, and the death of your own parents?

ROTH: Why not ask about the relationship between the death of my parents and the death of Gabe Wallach's mother, the germinating incident in my 1962 novel, *Letting Go?* Or ask about the death and funeral of the father, which is at the heart of "The Day It Snowed," my first published story in the *Chicago Review* in 1955? Or ask about the death of Kepesh's mother, wife of the owner of a Catskills hotel, which is the turning point in *The Professor of Desire?* The terrible blow of the death of a parent is something I began writing about long before any parent of mine had died. Novelists are frequently as interested in what hasn't happened to them as in what has. What may be taken by the innocent for naked autobiography is, as I've been suggesting, more than likely mock-autobiography or hypothetical autobiography or autobiography grandiosely enlarged. We know about the people who walk into the police station and confess to crimes they haven't committed. Well, the false confession appeals to writers, too. Novelists are even interested in what happens to other people and, like liars and con men everywhere, will pretend that something dramatic or awful or hair-raising or splendid that happened to someone else actually happened to them. The physical particulars and moral circumstances of Zuckerman's mother's death have practically nothing to do with the death of my own mother. The death of the mother of one of my dearest friends —whose account of her suffering stuck in my mind long after he'd told me about it—furnished the most telling details for the mother's death in *The Anatomy Lesson.* The black cleaning woman who commiserates with Zuckerman in Miami Beach about his mother's death is modeled on the housekeeper of old friends in Philadelphia, a woman I haven't seen for ten years and who never laid eyes on anybody in my family but me. I was always entranced by her tangy style of speech, and when the right moment came, I used it. But the words in her mouth I invented. Olivia, the eighty-three-year-old black Florida cleaning woman, *c'est moi.*

As you well know, the intriguing biographical issue—and critical issue, for that matter—isn't that a writer will write about some of what has happened to him, but *how* he writes about it, which, when understood properly, takes us a long way to understanding *why* he writes about it. A more intriguing question is why and how he writes about what hasn't happened

—how he feeds what's hypothetical or imagined into what's inspired and controlled by recollection, and how what's recollected spawns the overall fantasy. I suggest, by the way, that the best person to ask about the autobiographical relevance of the climactic death of the father in *Zuckerman Unbound* is my own father, who lives in Elizabeth, New Jersey. I'll give you his phone number.

INTERVIEWER: Then what is the relationship between your experience of psychoanalysis and the use of psychoanalysis as a literary stratagem?

ROTH: If I hadn't been analyzed I wouldn't have written *Portnoy's Complaint* as I wrote it, or *My Life as a Man* as I wrote it, nor would *The Breast* resemble itself. Nor would I resemble myself. The experience of psychoanalysis was probably more useful to me as a writer than as a neurotic, although there may be a false distinction there. It's an experience that I shared with tens of thousands of baffled people, and anything that powerful in the private domain that joins a writer to his generation, to his class, to his moment, is tremendously important for him, providing that afterwards he can separate himself enough to examine the experience objectively, imaginatively, in the writing clinic. You have to be able to become your doctor's doctor, even if only to write about patienthood, which was, certainly in part, a subject in *My Life as a Man*. Why patienthood interested me—and as far back as *Letting Go*, written four or five years before my own analysis—was because so many enlightened contemporaries had come to accept the view of themselves as patients, and the ideas of psychic disease, cure, and recovery. You're asking me about the relationship between art and life? It's like the relationship between the eight hundred or so hours that it took to be psychoanalyzed, and the eight or so hours that it would take to read *Portnoy's Complaint* aloud. Life is long and art is shorter.

INTERVIEWER: Can you talk about your marriage?

ROTH: It took place so long ago that I no longer trust my

memory of it. The problem is complicated further by *My Life as a Man*, which diverges so dramatically in so many places from its origin in my own nasty situation that I'm hard put, some twenty-five years later, to sort out the invention of 1974 from the facts of 1959. You might as well ask the author of *The Naked and the Dead* what happened to him in the Philippines. I can only tell you that that was my time as an infantryman, and that *My Life as a Man* is the war novel I wrote some years after failing to receive the Distinguished Service Cross.

INTERVIEWER: Do you have painful feelings on looking back?

ROTH: Looking back I see these as fascinating years—as people of fifty often do contemplating the youthful adventure for which they paid with a decade of their lives a comfortingly long time ago. I was more aggressive then than I am today, some people were even said to be intimidated by me, but I was an easy target, all the same. We're easy targets at twenty-five, if only someone discovers the enormous bull's-eye.

INTERVIEWER: And where was it?

ROTH: Oh, where it can usually be found in self-confessed budding literary geniuses. My idealism. My romanticism. My passion to capitalize the L in life. I wanted something difficult and dangerous to happen to me. I wanted a hard time. Well, I got it. I'd come from a small, safe, relatively happy provincial background—my Newark neighborhood in the thirties and forties was just a Jewish Terre Haute—and I'd absorbed, along with the ambition and drive, the fears and phobias of my generation of American Jewish children. In my early twenties, I wanted to prove to myself that I wasn't afraid of all those things. It wasn't a mistake to want to prove that, even though, after the ball was over, I was virtually unable to write for three or four years. From 1962 to 1967 is the longest I've gone, since becoming a writer, without publishing a book. Alimony and recurrent court costs had bled me of every penny I could earn by teaching and writing, and, hardly into my thirties, I was thousands of dollars in debt to my friend and editor, Joe Fox.

The loan was to help pay for my analysis, which I needed primarily to prevent me from going out and committing murder because of the alimony and court costs incurred for having served two years in a childless marriage. The image that teased me during those years was of a train that had been shunted onto the wrong track. In my early twenties, I had been zipping right along there, you know—on schedule, express stops only, final destination clearly in mind; and then suddenly I was on the wrong track, speeding off into the wilds. I'd ask myself, "How the hell do you get this thing back on the right track?" Well, you can't. I've continued to be surprised, over the years, whenever I discover myself, late at night, pulling into the wrong station.

INTERVIEWER: But not getting back on the same track was a great thing for you, presumably.

ROTH: John Berryman said that for a writer any ordeal that doesn't kill him is terrific. The fact that his ordeal did finally kill him doesn't make what he was saying wrong.

INTERVIEWER: What do you feel about feminism, particularly the feminist attack on you?

ROTH: What is it?

INTERVIEWER: The force of the attack would be, in part, that the female characters are unsympathetically treated, for instance that Lucy Nelson in *When She Was Good* is hostilely presented.

ROTH: Don't elevate that by calling it a "feminist" attack. That's just stupid reading. Lucy Nelson is a furious adolescent who wants a decent life. She is presented as better than her world and conscious of being better. She is confronted and opposed by men who typify deeply irritating types to many women. She is the protector of a passive, defenseless mother whose vulnerability drives her crazy. She happens to be raging against aspects of middle-class American life that the new militant feminism was to identify as the enemy only a few years after Lucy's appearance in print—hers might even be thought of as a case of premature feminist rage. *When She Was Good* deals with Lucy's struggle to free herself from the terrible disappointment engendered in a daughter by an irresponsible father. It deals with her hatred of the father he was and her yearning for the father he couldn't be. It would be sheer idiocy, particularly if this *were* a feminist attack, to contend that such powerful feelings of loss and contempt and shame do not exist in the daughters of drunks, cowards, and criminals. There is also the helpless Mama's boy Lucy marries, and her hatred of his incompetence and professional innocence. Is there no such thing in the world as marital hatred? That will come as news to all the rich divorce lawyers, not to mention to Thomas Hardy and Gustave Flaubert. By the way, is Lucy's father treated "hostilely" because he's a drunk and a petty thief who ends up in jail? Is Lucy's husband treated "hostilely" because he happens to be a big baby? Is the uncle who tries to destroy Lucy "hostilely" treated because he's a brute? This is a novel about a wounded daughter who has more than sufficient cause to be enraged with the men in her life. She is only 'hostilely" presented if it's an act of hostility to recognize that young women can be wounded and young women can be enraged. I'd bet there are even some enraged and wounded women who are feminists. You know, the dirty little secret is no longer sex; the dirty little secret is hatred and rage. It's the tirade that's taboo. Odd that this should be so a hundred years after Dostoyevsky (and fifty after Freud), but nobody nice likes to be identified with the stuff. It's the way folks used to feel about fellatio in the good old days. "Me? Never heard of it. Disgusting." But is it "hostile," really, to take a look at the ferocity of the emotion they call "hostility"? *When She Was Good* is not serving the cause—that's true. The anger of this young woman isn't presented to be endorsed with a hearty "Right on!" that will move the populace to action. The nature of the anger is examined, as is the depth of the wound. So are the consequences of the anger, for Lucy as for everyone. I hate to have to be the one to say it, but the portrait isn't without its poignancy. I don't mean by poignancy what the compassionate book reviewers call "compassion." I mean you see the suffering that real rage is.

INTERVIEWER: But supposing I say to you that nearly all the women in the books are there to obstruct, or to help, or to console the male characters. There's the woman who cooks and consoles and is sane and calming, or the other kind of woman, the dangerous maniac, the obstructor. They occur as means of helping or obstructing Kepesh or Zuckerman or Tarnopol. And that could be seen as a limited view of women.

ROTH: Let's face it, some women who are sane also happen to know how to cook. So do some of the dangerous maniacs. Let's leave out the sin of cooking. A great book on the order of *Oblomov* could be written about a man allying himself with woman after woman who gorges him with marvelous meals, but I haven't written it. If your description of the "sane," "calm," and "consoling" woman applies to anyone, it's to Claire Ovington in *The Professor of Desire*, with whom Kepesh establishes a tender liaison some years after the breakup of his marriage. Now, I'd have no objection to your writing a novel about this relationship from the point of view of Claire Ovington—I'd be intrigued to see how she saw it—so why do you take a slightly critical tone about my writing the novel from the point of view of David Kepesh?

INTERVIEWER: There's nothing wrong with the novel's being written from David Kepesh's point of view. What might cause difficulties for some readers is that Claire, and the other women in the novel, are there to help or hinder him.

ROTH: I'm not pretending to give you anything other than his sense of his life with this young woman. My book doesn't stand or fall on the fact that Claire Ovington is calm and sane, but on whether I am able to depict what calmness and sanity are like, and what it is to have a mate—and why it is one would want a mate—who possesses those and other vir-

tues in abundance. She is also vulnerable to jealousy when
Kepesh's ex-wife turns up uninvited, and she carries with her
a certain sadness about her family background. She isn't
there "as a means" of helping Kepesh. She *helps* him—and
he helps her. *They are in love.* She is there because Kepesh
has fallen in love with a sane and calm and consoling woman
after having been unhappily married to a difficult and exciting woman he was unable to handle. Don't people do that?
Someone more doctrinaire than you might tell me that the
state of being in love, particularly of being passionately in
love, is no basis for establishing permanent relationships between men and women. But, alas, people, even people of intelligence and experience, *will* do it—have done it and seem
intent on going on doing it—and I am not interested in writing about what people *should* do for the good of the human
race and pretending that's what they *do* do, but writing
about what they do indeed do, lacking the programmatic effi-
ciency of the infallible theorists. The irony of Kepesh's situation is that having found the calm and consoling woman he
can live with, a woman of *numerous* qualities, he then finds
his desire for her perversely seeping away, and realizes that
unless this involuntary diminution of passion can be arrested,
he'll become alienated from the best thing in his life. Doesn't
that happen either? From what I hear this damn seeping
away of desire happens all the time and is extremely distress-
ing to the people involved. Look, I didn't invent the loss of
desire, and I didn't invent the lure of passion, and I didn't
invent sane companions, and I didn't invent maniacs. I'm
sorry if my men don't have the correct feelings about women,
or the universal range of feelings about women, or the feelings about women that it will be okay for men to have in
1995, but I do insist that there is some morsel of truth in my
depiction of what it might be like for a man to be a Kepesh,
or a Portnoy, or a breast.

INTERVIEWER: Why have you never reused the character of

Portnoy in another book, the way that you have used Kepesh and Zuckerman?

ROTH: But I did use Portnoy in another book. *Our Gang* and *The Great American Novel* are Portnoy in another book. Portnoy wasn't a character for me, he was an explosion, and I wasn't finished exploding after *Portnoy's Complaint*. The first thing I wrote after *Portnoy's Complaint* was a long story that appeared in Ted Solotaroff's *American Review* called "On the Air." John Updike was here a while ago and while we were all having dinner one night, he said, "How come you've never reprinted that story?" I said, "It's too disgusting." John laughed. He said, "It is, it's a truly disgusting story." And I said, "I didn't know what I was thinking about when I wrote it." And that is true to some degree—I didn't want to know; the idea was *not* to know. But I also did know. I looked in the arsenal and found another dynamite stick, and I thought, "Light the fuse and see what happens." I was trying to blow up more of myself. This phenomenon is known to students of literary survey courses as the writer changing his style. I was blowing up a lot of old loyalties and inhibitions, literary as well as personal. I think this may be why so many Jews were incensed by *Portnoy's Complaint*. It wasn't that they'd never heard about kids masturbating before, or about Jewish family fighting. It was, rather, that if they couldn't even control someone like me anymore, with all my respectable affiliations and credentials, all my Seriousness of Purpose, something had gone wrong. After all, I wasn't Abbie Hoffman or Lenny Bruce, I was a university teacher who had published in *Commentary*. But at the time it seemed to me that the next thing to be serious about was not being so God damn serious. As Zuckerman reminds Appel, "Seriousness can be as stupid as anything else."

INTERVIEWER: Weren't you also looking for a fight, writing *Portnoy's Complaint?*

ROTH: I'd found a fight without looking for it long before

that. They'd never really got off my ass for publishing *Goodbye, Columbus,* which was considered in some circles to be my *Mein Kampf.* Unlike Alexander Portnoy, my education in petit bourgeois morality didn't come at home, but after I'd left home and begun to publish my first short stories. My own household environment as a youngster was much closer to Zuckerman's than to Portnoy's. It had its constraints, but there was nothing resembling the censorious small-mindedness and shame-ridden xenophobia that I ran into from the official Jews who wanted me to shut up. The moral atmosphere of the Portnoy household, in its repressive aspects, owes a lot to the response of persistent voices within the official Jewish community to my debut. They did much to help make it seem auspicious.

INTERVIEWER: You've been talking about the opposition to *Portnoy's Complaint.* What about the recognition—how did its enormous success affect you?

ROTH: It was too big, on a larger and much crazier scale than I could begin to deal with, so I took off. A few weeks after publication, I boarded a bus at the Port Authority terminal for Saratoga Springs, and holed up at Yaddo, the writers' colony, for three months. Precisely what Zuckerman should have done after *Carnovsky*—but he hung around, the fool, and look what happened to him. He would have enjoyed Yaddo more than he enjoyed Alvin Pepler. But it made *Zuckerman Unbound* funnier keeping him in Manhattan, and it made my own life easier, not being there.

INTERVIEWER: Do you dislike New York?

ROTH: I lived there from 1962 until I moved to the country after *Portnoy's Complaint,* and I wouldn't trade those years for anything. New York *gave* me *Portnoy's Complaint* in a way. When I was living and teaching in Iowa City and Princeton, I didn't ever feel so free as I did in New York, in the sixties, to indulge myself in comic performance, on paper and with friends. There were raucous evenings with my New York

friends, there was uncensored shamelessness in my psy-
choanalytic sessions, there was the dramatic, stagy atmosphere
of the city itself in the years after Kennedy's assassination—all
this inspired me to try out a new voice, a fourth voice, a less
page-bound voice than the voice of *Goodbye, Columbus,* or of
Letting Go, or of *When She Was Good.* So did the opposition
to the war in Vietnam. There's always something behind a
book to which it has no seeming connection, something invisible to the reader which has helped to release the writer's initial
impulse. I'm thinking about the rage and rebelliousness that
were in the air, the vivid examples I saw around me of angry
defiance and hysterical opposition. This gave me a few ideas for
my act.

INTERVIEWER: Did you feel you were part of what was going
on in the sixties?

ROTH: I felt the power of the life around me. I believed
myself to be feeling the full consciousness of a place—this time
New York—for the first time really since childhood. I was also,
like others, receiving a stunning education in moral, political,
and cultural possibilities from the country's eventful public life
and from what was happening in Vietnam.

INTERVIEWER: But you published a famous essay in *Commentary* in 1960 called "Writing American Fiction" about the
way that intellectuals or thinking people in America felt that
they were living in a foreign country, a country in whose
communal life they were *not* involved.

ROTH: Well, that's the difference between 1960 and 1968.
(Being published in *Commentary* is another difference.) Alienated in America, a stranger to its pleasures and preoccupations
—that was how many young people like me saw their situation
in the fifties. It was a perfectly honorable stance, I think,
shaped by our literary aspirations and modernist enthusiasms,
the high-minded of the second post-immigrant generation
coming into conflict with the first great eruption of postwar
media garbage. Little did we know that some twenty years later

the philistine ignorance on which we would have liked to turn our backs would infect the country like Camus's plague. Any satirist writing a futuristic novel who had imagined a President Reagan during the Eisenhower years would have been accused of perpetrating a piece of crude, contemptible, adolescent, anti-American wickedness, when, in fact, he would have succeeded, as prophetic sentry, just where Orwell failed; he would have seen that the grotesquerie to be visited upon the English-speaking world would not be an extension of the repressive Eastern totalitarian nightmare but a proliferation of the Western farce of media stupidity and cynical commercialism— American-style philistinism run amok. It wasn't Big Brother who'd be watching us from the screen, but we who'd be watching a terrifyingly powerful world leader with the soul of an amiable, soap opera grandmother, the values of a civic-minded Beverly Hills Cadillac dealer, and the historical background and intellectual equipment of a high school senior in a June Allyson musical.

INTERVIEWER: What happened to you later, in the seventies? Did what was happening in the country continue to mean much to someone like you?

ROTH: I have to remember what book I was writing and then I can remember what happened to me—though what was happening to me was largely the book I was writing. Nixon came and went in '73, and while Nixon was coming and going I was being driven quite crazy by *My Life as a Man.* In a way I had been writing that book on and off since 1964. I kept looking for a setting for the sordid scene in which Maureen buys a urine specimen from a poor pregnant black woman in order to get Tarnopol to think he's impregnated her. I thought of it first as a scene for *When She Was Good,* but it was all wrong for Lucy and Roy in Liberty Center. Then I thought it might go into *Portnoy's Complaint,* but it was too malevolent for that kind of comedy. Then I wrote cartons and cartons of drafts of what eventually turned out to be *My Life as a Man*

—eventually, after I finally realized that my solution lay in the very problem I couldn't overcome: my inability to find the setting appropriate to the sordid event, rather than the sordid event itself, was really at the heart of the novel. Watergate made life interesting when I wasn't writing, but from nine to five every day I didn't think too much about Nixon or about Vietnam. I was trying to solve the problem of this book. When it seemed I never would, I stopped and wrote *Our Gang;* when I tried again and still couldn't write it, I stopped and wrote the baseball book; then while finishing the baseball book, I stopped to write *The Breast.* It was as though I were blasting my way through a tunnel to reach the novel that I couldn't write. Each of one's books *is* a blast, clearing the way for what's next. It's all one book you write anyway. At night you dream six dreams. But *are* they six dreams? One dream prefigures or anticipates the next, or somehow concludes what hasn't yet even been fully dreamed. Then comes the next dream, the corrective of the dream before—the alternative dream, the antidote dream— enlarging upon it, or laughing at it, or contradicting it, or trying just to get the dream dreamed *right.* You can go on trying all night long.

INTERVIEWER: After *Portnoy,* after leaving New York, you moved to the country. What about rural life? Obviously it was used as material in *The Ghost Writer.*

ROTH: I might never have become interested in writing about a reclusive writer if I hadn't first had my own small taste of E. I. Lonoff's thirty-five years of rural splendor. I need something solid under my feet to kick off my imagination. But aside from giving me a sense of the Lonoffs' lives, the country existence hasn't offered anything as yet in the way of subject. Probably it never will and I should get the hell out. Only I happen to love living there, and I can't make *every* choice conform to the needs of my work.

INTERVIEWER: What about England, where you spend part of each year? Is that a possible source of fiction?

ROTH: Ask me twenty years from now. That's about how long it took Isaac Singer to get enough of Poland out of his system —and to let enough of America in—to begin, little by little, as a writer, to see and depict his upper Broadway cafeterias. If you don't know the fantasy life of a country, it's hard to write fiction about it that isn't just description of the decor, human and otherwise. Little things trickle through when I see the country dreaming out loud—in the theater, at an election, during the Falklands crisis, but I know nothing really about what means what to people here. It's very hard for me to understand who people are, even when they tell me, and I don't even know if that's *because* of who they are or because of me. I don't know who is impersonating what, if I'm necessarily seeing the real thing or just a fabrication, nor can I easily see where the two overlap. My perceptions are clouded by the fact that I speak the language. I believe I know what's being said, you see, even if I don't. Worst of all, I don't hate anything here. What a relief it is to have no culture-grievances, not to have to hear the sound of one's voice taking positions and having opinions and recounting all that's wrong! What bliss— but for the writing that's no asset. Nothing drives me crazy here, and a writer *has* to be driven crazy to help him to *see.* A writer needs his poisons. The antidote to his poisons is often a book. Now if I *had* to live here, if for some reason I were forbidden ever to return to America, if my position and my personal well-being were suddenly to become permanently bound up with England, well, what was maddening and meaningful might begin to come into focus, and yes, in about the year 2005, maybe 2010, little by little I'd stop writing about Newark and I would dare to set a story at a table in a wine bar on Kensington Park Road. A story about an elderly exiled foreign writer, in this instance reading not the *Jewish Daily Forward,* but the *Herald Tribune.*

INTERVIEWER: In these last three books, the Zuckerman novels, there has been a reiteration of the struggle with Jewishness and Jewish criticism. Why do you think these books go over the past as much as they do? Why is that happening now?

ROTH: In the early seventies, I began to be a regular visitor to Czechoslovakia. I went to Prague every spring and took a little crash course in political repression. I'd only known repression firsthand in somewhat more benign and covert forms—as psychosexual constraint or as social restriction. I knew less about anti-Semitic repression from personal experience than I did about the repressions Jews practiced upon themselves, and upon one another, as a consequence of the history of anti-Semitism. Portnoy, you remember, considers himself just such a practicing Jew. Anyway, I became highly attuned to the differences between the writer's life in totalitarian Prague and in freewheeling New York, and I decided, after some initial uncertainty, to focus on the unreckoned consequences of a life in art in the world that I knew best. I realized that there were already many wonderful and famous stories and novels by Henry James and Thomas Mann and James Joyce about the life of the artist, but none I knew of about the comedy that an artistic vocation can turn out to be in the U.S.A. When Thomas Wolfe tackled the subject he was rather rhapsodic. Zuckerman's struggle with Jewishness and Jewish criticism is seen in the context of his comical career as an American writer, ousted by his family, alienated from his fans, and finally at odds with his own nerve endings. The Jewish quality of books like mine doesn't really reside in their subject matter. Talking about Jewishness hardly interests me at all. It's a kind of sensibility that makes, say, *The Anatomy Lesson* Jewish, if anything does: the nervousness, the excitability, the arguing, the dramatizing, the indignation, the obsessiveness, the touchiness, the playacting—above all the *talking.* The talking and the shouting. Jews will go on, you know. It isn't what it's talking *about* that makes a book Jewish—it's that the book won't shut up. The book won't leave you alone. Won't let up. Gets too close. "Listen, listen—that's only the half of it!" I knew what I was doing when I broke Zuckerman's jaw. For a Jew a broken jaw is a terrible tragedy. It was to avoid this that so many of us went into teaching rather than prizefighting.

INTERVIEWER: Why is Milton Appel, the good, high-minded Jew who was a guru for Zuckerman in his early years, a punching-bag in *The Anatomy Lesson*, someone that Zuckerman wants to desanctify?

ROTH: If I were not myself, if someone else had been assigned the role of being Roth and writing his books, I might very well, in this other incarnation, have been his Milton Appel.

INTERVIEWER: Is Zuckerman's rage at Milton Appel the expression of a kind of guilt on your part?

ROTH: Guilt? Not at all. As a matter of fact, in an earlier draft of the book, Zuckerman and his young girlfriend Diana took exactly opposite positions in their argument about Appel. She, with all her feisty inexperience, said to Zuckerman, "Why do you let him push you around, why do you take this shit sitting down?" and Zuckerman, the older man, said to her, "Don't be ridiculous, dear, calm down, he doesn't matter." There was the real autobiographical scene, and it had no life at all. I had to absorb the rage into the main character even if my own rage on this topic had long since subsided. By being true to life I was actually ducking the issue. So I reversed their positions, and had the twenty-year-old college girl telling Zuckerman to grow up, and gave Zuckerman the tantrum. Much more fun. I wasn't going to get anywhere with a Zuckerman as eminently reasonable as myself.

INTERVIEWER: So your hero always has to be enraged or in trouble or complaining.

ROTH: My hero has to be in a state of vivid transformation or radical displacement. "I am not what I am—I am, if anything, what I am not." The litany begins something like that.

INTERVIEWER: How conscious are you as you are writing of

whether you are moving from a third- to a first-person narrative?

ROTH: It's not conscious or unconscious—the movement is spontaneous.

INTERVIEWER: But how does it feel, to be writing in the third person as opposed to the first person?

ROTH: How does it feel looking through a microscope, when you adjust the focus? Everything depends upon how close you want to bring the naked object to the naked eye. And vice versa. Depends on what you want to magnify, and to what power.

INTERVIEWER: But do you free yourself in certain ways by putting Zuckerman in the third person?

ROTH: I free myself to say about Zuckerman what it would be inappropriate for him to say about himself in quite the same way. The irony would be lost in the first person, or the comedy; I can introduce a note of gravity that might be jarring coming from him. The shifting within a single narrative from the one voice to the other is how a reader's moral perspective is determined. It's something like this that we all want to do in ordinary conversation when we employ the indefinite pronoun "one" in speaking of ourselves. Using "one" places your observation in a looser relationship to the self that's uttering it. Look, sometimes it's more telling to let him speak for himself, sometimes it's more telling to speak about him; sometimes it's more telling to narrate obliquely, sometimes not. *The Ghost Writer* is narrated in the first person, probably because what's being described is largely a world Zuckerman's discovered outside of himself, the book of a young explorer. The older and more scarred he gets, the more *inward*-looking he gets, the further out *I* have to get. The crisis of solipsism he suffers in *The Anatomy Lesson* is better seen from a bit of a distance.

INTERVIEWER: Do you direct yourself as you are writing to make distinctions between what is spoken and what is narrative?

ROTH: I don't "direct" myself. I respond to what seem the

liveliest possibilities. There's no necessary balance to be achieved between what is spoken and what is narrated. You go with what's alive. Two thousand pages of narrative and six lines of dialogue may be just the ticket for one writer, and two thousand pages of dialogue and six lines of narrative the solution for another.

INTERVIEWER: Do you ever take long chunks that have been dialogue and make them into narrative, or the other way around?

ROTH: Sure. I did that with the Anne Frank section of *The Ghost Writer*. I had trouble getting that right. When I began, in the third person, I was somehow *revering* the material. I was taking a high elegiac tone in telling the story of Anne Frank surviving and coming to America. I didn't know where I was going so I began by doing what you're supposed to do when writing the life of a saint. It was the tone appropriate to hagiography. Instead of Anne Frank gaining new meaning within the context of my story, I was trying to draw from the ready store of stock emotions that everybody is supposed to have about her. It's what even good actors sometimes will do during the first weeks of rehearsing a play—gravitate to the conventional form of presentation, cling to the cliché while anxiously waiting for something authentic to take hold. In retrospect, my difficulties look somewhat bizarre, because just what Zuckerman was fighting against, I was in fact succumbing to—the officially authorized and most consoling legend. I tell you, no one who later complained that in *The Ghost Writer* I had abused the memory of Anne Frank would have batted an eye had I let those banalities out into the world. That would have been just fine; I might even have got a citation. But I couldn't have given myself any prizes for it. The difficulties of telling a Jewish story—How should it be told? In what tone? To whom should it be told? To what end? Should it be told at all?—was finally to become *The Ghost Writer*'s theme. But before it became a theme, it apparently had to be an ordeal.

It often happens, at least with me, that the struggles that generate a book's moral life are naively enacted upon the body of the book during the early, uncertain stages of writing. That *is* the ordeal, and it ended when I took that whole section and recast it in the first person—Anne Frank's story told by Amy Bellette. The victim wasn't herself going to talk about her plight in the voice of "The March of Time." She hadn't in the *Diary,* so why should she in life? I didn't want this section to *appear* as first-person narration, but I knew that by passing it through the first-person sieve, I stood a good chance of getting rid of this terrible tone, which wasn't hers, but mine. I did get rid of it. The impassioned cadences, the straining emotions, the somber, overdramatized, archaic diction—I cleared it all out, thanks to Amy Bellette. Rather straightforwardly, I then cast the section *back* into the third person, and then I was able to get to work on it—to write rather than to rhapsodize or eulogize.

INTERVIEWER: How do you think you have influenced the environment, the culture, as a writer?

ROTH: Not at all. If I had followed my early college plans to become an attorney, I don't see where it would matter to the culture.

INTERVIEWER: Do you say that with bitterness or with glee?

ROTH: Neither. It's a fact of life. In an enormous commercial society that demands complete freedom of expression, the culture is a maw. Recently, the first American novelist to receive a special Congressional Gold Medal for his "contribution to the nation" was Louis L'Amour. It was presented to him at the White House by the President. The only other country in the world where such a writer would receive his government's highest award is the Soviet Union. In a totalitarian state, however, *all* culture is dictated by the regime; fortunately we in America live in Reagan's and not Plato's Republic, and aside from their stupid medal, culture is almost entirely ignored. And that is preferable by far. As long as those on top keep giving the honors to Louis L'Amour and couldn't care less about anything else, everything will be just fine. When I was first in Czechoslovakia, it occurred to me that I work in a society where as a writer everything goes and nothing matters, while for the Czech writers I met in Prague, nothing goes and everything matters. This isn't to say I wished to change places. I didn't envy them their persecution and the way in which it heightens their social importance. I didn't even envy them their seemingly more valuable and serious themes. The trivialization, in the West, of much that's deadly serious in the East is itself a subject, one requiring considerable imaginative ingenuity to transform into compelling fiction. To write a serious book that doesn't signal its seriousness with the rhetorical cues or thematic gravity that's traditionally associated with seriousness is a worthy undertaking too. To do justice to a spiritual predicament which is *not* blatantly shocking and monstrously horrible, which does *not* elicit universal compassion, or occur on a large historical stage, or on the grandest scale of twentieth-century suffering—well, that's the lot that has fallen to those who write where everything goes and nothing matters. I recently heard the critic George Steiner, on English television, denouncing contemporary Western literature as utterly worthless and without quality, and claiming that the great documents of the human soul, the masterpieces, could only arise from souls being crushed by regimes like those in Czechoslovakia. I wonder then why all the writers I know in Czechoslovakia loathe the regime and passionately wish that it would disappear from the face of the earth. Don't they understand, as Steiner does, that this is their chance to be great? Sometimes one or two writers with colossal brute strength do manage, miraculously, to survive and, taking the system as their subject, to make art of a very high order out of their persecution. But most of them who remain sealed up inside totalitarian states are, as writers, destroyed by the system. That system doesn't make masterpieces; it makes coronaries, ulcers, and asthma, it makes alcoholics, it makes depressives, it makes bitterness and desperation and insanity. The writers are intellectually disfigured, spiritually demoralized, physically sickened, and culturally bored. Frequently they are silenced completely. Ninetenths of the best of them will never do their best work just because of the system. The writers nourished by this system are the party hacks. When such a system prevails for two or three generations, relentlessly grinding away at a community of writers for twenty, thirty, or forty years, the obsessions become fixed, the language grows stale, the readership slowly dies out from starvation, and the existence of a national literature of originality, variety, vibrancy (which is very different from the brute survival of a single powerful voice) is nearly impossible. A literature that has the misfortune of remaining isolated underground for too long will inevitably become provincial, backwards, even naive, despite the fund of dark experience that may inspire it. By contrast, our work here hasn't been deprived of authenticity because as writers we haven't been stomped on by a totalitarian government. I don't know of any Western writer, aside from George Steiner, who is so grandiosely and sentimentally deluded about human suffering—and "masterpieces"— that he's come back from behind the Iron Curtain thinking himself devalued because he hasn't had to contend with such a wretched intellectual and literary environment. If the choice is between Louis L'Amour and our literary freedom and our extensive, lively, national literature on the one hand, and Solzhenitsyn and that cultural desert and crushing suppression on the other, I'll take L'Amour.

INTERVIEWER: But don't you feel powerless as a writer in America?

ROTH: Writing novels is not the road to power. I don't believe that, in my society, novels effect serious changes in anyone other than the handful of people who are writers, whose own novels are of course seriously affected by other novelists' novels. I can't see anything like that happening to the ordinary reader, nor would I expect it to.

INTERVIEWER: What do novels do then?

ROTH: To the ordinary reader? Novels provide readers with something to read. At their best writers change the *way* readers read. That seems to me the only realistic expectation. It also seems to me quite enough. Reading novels is a deep and singular pleasure, a gripping and mysterious human activity that does not require any more moral or political justification than sex.

INTERVIEWER: But are there no other after-effects?

ROTH: You asked if I thought my fiction had changed anything in the culture and the answer is no. Sure, there's been some scandal, but people are scandalized all the time; it's a way of life for them. It doesn't mean a thing. If you ask if I *want* my fiction to change anything in the culture, the answer is still no. What I want is to possess my readers while they are reading my book—if I can, to possess them in ways that other writers don't. Then let them return, just as they were, to a world where everybody else is working to change, persuade, tempt, and control them. The best readers come to fiction to be free of all that noise, to have set loose in them the consciousness that's otherwise conditioned and hemmed in by all that *isn't* fiction. This is something that every child, smitten by books, understands immediately, though it's not at all a childish idea about the importance of reading.

INTERVIEWER: Last question. How would you describe yourself? What do you think you are like, compared with those vividly transforming heroes of yours?

ROTH: I am like somebody who is trying vividly to transform himself out of himself and into his vividly transforming heroes. I am very much like somebody who spends all day writing.

HERMIONE LEE
Summer 1983–Winter 1984

13. Raymond Carver

Raymond Carver was born in Clatskanie, Oregon, on May 25, 1938, the son of a sawmill worker. He received his bachelor's degree from Humboldt State University in Arcata, California, and studied at the University of Iowa in 1963 and 1964.

A central figure in the recent revival of interest in the short-story form, Carver's collections include *Will You Please Be Quiet, Please?* (1976), *What We Talk About When We Talk About Love* (1981), and *Cathedral* (1983). He is also the author of *Fires: Essays, Poems, Stories* (1984), and, most recently, two books of poetry: *Where Water Comes Together with Other Water* (1985) and *Ultramarine* (1986). He is the recipient of many honors, including the Mildred and Harold Strauss Living Award. He has taught at the University of California at Santa Cruz and at Berkeley, the University of Iowa Writers' Workshop, and Syracuse University.

Carver lives with the writer Tess Gallagher in Port Angeles, Washington, and in Syracuse, New York.

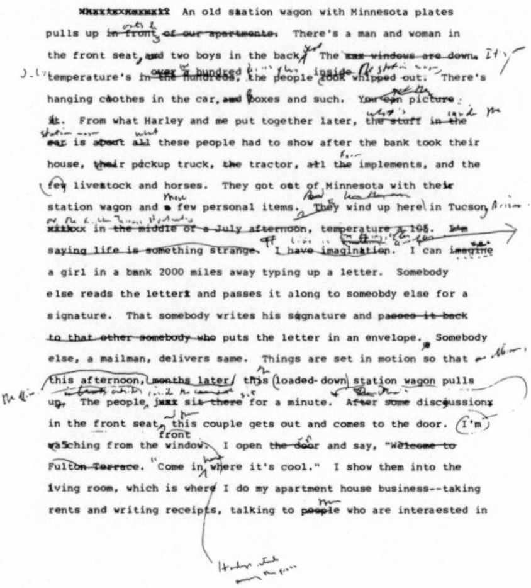

[Draft 1 — top left]

Wherexxxxxxxxx An old station wagon with Minnesota plates
pulls up in front of our apartments. There's a man and woman in
the front seat, and two boys in the back. The xxx windows are down. It's
temperature's in the hundreds, the people look whipped out. There's
hanging clothes in the car, and boxes and such. You can picture
it. From what Harley and me put together later, the stuff in the
car is about all these people had to show after the bank took their
house, their pickup truck, the tractor, all the implements, and the
few livestock and horses. They got out of Minnesota with their
station wagon and a few personal items. They wind up here in Tucson
xxxxxx in the middle of a July afternoon, temperature 105. I'm
saying life is something strange. I have imagination. I can imagine
a girl in a bank 2000 miles away typing up a letter. Somebody
else reads the letter and passes it along to somebody else for a
signature. That somebody writes his signature and passes it back
to that other somebody who puts the letter in an envelope. Somebody
else, a mailman, delivers same. Things are set in motion so that
this afternoon, months later, this (loaded-down) station wagon pulls
up. The people, just six there for a minute. After some discussion
in the front seat, this couple gets out and comes to the door. (I'm
watching from the window.) I open the door and say, "Welcome to
Fulton Terrace. "Come in, where it's cool." I show them into the
living room, which is where I do my apartment house business--taking
rents and writing receipts, talking to people who are interested in

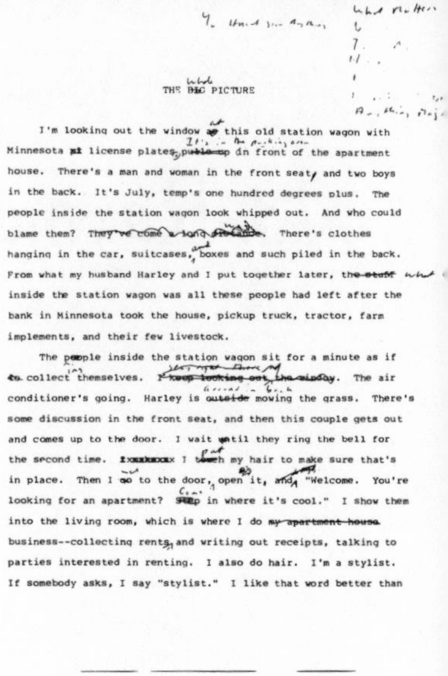

[Draft 2 — top right]

I'm looking out the window at this old station wagon with
Minnesota at license plates, pulls up in front of the apartment
house. There's a man and woman in the front seat, and two boys
in the back. It's July, temp's one hundred degrees plus. The
people inside the station wagon look whipped out. And who could
blame them? They've come a long distance. There's clothes
hanging in the car, suitcases, boxes and such piled in the back.
From what my husband Harley and I put together later, the stuff
inside the station wagon was all these people had left after the
bank in Minnesota took the house, pickup truck, tractor, farm
implements, and their few livestock.
The people inside the station wagon sit for a minute as if
to collect themselves. The air
conditioner's going. Harley is outside mowing the grass. There's
some discussion in the front seat, and then this couple gets out
and comes up to the door. I wait until they ring the bell for
the second time. Then I brush my hair to make sure that's
in place. Then I go to the door, open it, and "Welcome. You're
looking for an apartment? Step in where it's cool." I show them
into the living room, which is where I do my apartment house
business--collecting rents, and writing out receipts, talking to
parties interested in renting. I also do hair. I'm a stylist.
If somebody asks, I say "stylist." I like that word better than

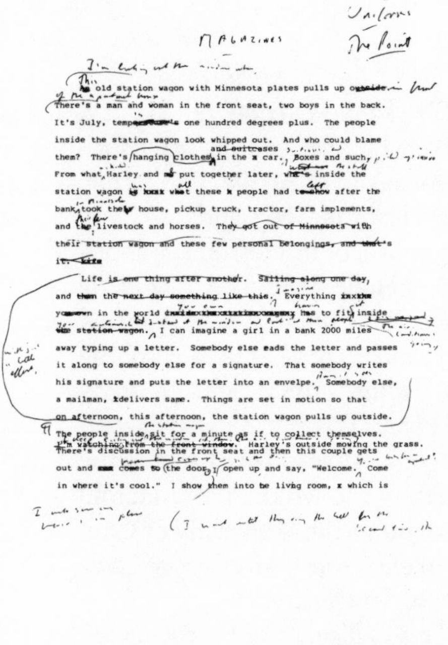

[Draft 3 — bottom left] MAGAZINES / The Point

An old station wagon with Minnesota plates pulls up outside
There's a man and woman in the front seat, two boys in the back.
It's July, temperature's one hundred degrees plus. The people
inside the station wagon look whipped out. And who could blame
them? There's hanging clothes in the car, and suitcases. Boxes and such,
From what Harley and me put together later, this
station wagon was what these people had to show after the
bank took the house, pickup truck, tractor, farm implements,
and the livestock and horses. They got out of Minnesota with
their station wagon and these few personal belongings, and that's
it. Life
Life is one thing after another. Sailing along one day,
and then the next day something like this. Everything
you own in the world has to fit inside
the station wagon. I can imagine a girl in a bank 2000 miles
away typing up a letter. Somebody else reads the letter and passes
it along to somebody else for a signature. That somebody writes
his signature and puts the letter into an envelpe. Somebody else,
a mailman, delivers same. Things are set in motion so that
on afternoon, this afternoon, the station wagon pulls up outside.
The people inside sit for a minute as if to collect themselves.
I'm watching from the front window. Harley's outside mowing the grass.
There's discussion in the front seat and then this couple gets
out and comes to the door, open up and say, "Welcome. Come
in where it's cool." I show them into the living room, which is

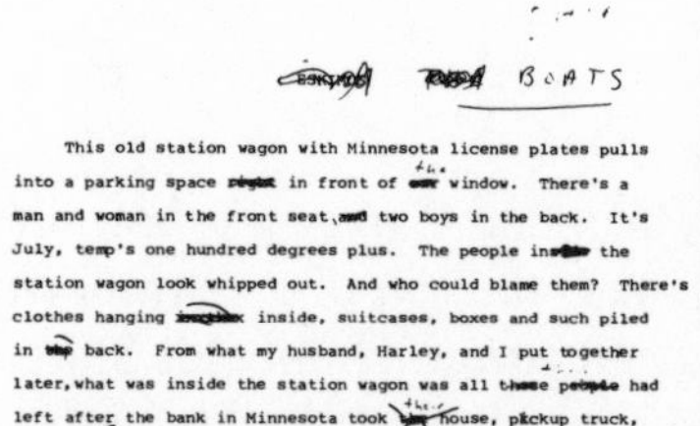

[Draft 4 — bottom right] BOATS

This old station wagon with Minnesota license plates pulls
into a parking space right in front of our window. There's a
man and woman in the front seat, and two boys in the back. It's
July, temp's one hundred degrees plus. The people inside the
station wagon look whipped out. And who could blame them? There's
clothes hanging inside, suitcases, boxes and such piled
in the back. From what my husband, Harley, and I put together
later, what was inside the station wagon was all these people had
left after the bank in Minnesota took the house, pickup truck,
tractor, farm implements, and their few livestock.
The people inside the station wagon sit for a minute, as if
collecting themselves. The air conditioner in our apartment is
running full-blast. Harley's around in back of the house mowing
the grass. There's some discussion in the front seat, and then
this the couple get out and start for the front door. I pat my
hair to make sure that's in place and wait til they push the
doorbell for the second time. Then I go open the door.
"You're looking for an apartment?X Come on in here where
it's cool." I show them into the living room. That's where I
do my business. It's where I collect rents, write out the
receipts, and talk to parties interested in renting. I also
do hair. If somebody asks, I say "hair stylist." I like that

Four drafts of the opening page of Raymond Carver's "The Bridle."

Raymond Carver

Raymond Carver lives in a large, two-story, wood-shingled house on a quiet street in Syracuse, New York. The front lawn slopes down to the sidewalk. A new Mercedes sits in the driveway. An older VW, the other household car, gets parked on the street.

The entrance to the house is through a large, screened-in porch. Inside, the furnishings are almost without character. Everything matches—cream-colored couches, a glass coffee table. Tess Gallagher, the writer with whom Raymond Carver lives, collects peacock feathers and sets them in vases throughout the house—the most noticeable decorative attempt. Our suspicions were confirmed; Carver told us that all the furniture was purchased and delivered in one day.

Gallagher has painted a detachable wood "No Visitors" sign, the lettering surrounded by yellow and orange eyelashes, which

*hangs on the screen door. Sometimes the phone is unplugged
and the sign stays up for days at a time.*

*Carver works in a large room on the top floor. The surface of
the long oak desk is clear; his typewriter is set to the side, on
an L-shaped wing. There are no knicknacks, charms, or toys of
any kind on Carver's desk. He is not a collector or a man prone
to mementos and nostalgia. Occasionally, one manila folder lies
on the oak desk, containing the story currently in the process of
revision. His files are well in order. He can extract a story and
all its previous versions at a moment's notice. The walls of the
study are painted white like the rest of the house, and, like the
rest of the house, they are mostly bare. Through a high rectangu-
lar window above Carver's desk, light filters into the room in
slanted beams, like light from high church windows.*

*Carver is a large man who wears simple clothes—flannel
shirts, khakis or jeans. He seems to live and dress as the characters in his stories live and dress. For someone of his size, he has
a remarkably low and indistinct voice; we found ourselves bend-
ing closer every few minutes to catch his words and asking the
irritating "What, what?"*

*Portions of the interview were conducted through the mail,
during 1981–82. When we met Carver, the "No Visitors" sign
was not up and several Syracuse students dropped by to visit
during the course of the interview, including Carver's son, a
senior. For lunch, Carver made us sandwiches with salmon he
had caught off the coast of Washington. Both he and Gallagher
are from Washington state and at the time of the interview, they
were having a house built in Port Angeles, where they plan to
live part of each year. We asked Carver if that house would feel
more like a home to him. He replied, "No, wherever I am is fine.
This is fine."*

INTERVIEWER: What was your early life like, and what made
you want to write?

CARVER: I grew up in a small town in eastern Washington,

a place called Yakima. My dad worked at the sawmill there. He was a saw-filer and helped take care of the saws that were used to cut and plane the logs. My mother worked as a retail clerk or a waitress or else stayed at home, but she didn't keep any job for very long. I remember talk concerning her "nerves." In the cabinet under the kitchen sink, she kept a bottle of patent "nerve medicine," and she'd take a couple of tablespoons of this every morning. My dad's nerve medicine was whiskey. Most often he kept a bottle of it under that same sink, or else outside in the woodshed. I remember sneaking a taste of it once and hating it, and wondering how anybody could drink the stuff. Home was a little two-bedroom house. We moved a lot when I was a kid, but it was always into another little two-bedroom house. The first house I can remember living in, near the fairgrounds in Yakima, had an outdoor toilet. This was in the late 1940s. I was eight or ten years old then. I used to wait at the bus stop for my dad to come home from work. Usually he was as regular as clockwork. But every two weeks or so, he wouldn't be on the bus. I'd stick around then and wait for the next bus, but I already knew he wasn't going to be on that one, either. When this happened, it meant he'd gone drinking with friends of his from the sawmill. I still remember the sense of doom and hopelessness that hung over the supper table when my mother and I and my kid brother sat down to eat.

INTERVIEWER: But what made you want to write?

CARVER: The only explanation I can give you is that my dad told me lots of stories about himself when he was a kid, and about his dad and his grandfather. His grandfather had fought in the Civil War. He fought for both sides! He was a turncoat. When the South began losing the war, he crossed over to the North and began fighting for the Union forces. My dad laughed when he told this story. He didn't see anything wrong with it, and I guess I didn't either. Anyway, my dad would tell me stories, anecdotes really, no moral to them, about tramping around in the woods, or else riding the rails and having to look out for railroad bulls. I loved his company and loved to listen to him tell me these stories. Once in a while he'd read something to me from what he was reading. Zane Grey westerns. These were the first real hardback books, outside of grade-school texts, and the Bible, that I'd ever seen. It wouldn't happen very often, but now and again I'd see him lying on the bed of an evening and reading from Zane Grey. It seemed a very private act in a house and family that were not given to privacy. I realized that he had this private side to him, something I didn't understand or know anything about, but something that found expression through this occasional reading. I was interested in that side of him and interested in the act itself. I'd ask him to read me what he was reading, and he'd oblige by just reading from wherever he happened to be in the book. After a while he'd say, "Junior, go do something else now." Well, there were plenty of things to do. In those days, I went fishing in this creek that was not too far from our house. A little later, I started hunting ducks and geese and upland game. That's what excited me in those days, hunting and fishing. That's what made a dent in my emotional life, and that's what I wanted to write about. My reading fare in those days, aside from an occasional historical novel or Mickey Spillane mystery, consisted of *Sports Afield* and *Outdoor Life,* and *Field & Stream.* I wrote a longish thing about the fish that got away, or the fish I caught, one or the other, and asked my mother if she would type it up for me. She couldn't type, but she did go rent a typewriter, bless her heart, and between the two of us, we typed it up in some terrible fashion and sent it out. I remember there were two addresses on the masthead of the outdoors magazine; so we sent it to the office closest to us, to Boulder, Colorado, the circulation department. The piece came back, finally, but that was fine. It had gone out in the world, that manuscript—it had been places. Somebody had read it besides my mother, or so I hoped anyway. Then I saw an ad in *Writer's Digest.* It was a photograph of a man, a successful author, obviously, testifying to something called the Palmer Institute of Authorship. That seemed like just the thing for me. There was a monthly payment plan involved. Twenty dollars down, ten or fifteen dollars a month for three years or thirty years, one of those things. There were weekly assignments with personal responses to the assignments. I stayed with it for a few months. Then, maybe I got bored; I stopped doing the work. My folks stopped making the payments. Pretty soon a letter arrived from the Palmer Institute telling me that if I paid them up in full, I could still get the certificate of completion. This seemed more than fair. Somehow I talked my folks into paying the rest of the money, and in due time I got the certificate and hung it up on my bedroom wall. But all through high school it was assumed that I'd graduate and go to work at the sawmill. For a long time I wanted to do the kind of work my dad did. He was going to ask his foreman at the mill to put me on after I graduated. So I worked at the mill for about six months. But I hated the work and knew from the first day I didn't want to do that for the rest of my life. I worked long enough to save the money for a car, buy some clothes, and so I could move out and get married.

INTERVIEWER: Somehow, for whatever reasons, you went to college. Was it your wife who wanted you to go on to college? Did she encourage you in this respect? Did she want to go to college and that made you want to go? How old were you at this point? She must have been pretty young, too.

CARVER: I was eighteen. She was sixteen and pregnant and had just graduated from an Episcopalian private school for girls in Walla Walla, Washington. At school she'd learned the right way to hold a teacup; she'd had religious instruction and gym and such, but she also learned about physics and literature and foreign languages. I was terrifically impressed that she knew Latin. Latin! She tried off and on to go to college during those first years, but it was too hard to do that; it was impossible to do that and raise a family and be broke all the time, too. I mean

broke. Her family didn't have any money. She was going to that
school on a scholarship. Her mother hated me and still does.
My wife was supposed to graduate and go on to the University
of Washington to study law on a fellowship. Instead, I made
her pregnant, and we got married and began our life together.
She was seventeen when the first child was born, eighteen
when the second was born. What shall I say at this point? We
didn't have any youth. We found ourselves in roles we didn't
know how to play. But we did the best we could. Better than
that, I want to think. She did finish college finally. She got her
B.A. degree at San Jose State twelve or fourteen years after we
married.

INTERVIEWER: Were you writing during these early, difficult
years?

CARVER: I worked nights and went to school days. We were
always working. She was working and trying to raise the kids
and manage a household. She worked for the telephone company. The kids were with a babysitter during the day. Finally,
I graduated with the B.A. degree from Humboldt State College and we put everything into the car and in one of those
carryalls that fits on top of your car, and we went to Iowa City.
A teacher named Dick Day at Humboldt State had told me
about the Iowa Writers' Workshop. Day had sent along a story
of mine and three or four poems to Don Justice, who was
responsible for getting me a five-hundred-dollar grant at Iowa.

INTERVIEWER: Five hundred dollars?

CARVER: That's all they had, they said. It seemed like a lot
at the time. But I didn't finish at Iowa. They offered me more
money to stay on the second year, but we just couldn't do it.
I was working in the library for a dollar or two an hour, and
my wife was working as a waitress. It was going to take me
another year to get a degree, and we just couldn't stick it out.
So we moved back to California. This time it was Sacramento.
I found work as a night janitor at Mercy Hospital. I kept the
job for three years. It was a pretty good job. I only had to work

two or three hours a night, but I was paid for eight hours. There was a certain amount of work that had to get done, but once it was done, that was it—I could go home or do anything I wanted. The first year or two I went home every night and would be in bed at a reasonable hour and be able to get up in the morning and write. The kids would be off at the babysitter's and my wife would have gone to her job—a door-to-door sales job. I'd have all day in front of me. This was fine for a while. Then I began getting off work at night and going drinking instead of going home. By this time it was 1967 or 1968.

INTERVIEWER: When did you first get published?

CARVER: When I was an undergraduate at Humboldt State in Arcata, California. One day, I had a short story taken at one magazine and a poem taken at another. It was a terrific day! Maybe one of the best days ever. My wife and I drove around town and showed the letters of acceptance to all of our friends. It gave some much-needed validation to our lives.

INTERVIEWER: What was the first story you ever published? And the first poem?

CARVER: It was a story called "Pastoral" and it was published in the *Western Humanities Review.* It's a good literary magazine and it's still being published by the University of Utah. They didn't pay me anything for the story, but that didn't matter. The poem was called "The Brass Ring," and it was published by a magazine in Arizona, now defunct, called *Targets.* Charles Bukowski had a poem in the same issue, and I was pleased to be in the same magazine with him. He was a kind of hero to me then.

INTERVIEWER: Is it true—a friend of yours told me this—that you celebrated your first publication by taking the magazine to bed with you?

CARVER: That's partly true. Actually, it was a book, the *Best American Short Stories* annual. My story "Will You Please Be Quiet, Please?" had just appeared in the collection. That was back in the late sixties, when it was edited every year by Martha

Foley and people used to call it that—simply, "The Foley Collection." The story had been published in an obscure little magazine out of Chicago called *December.* The day the anthology came in the mail I took it to bed to read and just to look at, you know, and hold it, but I did more looking and holding than actual reading. I fell asleep and woke up the next morning with the book there in bed beside me, along with my wife.

INTERVIEWER: In an article you did for *The New York Times Book Review* you mentioned a story "too tedious to talk about here"—about why you choose to write short stories over novels. Do you want to go into that story now?

CARVER: The story that was "too tedious to talk about" has to do with a number of things that aren't very pleasant to talk about. I did finally talk about some of these things in the essay "Fires," which was published in *Antaeus.* In it I said that finally, a writer is judged by what he writes, and that's the way it should be. The circumstances surrounding the writing are something else, something extraliterary. Nobody ever asked me to be a writer. But it *was* tough to stay alive and pay bills and put food on the table and at the same time to think of myself as a writer and to *learn* to write. After years of working crap jobs and raising kids and trying to write, I realized I needed to write things I could finish and be done with in a hurry. There was no way I could undertake a novel, a two- or three-year stretch of work on a single project. I needed to write something I could get some kind of a payoff from immediately, not next year, or three years from now. Hence, poems and stories. I was beginning to see that my life was not—let's say it was not what I wanted it to be. There was always a wagonload of frustration to deal with—wanting to write and not being able to find the time or the place for it. I used to go out and sit in the car and try to write something on a pad on my knee. This was when the kids were in their adolescence. I was in my late twenties or early thirties. We were still in a state of penury, we had one bankruptcy behind us, and years of hard work with nothing to show for it except an old car, a rented house, and new creditors on our backs. It was depressing, and I felt spiritually obliterated. Alcohol became a problem. I more or less gave up, threw in the towel, and took to full-time drinking as a serious pursuit. That's part of what I was talking about when I was talking about things "too tedious to talk about."

INTERVIEWER: Could you talk a little more about the drinking? So many writers, even if they're not alcoholics, drink so much.

CARVER: Probably not a whole lot more than any other group of professionals. You'd be surprised. Of course there's a mythology that goes along with the drinking, but I was never into that. I was into the drinking itself. I suppose I began to drink heavily after I'd realized that the things I'd wanted most in life for myself and my writing, and my wife and children, were simply not going to happen. It's strange. You never start out in life with the intention of becoming a bankrupt or an alcoholic or a cheat and a thief. Or a liar.

INTERVIEWER: And you were all those things?

CARVER: I was. I'm not any longer. Oh, I lie a little from time to time, like everyone else.

INTERVIEWER: How long since you quit drinking?

CARVER: June second, 1977. If you want the truth, I'm prouder of that, that I've quit drinking, than I am of anything in my life. I'm a recovered alcoholic. I'll always be an alcoholic, but I'm no longer a practicing alcoholic.

INTERVIEWER: How bad did the drinking get?

CARVER: It's very painful to think about some of the things that happened back then. I made a wasteland out of everything I touched. But I might add that towards the end of the drinking there wasn't much left anyway. But specific things? Let's just say, on occasion, the police were involved and emergency rooms and courtrooms.

INTERVIEWER: How did you stop? What made you able to stop?

CARVER: The last year of my drinking, 1977, I was in a recovery center twice, as well as one hospital; and I spent a few days in a place called DeWitt near San Jose, California. De-Witt used to be, appropriately enough, a hospital for the criminally insane. Toward the end of my drinking career I was completely out of control and in a very grave place. Blackouts, the whole business—points where you can't remember anything you say or do during a certain period of time. You might drive a car, give a reading, teach a class, set a broken leg, go to bed with someone, and not have any memory of it later. You're on some kind of automatic pilot. I have an image of myself sitting in my living room with a glass of whiskey in my hand and my head bandaged from a fall caused by an alcoholic seizure. Crazy! Two weeks later I was back in a recovery center, this time at a place called Duffy's, in Calistoga, California, up in the wine country. I was at Duffy's on two different occasions; in the place called DeWitt, in San Jose; and in a hospital in San Francisco—all in the space of twelve months. I guess that's pretty bad. I was dying from it, plain and simple, and I'm not exaggerating.

INTERVIEWER: What brought you to the point where you could stop drinking for good?

CARVER: It was late May 1977. I was living by myself in a house in a little town in northern California, and I'd been sober for about three weeks. I drove to San Francisco, where they were having this publishers' convention. Fred Hills, at that time editor-in-chief at McGraw-Hill, wanted to take me to lunch and offer me money to write a novel. But a couple of nights before the lunch, one of my friends had a party. Midway through, I picked up a glass of wine and drank it, and that's the last thing I remember. Blackout time. The next morning when the stores opened, I was waiting to buy a bottle. The dinner that night was a disaster; it was terrible, people quarreling and disappearing from the table. And the next morning I had to get up and go have this lunch with Fred Hills. I was so hung over when I woke up I could hardly hold my head up. But I drank a half pint of vodka before I picked up Hills and that helped, for the short run. And then he wanted to drive over to Sausalito for lunch! That took us at least an hour in heavy traffic, and I was drunk and hung over both, you understand. But for some reason he went ahead and offered me this money to write a novel.

INTERVIEWER: Did you ever write the novel?

CARVER: Not yet! Anyway, I managed to get out of San Francisco back up to where I lived. I stayed drunk for a couple more days. And then I woke up, feeling terrible, but I didn't drink anything that morning. Nothing alcoholic, I mean. I felt terrible physically—mentally, too, of course—but I didn't drink anything. I didn't drink for three days, and when the third day had passed, I began to feel some better. Then I just kept not drinking. Gradually I began to put a little distance between myself and the booze. A week. Two weeks. Suddenly it was a month. I'd been sober for a month, and I was slowly starting to get well.

INTERVIEWER: Did AA help?

CARVER: It helped a lot. I went to at least one and sometimes two meetings a day for the first month.

INTERVIEWER: Did you ever feel that alcohol was in any way an inspiration? I'm thinking of your poem "Vodka," published in *Esquire.*

CARVER: My God, no! I hope I've made that clear. Cheever remarked that he could always recognize "an alcoholic line" in a writer's work. I'm not exactly sure what he meant by this but I think I know. When we were teaching in the Iowa Writers' Workshop in the fall semester of 1973, he and I did nothing *but* drink. I mean we met our classes, in a manner of speaking. But the entire time we were there—we were living in this hotel they have on campus, the Iowa House—I don't think either of us ever took the covers off our typewriters. We made trips to a liquor store twice a week in my car.

INTERVIEWER: To stock up?

CARVER: Yes, stock up. But the store didn't open until ten A.M. Once we planned an early morning run, a ten o'clock run, and we were going to meet in the lobby of the hotel. I came down early to get some cigarettes and John was pacing up and down in the lobby. He was wearing loafers, but he didn't have any socks on. Anyway, we headed out a little early. By the time we got to the liquor store the clerk was just unlocking the front door. On this particular morning, John got out of the car before I could get it properly parked. By the time I got inside the store he was already at the checkout stand with a half gallon of Scotch. He lived on the fourth floor of the hotel and I lived on the second. Our rooms were identical, right down to the same reproduction of the same painting hanging on the wall. But when we drank together, we always drank in his room. He said he was afraid to come down to drink on the second floor. He said there was always a chance of him getting mugged in the hallway! But you know, of course, that fortunately, not too long after Cheever left Iowa City, he went to a treatment center and got sober and stayed sober until he died.

INTERVIEWER: Do you feel the spoken confessions at Alcoholics Anonymous meetings have influenced your writing?

CARVER: There are different kinds of meetings—speaker meetings where just one speaker will get up and talk for fifty minutes or so about what it was like then, and maybe what it's like now. And there are meetings where everyone in the room has a chance to say something. But I can't honestly say I've ever consciously or otherwise patterned any of my stories on things I've heard at the meetings.

INTERVIEWER: Where do your stories come from, then? I'm especially asking about the stories that have something to do with drinking.

CARVER: The fiction I'm most interested in has lines of reference to the real world. None of my stories really *happened*, of course. But there's always something, some element, some-

thing said to me or that I witnessed, that may be the starting
place. Here's an example: "That's the last Christmas you'll ever
ruin for us!" I was drunk when I heard that, but I remembered
it. And later, much later, when I was sober, using only that one
line and other things I imagined, imagined so accurately that
they *could* have happened, I made a story—"A Serious Talk."
But the fiction I'm most interested in, whether it's Tolstoy's
fiction, Chekhov, Barry Hannah, Richard Ford, Hemingway,
Isaac Babel, Ann Beattie, or Anne Tyler, strikes me as autobiographical to some extent. At the very least it's referential.
Stories long or short don't just come out of thin air. I'm reminded of a conversation involving John Cheever. We were
sitting around a table in Iowa City with some people and he
happened to remark that after a family fracas at his home one
night, he got up the next morning and went into the bathroom
to find something his daughter had written in lipstick on the
bathroom mirror: "D-e-r-e daddy, don't leave us." Someone at
the table spoke up and said, "I recognize that from one of your
stories." Cheever said, "Probably so. Everything I write is
autobiographical." Now of course that's not literally true. But
everything we write is, in some way, autobiographical. I'm not
in the least bothered by "autobiographical" fiction. To the
contrary. *On the Road*. Céline. Roth. Lawrence Durrell in *The
Alexandria Quartet.* So much of Hemingway in the Nick
Adams stories. Updike, too, you bet. Jim McConkey. Clark
Blaise is a contemporary writer whose fiction is out-and-out
autobiography. Of course, you have to know what you're doing
when you turn your life's stories into fiction. You have to be
immensely daring, very skilled and imaginative and willing to
tell everything on yourself. You're told time and again when
you're young to write about what you know, and what do you
know better than your own secrets? But unless you're a special
kind of writer, and a very talented one, it's dangerous to try and
write volume after volume on The Story of My Life. A great
danger, or at least a great temptation, for many writers is to

become too autobiographical in their approach to their fiction. A little autobiography and a lot of imagination are best.

INTERVIEWER: Are your characters trying to do what matters?

CARVER: I think they are trying. But trying and succeeding are two different matters. In some lives, people always succeed; and I think it's grand when that happens. In other lives, people don't succeed at what they try to do, at the things they want most to do, the large or small things that support the life. These lives are, of course, valid to write about, the lives of the people who don't succeed. Most of my own experience, direct or indirect, has to do with the latter situation. I think most of my characters would like their actions to count for something. But at the same time they've reached the point—as so many people do—that they know it isn't so. It doesn't add up any longer. The things you once thought important or even worth dying for aren't worth a nickel now. It's their lives they've become uncomfortable with, lives they see breaking down. They'd like to set things right, but they can't. And usually they do know it, I think, and after that they just do the best they can.

INTERVIEWER: Could you say something about one of my favorite stories in your most recent collection? Where did the idea for "Why Don't You Dance?" originate?

CARVER: I was visiting some writer friends in Missoula back in the mid-1970s. We were all sitting around drinking and someone told a story about a barmaid named Linda who got drunk with her boyfriend one night and decided to move all of her bedroom furnishings into the backyard. They did it, too, right down to the carpet and the bedroom lamp, the bed, the nightstand, everything. There were about four or five writers in the room, and after the guy finished telling the story, someone said, "Well, who's going to write it?" I don't know who else might have written it, but I wrote it. Not then, but later. About four or five years later, I think. I changed and added things to it, of course. Actually, it was the first story I wrote after I finally stopped drinking.

INTERVIEWER: What are your writing habits like? Are you always working on a story?

CARVER: When I'm writing, I write every day. It's lovely when that's happening. One day dovetailing into the next. Sometimes I don't even know what day of the week it is. The "paddle-wheel of days," John Ashbery has called it. When I'm not writing, like now, when I'm tied up with teaching duties as I have been the last while, it's as if I've never written a word or had any desire to write. I fall into bad habits. I stay up too late and sleep in too long. But it's okay. I've learned to be patient and to bide my time. I had to learn that a long time ago. Patience. If I believed in signs, I suppose my sign would be the sign of the turtle. I write in fits and starts. But when I'm writing, I put in a lot of hours at the desk, ten or twelve or fifteen hours at a stretch, day after day. I love that, when that's happening. Much of this work time, understand, is given over to revising and rewriting. There's not much that I like better than to take a story that I've had around the house for a while and work it over again. It's the same with the poems I write. I'm in no hurry to send something off just after I write it, and I sometimes keep it around the house for months doing this or that to it, taking this out and putting that in. It doesn't take that long to do the first draft of the story, that usually happens in one sitting, but it does take a while to do the various versions of the story. I've done as many as twenty or thirty drafts of a story. Never less than ten or twelve drafts. It's instructive, and heartening both, to look at the early drafts of great writers. I'm thinking of the photographs of galleys belonging to Tolstoy, to name one writer who loved to revise. I mean, I don't know if he loved it or not, but he did a great deal of it. He was always revising, right down to the time of page proofs. He went through and rewrote *War and Peace* eight times and was still making corrections in the galleys. Things like this should hearten every writer whose first drafts are dreadful, like mine are.

INTERVIEWER: Describe what happens when you write a story.

CARVER: I write the first draft quickly, as I said. This is most often done in longhand. I simply fill up the pages as rapidly as I can. In some cases, there's a kind of personal shorthand, notes to myself for what I will do later when I come back to it. Some scenes I have to leave unfinished, unwritten in some cases; the scenes that will require meticulous care later. I mean all of it requires meticulous care—but some scenes I save until the second or third draft, because to do them and do them right would take too much time on the first draft. With the first draft it's a question of getting down the outline, the scaffolding of the story. Then on subsequent revisions I'll see to the rest of it. When I've finished the longhand draft I'll type a version of the story and go from there. It always looks different to me, better, of course, after it's typed up. When I'm typing the first draft, I'll begin to rewrite and add and delete a little then. The real work comes later, after I've done three or four drafts of the story. It's the same with the poems, only the poems may go through forty or fifty drafts. Donald Hall told me he sometimes writes a hundred or so drafts of his poems. Can you imagine?

INTERVIEWER: Has your way of working changed?

CARVER: The stories in *What We Talk About* are different to an extent. For one thing, it's a much more self-conscious book in the sense of how intentional every move was, how calculated. I pushed and pulled and worked with those stories before they went into the book to an extent I'd never done with any other stories. When the book was put together and in the hands of my publisher, I didn't write anything at all for six months. And then the first story I wrote was "Cathedral," which I feel is totally different in conception and execution from any stories that have come before. I suppose it reflects a change in my life as much as it does in my way of writing. When I wrote "Cathedral" I experienced this rush and I felt, "This is what it's all about, this is the reason we do this." It was different than the stories that had come before. There was an opening up when I wrote the story. I knew I'd gone as far the other way as I could or wanted to go, cutting everything down to the marrow, not just to the bone. Any farther in that direction and I'd be at a dead end—writing stuff and publishing stuff I wouldn't want to read myself, and that's the truth. In a review of the last book, somebody called me a "minimalist" writer. The reviewer meant it as a compliment. But I didn't like it. There's something about "minimalist" that smacks of smallness of vision and execution that I don't like. But all of the stories in the new book, the one called *Cathedral*, were written within an eighteen-month period; and in every one of them I feel this difference.

INTERVIEWER: Do you have any sense of an audience? Updike described his ideal reader as a young boy in a small midwestern town finding one of his books on a library shelf.

CARVER: It's nice to think of Updike's idealized reader. But except for the early stories, I don't think it's a young boy in a small midwestern town who's reading Updike. What would this young boy make of *The Centaur* or *Couples* or *Rabbit Redux* or *The Coup*? I think Updike is writing for the audience that John Cheever said he was writing for, "intelligent, adult men and women," wherever they live. Any writer worth his salt writes as well and as truly as he can and hopes for as large and perceptive a readership as possible. So you write as well as you can and hope for good readers. But I think you're also writing for other writers to an extent—the dead writers whose work you admire, as well as the living writers you like to read. If they like it, the other writers, there's a good chance other "intelligent, adult men and women" may like it, too. But I don't have that boy you mentioned in mind, or anyone else for that matter, when I'm doing the writing itself.

INTERVIEWER: How much of what you write do you finally throw away?

CARVER: Lots. If the first draft of the story is forty pages long, it'll usually be half that by the time I'm finished with it. And it's not just a question of taking out or bringing it down. I take out a lot, but I also add things and then add some more and take out some more. It's something I love to do, putting words in and taking words out.

INTERVIEWER: Has the process of revision changed now that the stories seem to be longer and more generous?

CARVER: Generous, yes, that's a good word for them. Yes, and I'll tell you why. Up at school there's a typist who has one of those space-age typewriters, a word processor, and I can give her a story to type and once she has it typed and I get back the fair copy, I can mark it up to my heart's content and give it back to her; and the next day I can have my story back, all fair copy once more. Then I can mark it up again as much as I want, and the next day I'll have back a fair copy once more. I love it. It may seem like a small thing, really, but it's changed my life, that woman and her word processor.

INTERVIEWER: Did you ever have any time off from not having to earn a living?

CARVER: I had a year once. It was a very important year for me, too. I wrote most of the stories in *Will You Please Be Quiet, Please?* in that year. It was back in 1970 or 1971. I was working for this textbook publishing firm in Palo Alto. It was my first white-collar job, right after the period when I'd been a janitor at the hospital in Sacramento. I'd been working away there quietly as an editor when the company, it was called SRA, decided to do a major reorganization. I planned to quit, I was writing my letter of resignation, but then suddenly—I was fired. It was just wonderful the way it turned out. We invited all of our friends that weekend and had a firing party! For a year I didn't have to work. I drew unemployment and had my severance pay to live on. And that's the period when my wife finished her college degree. That was a turning point, that time. It was a good period.

INTERVIEWER: Are you religious?

CARVER: No, but I have to believe in miracles and the possibility of resurrection. No question about that. Every day that I wake up, I'm glad to wake up. That's why I like to wake up early. In my drinking days I would sleep until noon or whatever and I would usually wake up with the shakes.

INTERVIEWER: Do you regret a lot of things that happened back then when things were so bad?

CARVER: I can't change anything now. I can't afford to regret. That life is simply gone now, and I can't regret its passing. I have to live in the present. The life back then is gone just as surely—it's as remote to me as if it had happened to somebody I read about in a nineteenth-century novel. I don't spend more than five minutes a month in the past. The past really *is* a foreign country, and they do do things differently there. Things happen. I really do feel I've had two different lives.

INTERVIEWER: Can you talk a little about literary influences, or at least name some writers whose work you greatly admire?

CARVER: Ernest Hemingway is one. The early stories. "Big Two-Hearted River," "Cat in the Rain," "The Three-Day Blow," "Soldier's Home," lots more. Chekhov. I suppose he's the writer whose work I most admire. But who doesn't like Chekhov? I'm talking about his stories now, not the plays. His plays move too slowly for me. Tolstoy. Any of his short stories, novellas, and *Anna Karenina*. Not *War and Peace*. Too slow. But *The Death of Ivan Ilyich, Master and Man*, "How Much Land Does a Man Need?" Tolstoy is the best there is. Isaac Babel, Flannery O'Connor, Frank O'Connor. James Joyce's *Dubliners*. John Cheever. *Madame Bovary*. Last year I reread that book, along with a new translation of Flaubert's letters written while he was composing—no other word for it—*Madame Bovary*. Conrad. Updike's *Too Far to Go*. And there are wonderful writers I've come across in the last year or two like

Tobias Wolff. His book of stories *In the Garden of the North American Martyrs* is just wonderful. Max Schott. Bobbie Ann Mason. Did I mention her? Well, she's good and worth mentioning twice. Harold Pinter. V. S. Pritchett. Years ago I read something in a letter by Chekhov that impressed me. It was a piece of advice to one of his many correspondents, and it went something like this: Friend, you don't have to write about extraordinary people who accomplish extraordinary and memorable deeds. (Understand I was in college at the time and reading plays about princes and dukes and the overthrow of kingdoms. Quests and the like, large undertakings to establish heroes in their rightful places. Novels with larger-than-life heroes.) But reading what Chekhov had to say in that letter, and in other letters of his as well, and reading his stories, made me see things differently than I had before. Not long afterwards I read a play and a number of stories by Maxim Gorky, and he simply reinforced in his work what Chekhov had to say. Richard Ford is another fine writer. He's primarily a novelist, but he's also written stories and essays. He's a friend. I have a lot of friends who are good friends, and some of them are good writers. Some not so good.

INTERVIEWER: What do you do in that case? I mean, how do you handle that—if one of your friends publishes something you don't like?

CARVER: I don't say anything unless the friend asks me, and I hope he doesn't. But if you're asked you have to say it in a way that it doesn't wreck the friendship. You want your friends to do well and write the best they can. But sometimes their work is a disappointment. You want everything to go well for them, but you have this dread that maybe it won't and there's not much you can do.

INTERVIEWER: What do you think of moral fiction? I guess this has to lead into talk about John Gardner and his influence on you. I know you were his student many years ago at Humboldt State College.

CARVER: That's true. I've written about our relationship in the *Antaeus* piece and elaborated on it more in my introduction to a posthumous book of his called *On Becoming a Novelist.* I think *On Moral Fiction* is a wonderfully smart book. I don't agree with all of it, by any means, but generally he's right. Not so much in his assessments of living writers as in the aims, the aspirations of the book. It's a book that wants to affirm life rather than trash it. Gardner's definition of morality is life-affirming. And in that regard he believes good fiction is moral fiction. It's a book to argue with, if you like to argue. It's brilliant, in any case. I think he may argue his case even better in *On Becoming a Novelist.* And he doesn't go after other writers as he did in *On Moral Fiction.* We had been out of touch with each other for years when he published *On Moral Fiction,* but his influence, the things he stood for in my life when I was his student, were still so strong that for a long while I didn't want to read the book. I was afraid to find out that what I'd been writing all these years was immoral! You understand that we'd not seen each other for nearly twenty years and had only renewed our friendship after I'd moved to Syracuse and he was down there at Binghamton, seventy miles away. There was a lot of anger directed toward Gardner and the book when it was published. He touched nerves. I happen to think it's a remarkable piece of work.

INTERVIEWER: But after you read the book, what did you think then about your own work? Were you writing "moral" or "immoral" stories?

CARVER: I'm still not sure! But I heard from other people, and then he told me himself, that he liked my work. Especially the new work. That pleases me a great deal. Read *On Becoming a Novelist.*

INTERVIEWER: Do you still write poetry?

CARVER: Some, but not enough. I want to write more. If too long a period of time goes by, six months or so, I get nervous if I haven't written any poems. I find myself wondering if I've stopped being a poet or stopped being able to write poetry. It's usually then that I sit down and try to write some poems. This book of mine that's coming in the spring, *Fires*—that's got all of the poems of mine I want to keep.

INTERVIEWER: How do they influence each other? The writing of fiction and the writing of poetry?

CARVER: They don't any longer. For a long time I was equally interested in the writing of poetry and the writing of fiction. In magazines I always turned to the poems first before I read the stories. Finally, I had to make a choice, and I came down on the side of the fiction. It was the right choice for me. I'm not a "born" poet. I don't know if I'm a "born" anything except a white American male. Maybe I'll become an occasional poet. But I'll settle for that. That's better than not being any kind of poet at all.

INTERVIEWER: How has fame changed you?

CARVER: I feel uncomfortable with that word. You see, I started out with such low expectations in the first place—I mean, how far are you going to get in this life writing short stories? And I didn't have much self-esteem as a result of this drinking thing. So it's a continual amazement to me, this attention that's come along. But I can tell you that after the reception for *What We Talk About*, I felt a confidence that I've never felt before. Every good thing that's happened since has conjoined to make me want to do even more and better work. It's been a good spur. And all this is coming at a time in my life when I have more strength than I've ever had before. Do you know what I'm saying? I feel stronger and more certain of my direction now than ever before. So "fame"—or let's say this newfound attention and interest—has been a good thing. It bolstered my confidence, when my confidence needed bolstering.

INTERVIEWER: Who reads your writing first?

CARVER: Tess Gallagher. As you know, she's a poet and short-story writer herself. I show her everything I write except for letters, and I've even shown her a few of those. But she has a wonderful eye and a way of feeling herself into what I write. I don't show her anything until I've marked it up and taken it as far as I can. That's usually the fourth or fifth draft, and then she reads every subsequent draft thereafter. So far I've dedicated three books to her and those dedications are not just a token of love and affection; they also indicate the high esteem in which I hold her and an acknowledgment of the help and inspiration she's given me.

INTERVIEWER: Where does Gordon Lish enter into this? I know he's your editor at Knopf.

CARVER: Just as he was the editor who began publishing my stories at *Esquire* back in the early 1970s. But we had a friendship that went back before that time, back to 1967 or 1968, in Palo Alto. He was working for a textbook publishing firm right across the street from the firm where I worked. The one that fired me. He didn't keep any regular office hours. He did most of his work for the company at home. At least once a week he'd ask me over to his place for lunch. He wouldn't eat anything himself, he'd just cook something for me and then hover around the table watching me eat. It made me nervous, as you might imagine. I'd always wind up leaving something on my plate, and he'd always wind up eating it. Said it had to do with the way he was brought up. This is not an isolated example. He still does things like that. He'll take me to lunch now and won't order anything for himself except a drink and then he'll eat up whatever I leave in my plate! I saw him do it once in the Russian Tea Room. There were four of us for dinner, and after the food came he watched us eat. When he saw we were going to leave food on our plates, he cleaned it right up. Aside from this craziness, which is more funny than anything, he's remarkably smart and sensitive to the needs of a manuscript. He's a good editor. Maybe he's a great editor. All I know for sure is that he's my editor and my friend, and I'm glad on both counts.

INTERVIEWER: Would you consider doing more movie script work?

CARVER: If the subject could be as interesting as this one I just finished with Michael Cimino on the life of Dostoyevsky, yes, of course. Otherwise, no. But Dostoyevsky! You bet I would.

INTERVIEWER: And there was real money involved.

CARVER: Yes.

INTERVIEWER: That accounts for the Mercedes.

CARVER: That's it.

INTERVIEWER: What about *The New Yorker?* Did you ever send your stories to *The New Yorker* when you were first starting out?

CARVER: No, I didn't. I didn't read *The New Yorker.* I sent my stories and poems to the little magazines and once in a while something was accepted, and I was made happy by the acceptance. I had some kind of audience, you see, even though I never met any of my audience.

INTERVIEWER: Do you get letters from people who've read your work?

CARVER: Letters, tapes, sometimes photographs. Somebody just sent me a cassette—songs that had been made out of some of the stories.

INTERVIEWER: Do you write better on the West Coast—out in Washington—or here in the East? I guess I'm asking how important a sense of place is to your work.

CARVER: Once, it was important to see myself as a writer from a particular place. It was important for me to be a writer from the West. But that's not true any longer, for better or worse. I think I've moved around too much, lived in too many places, felt dislocated and displaced, to now have any firmly rooted sense of "place." If I've ever gone about consciously locating a story in a particular place and period, and I guess I have, especially in the first book, I suppose that place would be the Pacific Northwest. I admire the sense of place in such writers as Jim Welch, Wallace Stegner, John Keeble, William Eastlake, and William Kittredge. There are plenty of good writers with this sense of place you're talking about. But the majority of my stories are not set in any specific locale. I mean, they could take place in just about any city or urban area; here in Syracuse, but also Tucson, Sacramento, San Jose, San Francisco, Seattle, or Port Angeles, Washington. In any case, most of my stories are set indoors!

INTERVIEWER: Do you work in a particular place in your house?

CARVER: Yes, upstairs in my study. It's important to me to have my own place. Lots of days go by when we just unplug the telephone and put out our "No Visitors" sign. For many years I worked at the kitchen table, or in a library carrel, or else out in my car. This room of my own is a luxury *and* a necessity now.

INTERVIEWER: Do you still hunt and fish?

CARVER: Not so much anymore. I still fish a little, fish for salmon in the summer, if I'm out in Washington. But I don't hunt, I'm sorry to say. I don't know where to go! I guess I could find someone who'd take me, but I just haven't gotten around to it. But my friend Richard Ford is a hunter. When he was up here in the spring of 1981 to give a reading from his work, he took the proceeds from his reading and bought me a shotgun. Imagine that! And he had it inscribed, "For Raymond from Richard, April 1981." Richard is a hunter, you see, and I think he was trying to encourage me.

INTERVIEWER: How do you hope your stories will affect people? Do you think your writing will change anybody?

CARVER: I really don't know. I doubt it. Not change in any profound sense. Maybe not any change at all. After all, art is a form of entertainment, yes? For both the maker and the consumer. I mean in a way it's like shooting billiards or playing cards, or bowling—it's just a different, and I would say higher, form of amusement. I'm not saying there isn't spiritual nour-

ishment involved, too. There is, of course. Listening to a Beethoven concerto or spending time in front of a van Gogh
painting or reading a poem by Blake can be a profound experience on a scale that playing bridge or bowling a 220 game can
never be. Art is all the things art is supposed to be. But art is
also a superior amusement. Am I wrong in thinking this? I
don't know. But I remember in my twenties reading plays by
Strindberg, a novel by Max Frisch, Rilke's poetry, listening all
night to music by Bartók, watching a TV special on the Sistine
Chapel and Michelangelo and feeling in each case that my life
had to change after these experiences, it couldn't help but be
affected by these experiences and *changed*. There was simply
no way I would not become a different person. But then I
found out soon enough my life was not going to change after
all. Not in any way that I could see, perceptible or otherwise.
I understood then that art was something I could pursue when
I had the time for it, when I could afford to do so, and that's
all. Art was a luxury and it wasn't going to change me or my
life. I guess I came to the hard realization that art doesn't make
anything happen. No. I don't believe for a minute in that
absurd Shelleyan nonsense having to do with poets as the
"unacknowledged legislators" of this world. What an idea! Isak
Dinesen said that she wrote a little every day, without hope and
without despair. I like that. The days are gone, if they were ever
with us, when a novel or a play or a book of poems could change
people's ideas about the world they live in or even about themselves. Maybe writing fiction about particular kinds of people
living particular kinds of lives will allow certain areas of life to
be understood a little better than they were understood before.
But I'm afraid that's it, at least as far as I'm concerned. Perhaps
it's different in poetry. Tess has had letters from people who
have read her poems and say the poems saved them from
jumping off a cliff or drowning themselves, etc. But that's
something else. Good fiction is partly a bringing of the news
from one world to another. That end is good in and of itself,

I think. But changing things through fiction, changing some-body's political affiliation or the political system itself, or saving the whales or the redwood trees, no. Not if these are the kinds of changes you mean. And I don't think it should have to do any of these things, either. It doesn't *have* to do anything. It just has to be there for the fierce pleasure we take in doing it, and the different kind of pleasure that's taken in reading some-thing that's durable and made to last, as well as beautiful in and of itself. Something that throws off these sparks—a persistent and steady glow, however dim.

MONA SIMPSON
LEWIS BUZBEE
Winter 1983

Notes on the Contributors

LEWIS BUZBEE *(Interview with Raymond Carver)* is a bookseller. His fiction has appeared in *The Western Humanities Review*, the *Westbere Review*, and elsewhere. He reviews fiction for the *San Francisco Chronicle*.

DUNCAN FALLOWELL *(Interview with Arthur Koestler)* is a journalist and writer. He regularly contributes profiles to *The Times* of London and *Time Out*.

SHUSHA GUPPY *(Interviews with Eugene Ionesco and Edna O'Brien)* is the London editor of *The Paris Review* and a regular contributor to *The Daily Telegraph* (London), British *Vogue*, and other periodicals.

HERMIONE LEE *(Interview with Philip Roth)* is a lecturer in English at the University of York. She has published books on Virginia Woolf, Elizabeth Bowen, and Philip Roth. She reviews fiction for *The Observer*.

JOHN MCCALL *(Interview with Malcolm Cowley)* edits a weekly newspaper in New Jersey. He is a recipient of a 1983 New Jersey State Council for the Arts grant for fiction, and the 1984

International Society of Weekly Newspaper Editors' Golden Quill Award for editorial achievement.

ROBERT PHILLIPS *(Interview with Philip Larkin)* is a writer and critic whose most recent book is *Personal Accounts: New & Selected Poems*, 1966–1986 (Ontario Review Press). He recently edited *Letters of Delmore Schwartz* and *The Stories of Denton Welch.* He is a contributing editor of *The Paris Review.*

DARRYL PINCKNEY *(Interview with Elizabeth Hardwick)* is on the staff of *The New York Review of Books.*

GEORGE PLIMPTON *(Interviews with Malcolm Cowley, William Maxwell,* and *John Barth)* is the editor of *The Paris Review.* His most recent book is *Open Net* (W. W. Norton).

CHRISTIAN SALMON *(Interview with Milan Kundera)* is a researcher at the National Center for Scientific Research in Paris. DINAH LOUDA, the translator of the Kundera interview, is a graduate student in political science at Harvard University and a freelance journalist. AARON ASHER, Milan Kundera's editor at Harper and Row, contributed greatly to the final version of this interview.

KAREN SAUM *(Interview with May Sarton)* edits *This Time,* a newspaper in Orland, Maine, which features interviews with crafters and homesteaders.

JOHN SEABROOK *(Interview with William Maxwell)* is a staff writer for *Manhattan, Inc.* and an occasional contributor to *The Washington Post,* the *Village Voice,* the *Christian Science Monitor, The Nation,* and *Vanity Fair.*

MONA SIMPSON *(Interview with Raymond Carver)* is a senior editor of *The Paris Review.* Knopf will publish her first novel in the fall of 1986.

PETER STITT *(Interview with John Ashbery)* is Associate Professor of English at the University of Houston and the author of *The World's Hieroglyphic Beauty: Five American Poets* (University of Georgia Press), a collection of essays and interviews. He is a frequent contributor to *The Georgia Review,* the *Kenyon Review, Poetry,* and *The New York Times Book Review.*